W9-BTN-252

Education and the Integration of Ethnic Minorities

ST. JOSEPH'S UNIVERSITY

3 9353 00224 3721

Education and the Integration of Ethnic Minorities

Edited by

Dietmar Rothermund and John Simon

LC
3715
.E38
1986

St. Martin's Press, New York

© International Centre for Ethnic Studies, 1986

All rights reserved. For information, write:
Scholarly and Reference Division,
St. Martin's Press, Inc., 175 Fifth Avenue, New York, NY 10010

First published in the United States of America in 1986

Library of Congress Cataloging in Publication Data
Main entry under title:

Education and the integration of ethnic minorities.

  Bibliography: p.
  Includes index.
  1. Minorities — Education — Case studies. 2. Educational
equalization — Case studies. 3. Social integration — Case
studies. 4. Education and state — Case studies.
I. Rothermund, Dietmar. II. Simon, John B.
LC3715.E38   1985   370.19′342   85-19616
ISBN 0-312-23725-1

CONTENTS

PREFACE

The present volume contains the papers presented at a workshop on 'Education and the Integration of Ethnic Minorities' held at Bad Homburg, Germany on 3–6 June 1984. The workshop was convened on behalf of the International Centre for Ethnic Studies, Sri Lanka. This centre was founded in 1982 to promote comparative research and policy-oriented studies in ethnic minority–majority relations. The centre has sponsored many international workshops on specific issues such as the role of the judiciary in plural societies, the role of religion, the position of women, etc. In fact, the idea of establishing this centre grew out of two international workshops held in earlier years in Kenya and Sri Lanka, whose proceedings were published in Robert B. Goldmann and A. Jeyaratnam Wilson (eds), *From Independence to Statehood: Managing Ethnic Conflict in Five African and Asian States* (London: Frances Pinter, 1984).

The Sri Lanka workshop on affirmative action and equalization policies did touch upon education, too. The papers of K.M. de Silva, C.R. de Silva and N. Tiruchelvam in the above-mentioned volume are devoted to ethnic conflict with regard to educational institutions in Sri Lanka and are of special interest in the context of the theme of the present volume. But no attempt was made at that time to draw a more broad-based international comparison of minority–majority relations in the field of education. The Bad Homburg workshop tried to fill this gap by highlighting the great variety of social contexts in which conflicts may arise and conflict resolutions may be attempted in education. Significant case studies were presented, but they certainly do not constitute a representative cross-section of international research in this field. The introduction which follows this preface attempts to provide a synthesis of the proceedings of the workshop.

The International Centre for Ethnic Studies has established an Annual Lecture highlighting a theme of special relevance to the centre's work. The first of these lectures was given in Colombo in 1983 by the centre's chairman, Prof. K.M. de Silva. He spoke about the management of ethnic tensions in the context of the tragic events in Sri Lanka in that year. The convener of the Bad Homburg workshop was asked to deliver the Annual Lecture of 1984. A synthesis of the proceedings of that workshop seemed to be the most appropriate theme and the nearby University of Frankfurt the best venue for this lecture. Prof. Patrick Dias, who heads a department dealing with education in the Third World at Frankfurt University, kindly made the arrangements for that lecture. The text of the introduction is the revised lecture manuscript and has, therefore, retained the style of communication in keeping with its original purpose. We hope it will also prove useful to the readers of this volume by raising the main issues which were at the heart of our debates in the Bad Homburg workshop.

In addition to the authors who contributed papers to this volume, several other participants acted as discussants and panellists. The authors and editors wish to thank them for their very valuable contributions. We would also like to thank the Stiftung Volkswagen-werk, which provided the funds for this workshop, and the Werner Reimers Stiftung, which invited us to meet at their very hospitable conference centre at Bad Homburg.

After the exciting workshop ended the sobering task of revising and editing the papers had to be faced. The authors were very cooperative in this respect. The editors found it very helpful that they could share the burden of getting the manuscript ready for the press. Dietmar Rothermund, who had convened the workshop, established contact with the publisher and kept in touch with the authors while John Simon helped prepare the papers for publication.

Dietmar Rothermund, Heidelberg
John Simon, Helsinki
May 1985

1 INTRODUCTION

Dietmar Rothermund

Ethnic conflict is increasing in a rapidly changing world. Economic growth does not necessarily create equal opportunities but often accelerates the emergence of tensions, particularly in circumstances where such growth attracts migration or accentuates social differentiation among settled communities. The perception of inequality and discrimination may then contribute to a feeling of ethnic solidarity. This solidarity may be based on religion, language, common origin, etc. (factors of an ascribed rather than an achieved quality). Migrants who lead a segregated life in a more or less hostile or indifferent social environment may initially adopt an apologetic and defensive attitude, but their second- and third-generation descendants will often take a more assertive stance, stressing their ethnic identity and searching for their cultural roots. If the environment is sufficiently responsive and does not prevent the entrance of minorities into the mainstream of public life, the quest for ethnic roots may enrich the culture of the host, but if the environment is antagonistic this quest can prove to be explosive.

Generally the debate about ethnic minorities is focused on underprivileged groups, and their integration is discussed in terms of affirmative action, positive discrimination and other remedial measures. But, in fact, some of the most explosive issues in our world today are ethnic conflicts between privileged minorities and underprivileged or supposedly underprivileged majorities. In such cases the minority may adopt a militant position because of an acute sense of relative deprivation, that is to say, an expectation of declining opportunities, whereas the majority resorts to intimidation and official discrimination in order to attain what it considers to be its rightful place in the respective society. It is obvious that in this context integration poses a problem which is different from that of integrating the 'underdog'.

Education is considered to be an important instrument of integration in both cases. As far as underprivileged minorities are

1

concerned, it must help them to enter the mainstream of society and when there is a conflict between a privileged minority and an underprivileged majority, education must establish an equilibrium and ward off the forces of disintegration. Formal education has certain limitations and may fail in achieving those ends because it is essentially an instrument of the self-recruitment of the educated and as such a filter and not a medium of integration. It is designed so as to integrate only those who can play the game according to the prevalent rules. Attempts at redesigning the system of formal education so as to reduce the number of 'drop-outs' often degenerate into custodial activities, sidetracks of the system established merely to keep young people in school and off the street, sidetracks which then turn into blind alleys of unemployment.

While the educational system may 'sidetrack' the problem of coping with underprivileged minorities in this way, a straightforward collision may occur when it has to establish a balance between a privileged minority and an underprivileged majority. The majority will attack the very function of the system as an instrument of self-recruitment of the educated and will try to change the rules of the game. Those who supposedly have a head start due to the prevailing system of education are 'put in their place' by means of a deliberate policy of favouring the majority. This often involves acrimonious debates about the medium of instruction. The majority will try to impose a national language as medium of instruction, and the privileged minority will insist on the option of using either its own language or the language of the former colonial rulers.

Language: the problem of the medium of instruction

Language is, in fact, the most crucial issue in many debates about education and the integration of ethnic minorities. In the case of small underprivileged minorities there is usually no other option but the adoption of the language of the dominant society. But larger underprivileged minorities may stake a claim for bilingual education, and there are good reasons for supporting such a claim. Children who have learned one language properly and have gained some cognitive competence in this way acquire a second language more easily and also gain a proficiency in that language in keeping with that cognitive competence; children, on the other hand, who only pick up enough words for simple communication may never achieve enough cognitive competence in any language. Children of a minority may become permanently handicapped if they use their own language only for 'home consumption' but are taught in a different medium used only in that specific school context. Cognitive starvation leads to assimilation at a very low level of cultural communication and integration at an equally low level of social performance. Privileged minorities with a strong linguistic and educational tradition usually do not face such problems even if the majority imposes on them a new medium of instruction, but they will nevertheless resent this imposition, particularly if the new medium is deficient in modern scientific terminology and thus constitutes a handicap for advanced education.

The issues mentioned here indicate that education by itself cannot have an integrative effect unless the social and political context is conducive to it. Young people may grow up against the grain of society, but they cannot be formally educated against it. The legal and constitutional framework, the pattern of social behaviour, the lifestyle of the community must be attuned to integration if education is supposed to play an integrative role. If this is true, education must be regarded as a dependent variable and educational activists must be warned that their endeavours will be futile unless all other conditions are met by the social system. But the educational system has a certain autonomy because it is supposed to be a repository of values which transcend the pressures and preoccupations of everyday life. Usually such values are rooted in the past and this accounts for the innate conservatism of the educational system. However, if people do not expect educational values to be linked to the fleeting moment such values may also be informed by a premonition of a future society. This presents an opportunity for innovation in education. Integrative concepts developed in this way may in due course have an impact on social life.

There is a further reason for optimism. Social interaction usually extends beyond the conscious control of human beings. Educational systems may appear to be cumbersome and rigid, but they always afford an opportunity for a close and enduring encounter of different generations, an opportunity which, of course, may be missed in lifeless confrontation but which more often gives rise to a true dialogue.

The education of second-generation migrants

In the workshop in which the papers in this book were first presented, we tried to focus our attention on case studies which illuminated some of the points mentioned above. Challenges which may seem to be unique and unprecedented in one country — such as the present German problem of integrating the 'Young Turks' — are actually quite commonplace in terms of international experience. The United States of America, for instance, had to cope with many waves of immigrants, but the famous American 'melting pot' is also not such a powerful integrative mechanism as we were once led to believe.

The workshop could not produce a representative sample of the whole international scene so we had to select a few examples which seemed to be of specific relevance to our theme. We started with a presentation of the German problem of dealing with a large ethnic minority of recent migrants, the Turks. Ursula Mehrländer told us that the main group demanding attention are the Turkish adolescents, who have come to Germany to join their parents at a stage in their life when they have neither had a good dose of formal education in their home country nor are able to enter the German system in such a way as to make adequate use of it. For these young people the transition from school to work is a major problem. They will remain permanently disadvantaged.

Antje-Katrin Menk, in reporting on the linguistic training of Turkish youths in Germany also emphasized the fact that *Seiteneinsteiger*, i.e. youngsters who join the educational system at a later stage, face great difficulties but are better off if they have had sufficient formal education in Turkey to be able to adapt to the German educational system and not drop out in despair. In discussing the two papers on Turkish migrants our friends from Sri Lanka raised the pertinent question whether Germans would consider the possibility of Germany's becoming a plural society. Seen from this angle the whole issue becomes one of the social outlook of the majority rather than a mere problem of the minority. Not much thought has been given to this perspective in Germany so far.

Toru Umakoshi then enlightened us about a problem most of us did not even know existed: the education of the Korean minority in Japan. Here is a surprising case of reviving fading ethnicity among the second generation of migrants. Korean workers were brought to Japan when Korea was a Japanese colony. This immigration stopped after the Second World War. The Korean community in Japan is thus an old, settled community — about three-quarters of its members were born in Japan. The Turkish community in Germany may reach a similar stage by the year 2000. But the 660,000 Koreans in Japan are at present a much smaller part of the total population than the Turks are in Germany. Moreover, the Koreans look like the Japanese and cannot be distinguished from them if they change their names and style of dress. Many of them have done just that in order to avoid discrimination. Korean schools in Japan, however, emphasize ethnic identity and are largely supported by the North Korean government, which combines the message of ethnic solidarity with a powerful dose of political propaganda. As graduates of this system cannot enter Japanese universities, there is even a Korean university in Japan. But this ethnic exclusiveness reduces the career prospects of Korean youths and therefore enrolment is rapidly decreasing. This example reminds us that education aimed at restoring ethnic identity without fostering integration is bound to fail.

Ethnic identity versus integration

A different case of ethnic education which is not conducive to integration was presented by Mary Somers Heidhues, who reported on Chinese education in Malaysia and Indonesia. The Chinese minorities in these countries are not underprivileged but rich and powerful with a strong sense of ethnic identity. In both countries Chinese education was more or less suppressed by the imposition of the respective national language as the medium of instruction. At an earlier stage the insistence on Mandarin as the medium of instruction in Chinese schools — a language which was not the idiom of most Chinese settled in Southeast Asia — had contributed significantly to ethnic solidarity and educational uniformity among those Chinese. The new educational policy favouring the 'sons of the soil' (Bumiputra in Malaysia, Pribumi in Indonesia) is more or less the same in both countries. Because of the relatively small size of the Chinese minority in Indonesia this policy has resulted in an almost total suppression of Chinese education there, but the large Chinese minority in Malaysia (about one-third of the population) has been able to resist more effectively. Nevertheless, Chinese education is now limited to primary schools and turns out to be a dead end as far as the further education of Chinese children is concerned.

The lessons which can be derived from the chapters by Toru Umakoshi and Mary Somers Heidhues are that an ethnic education which enhances segregation rather than integration handicaps the minority concerned. Systems of minority ethnic education can prevail only as long as the respective minority groups retain a privileged position and can afford to look down upon the majority. The imposition of a new educational policy by the majority causes resentment, of course, and is therefore not conducive to harmonious integration.

A rather successful example of minority integration was presented to us by Chaim Adler, who spoke about the education of Jewish immigrants from Asia and Africa in Israel. In this case integration was deeply desired by everybody concerned, but even what is deeply desired may not be easily achieved. The uplift of the underprivileged immigrants from Asia and Africa by means of an efficient educational system is, therefore, an achievement to be proud of. This kind of integration, however, was deemed inappropriate for Israel's Arab minority. The medium of instruction is a major obstacle, tying up the Arab minority in its own system of ethnic education. Chaim Adler rightly emphasized that it is almost impossible for an educational system to provide access to avenues which are blocked by insurmountable social and cultural obstacles. In terms of primary education, the Arabs are on par with the other Israelis, but further education is often not pursued and career prospects are dim. Rising expectations meet with growing frustration, creating a potentially very explosive situation.

The pitfalls of positive discrimination

A different kind of frustration was described by Uma Eleazu in his paper on federal endeavours to establish a balance of educational opportunities in Nigeria. Creating equal chances for education in the great variety of federal states of Nigeria is a tall order indeed, in view of the glaring regional disparities. Moreover, education is mostly managed by these states, and there are only a few federal institutions which are supposed to perform this miracle. So-called 'disadvantaged states' get certain reservations in federal institutions, but they often cannot fill the respective quotas because sufficiently qualified candidates are not available. Keeping the reserved seats vacant causes resentment among those who are not admitted and raises the question whether a disadvantaged majority can force an advanced minority to stand still while waiting for the less developed groups to catch up with it. Such attempts at 'positive discrimination' risk a loss of skills and a lowering of national performance. They may also lead to violent reactions by those who are bottled up in their present position. However, if achieving minorities are not restrained, disparities are bound to increase and frustrations will grow among the 'disadvantaged'.

The same dilemma of 'positive discrimination' was evoked by Suma Chitnis when she described India's efforts to bring about the educational integration of the underprivileged scheduled castes and tribes. Even earmarking scholarships and lowering entrance qualifications have often proved inadequate means of filling the places available in higher education and government service. In both the Nigerian and the Indian cases it is the grinding poverty of the 'disadvantaged' which prevents educational integration. As a mere cure for the symptoms, 'positive discrimination' does not provide an adequate therapy for the disease it is supposed to fight. But it is useful as a political alibi and therefore is retained even if everybody knows that it is of no avail. Moreover, 'positive discrimination' creates vested interests and cannot be easily withdrawn after it has been practised for some time. The lesson to be derived from these two cases is that 'positive discrimination' of an ascriptive kind, singling out specific groups and reserving quotas for them in educational and other institutions, should be avoided.

Another interesting aspect of the problem of minority integration was discussed by Dagmar Hellmann-Rajanayagam, who described the social distance between two Tamil minorities in Sri Lanka. Her paper showed that common ethnic origin and language do not necessarily establish a sense of identity, especially if there are great disparities in social structure and educational standards. The old, settled Tamil community of northern Sri Lanka, which was for a long time a relatively privileged minority due to its active interest in modern education, is figuratively as well as literally miles apart from the underprivileged and largely uneducated minority of the Tamil plantation labourers in the tea estates of the highlands. Social distance often implies mutual distrust. Plantation Tamils nowadays often resent Jaffna Tamil teachers and would like to have them replaced by other staff. They are also ready to learn Sinhalese and aspire to integration whereas Jaffna Tamils would fight against it.

When this paper was discussed at the workshop we learned about the art of breeding 'Tamil Tigers'. University admission had become the main battleground between the Sinhalese and the Jaffna Tamils. For a long time the Jaffna Tamils living in an arid zone had looked to education and government jobs for advancement whereas the Sinhalese who owned land could rely on income from agriculture or look to private enterprise as a source of employment. As competition increased the Sinhalese also coveted government jobs and tried to restrict the university admission of the Tamils. Thus bottled up, many of the young Tamils who were denied the places they felt they deserved turned into 'Tigers'.

Hispanics: ethnic identity and bilingual education

An interesting contrast to the dichotomy of the two Tamil minorities was provided by Isaura Santiago Santiago's papers on American Hispanics and their quest for bilingual education. Unlike Sri Lanka's Tamils the American Hispanics are not an ethnic minority as such: they come from a variety of countries. A composite Hispanic identity emerges only as a common reaction to the proverbial American 'melting pot' in terms of the quest for bilingualism. Moreover, Puerto Rico as an ancient Hispanic settlement and politically an integral part of the United States acts as a catalyst for Hispanic cultural identity and has a much stronger and more enduring influence than the distant cultural centres of earlier immigrants.

In this context bilingual education cannot be conceived of as a transitional remedial measure — as the American majority would like to see it — but must be admitted as a potentially permanent feature and a full programme of cultural education. It should not be regarded as a crutch on which an underprivileged minority limps into the melting pot. It was an eye-opener for all of us when Isaura Santiago told us that at present the chances of employment for Hispanic drop-outs are much higher than those for Hispanic high-school graduates. This problem needs further investigation, because if this is not just a passing phase education becomes dysfunctional and is a curse rather than the boon it is expected to be. If such a situation is not remedied in a constructive way the breeding of Hispanic 'Tigers' may progress in the United States along the lines of the Tamil Tigers in Sri Lanka.

The drop-out whom society makes no effort to integrate at all was the main subject of John Simon's paper which took us 'Beyond the educational system'. He attacked the indifference towards the education of minority children who are dumped into inferior schools meant only to keep them off the streets rather than to educate them. This kind of custodial arrangement can only breed frustration. He also argued that there is a great discrepancy between schooling and real life for most minority children, and he suggested that it may be easier to change society so that it conforms to an educational vision than to create an effective educational programme if it is in conflict with the realities of daily life.

The panel discussions

In addition to our discussions of these papers at the workshop we had two panel discussions, one on 'The minority dilemma: identity or integration?' and the other on 'Affirmative action in support of the underprivileged'. The first session began with a keynote piece (see Chapter 12) by Hans-Joachim Hoffmann-Nowotny, who has done a great deal of research on the integration of migrant workers in Switzerland. He presented a model of structural integration and cultural assimilation which neatly summed up many of the issues discussed in the workshop but also provoked spirited reactions. These reactions were mostly due to the fact that he had outlined the contrast of two Utopias — the moral Utopia of an open plural society which, according to his verdict, could not be established and the pragmatic Utopia of a laminated society — a kind of layer cake — in which there is limited social interaction as buffer zones of indifference shield the respective members from exposure. Originally only presented as a panellist's statement this contribution was subsequently submitted in a form which could be included in this volume. John Simon's second contribution originated as an oral rejoinder to it (see Chapter 13).

The panellists addressed themselves to the central question of whether integration necessarily implies a loss of identity. Ethnic schools which serve as a means of preserving ethnic identity not only impede integration, they prove to be a dead end as far as further education and career prospects are concerned. On the other hand, if ethnic identity is not respected by the educational system, it may soon disappear. Actually, an educational system may be enriched by respecting ethnic identity. Bilingual education could be an important element in this process. It would also provide international and inter-ethnic links.

In the panel discussion about affirmative action we agreed that this type of action must avoid the pitfalls of 'positive discrimination' which is not really affirmative. It was suggested that affirmative action should be based on a comprehensive concept of social change. There should be a revival of voluntary action and build-up of supportive structures in order to make affirmative action a success. The mechanical application of quotas and reservations neglects these important measures.

One may ask what kind of conclusions could be derived from our discussions. We certainly did not intend to formulate policy recommendations, but nevertheless some tentative suggestions could be offered. First of all we need to pay much more attention to the specific context of majority–minority relations. The privileged minority is obviously placed in a position which is very different from that of a historically deprived minority which cannot even get a foothold on the path of advancement. However, we cannot recommend negative measures which simply retard the progress of achieving minorities in order to let the disadvantaged catch up with them. Nor could we recommend measures of 'positive discrimination' which just aim at providing a limited number of opportunities for members of underprivileged minorities to get on equal terms with other members of the society. Such positions are usually captured by minorities within the minority and tend to create vested interests in ascriptive 'backwardness'.

I arrived at a few additional conclusions while listening to the proceedings of the workshop. Further efforts to improve the position of any disadvantaged group — whether minority or majority — should emphasize carefully designed remedial measures which are planned so as to take the total social context into consideration. 'Displaced objectives' — to use a term introduced by Uma Eleazu — are the most common pitfall of affirmative action or 'positive discrimination'. The German problem of educating its young Turkish residents must be seen in this light. The view expressed at our workshop was that a good bilingual education should be offered to increase their cognitive competence by initially strengthening their command of their own language and then enabling them to acquire a good grasp of German. This should be done irrespective of any considerations of remigration, as a contribution to the full development of their abilities. Germany will not become a fully fledged plural society; very few Germans will ever become fluent in Turkish. Therefore it would be an illusion to ask for Turkish language training for Germans as a parallel to German instruction for Turkish children. But Germans should definitely be able to respect bilingual citizens who contribute to a diversified if not a plural society.

This is one insight I felt we could derive from the discussions at the workshop as far as a solution of the immediate problem in Germany is concerned. It is much more difficult to outline general conclusions applicable to the world at large. More comparative international studies are required. We deliberately focused this workshop on the field of education because it is a most crucial arena of ethnic conflict and at the same time a field providing institutional remedies for conflict resolution. But from time to time in our discussions we noticed the limitations of these institutional remedies. Whenever education is expected to cope with problems which are beyond its reach, such as widespread poverty and extreme social inequality or deeply ingrained ethnic differentiation in terms of region, religion and language, political solutions must be found before educational measures are adopted. Otherwise the educational field just turns into an arena of political conflict and actually accentuates conflict by providing an institutional focus for it rather than contributing to its resolution.

2 THE SECOND GENERATION OF MIGRANT WORKERS IN GERMANY: THE TRANSITION FROM SCHOOL TO WORK

Ursula Mehrländer

This contribution examines the economic adaptation and occupational achievement of Turkish adolescents in the Federal Republic of Germany using the data from a survey of 430 Turkish adolescents and 380 fathers and mothers carried out in twenty-two German cities.[1]

Statistical overview

The government of the Federal Republic of Germany (FRG) during the 1960s entered into bilateral agreements regarding the recruitment of foreign workers with the Spanish, Greek, Turkish, Portuguese and Yugoslav governments. These agreements and the free movement of workers among European Community member states led to a large increase in the employment of foreign labour in Germany after 1961. By 1973, the number of immigrant workers reached 2.6 million, constituting 11.6 per cent of the German labour force.[2]

In 1973, the German federal government stopped all labour recruitment abroad. Consequently, the number of foreign workers declined to 1.7 million or 9 per cent of the labour force by 1983. Although the number of foreign workers declined, the total foreign residential population remained stable between 1974 and 1978, implying a shift in age and family structure as a result of an influx of dependants. By 1981, the foreign population reached 4.6 million, its highest level ever. By 1983 the number had declined slightly to 4.5 million.

This general pattern is reflected in the personal experience of many Turkish workers and their families. Most Turkish workers migrated between 1968 and 1973. In 1968 Turkish workers accounted for 12.8 per cent of the total number of foreign workers; by 1975 this figure had risen to 27.1 per cent. In 1978 there were just over 590,000 Turkish workers (not including non-working family members); by 1983 this figure had fallen to 533,000, representing roughly 32 per cent of all foreign workers.

The growth of the total Turkish population in the FRG is impressive, having more than quadrupled between 1968 and 1973. By 1974 it exceeded 1 million, and by 1982 one-third of the entire foreign population in the FRG was Turkish. This growth is attributable to an influx of family members as well as to the increasing number of Turkish children born in Germany. Immigration during the last few years has largely consisted of women and adolescents. About 60 per cent of all Turkish migrants who entered between 1976 and 1978 were under 18 years of age. The number of Turks under the age of 15 in the FRG increased from about 160,000 in 1973 to approximately 523,000 in 1983.[3]

Influence of school attendance in the FRG on Turkish adolescents' occupational status

After their migration to the FRG, Turkish adolescents became part of a large ethnic minority. Unlike workers of other nationalities, only 38 per cent of the Turkish fathers had arranged migration for their families by 1971. This time-lag either caused or intensified various social problems for the Turkish children as well as for German society.[4]

One factor for successful integration of Turkish children is their age of entry. If they are young enough to attend kindergarten, which facilitates their acquiring the German language, integration is likely. The admission of Turkish children with no or insufficient command of the German language to the lower grades of primary school is obviously easier than their admission to upper grades. Few Turkish dependants were brought to the FRG as very young children. Only 6 per cent of them were under the age of 6, and 17 per cent were between 6 and 10 years of age. A large number (43 per cent) were in the 15 to 25 age group so did not attend German kindergarten nor, for that matter, any school. In the long run, this lack of German schooling limits their chances of obtaining occupational training in the FRG. Table 2.1 relates young Turkish immigrants' school attendance in Germany to age at the time of immigration. For those who attended

Table 2.1 Turkish adolescents school attendance in the FRG according to age at time of immigration (per cent), $N = 430$

	Age at immigration					
	Under 16	6–9	10–14	15–19	20–25	Total
Attended school	100.0	97.2	81.9	24.4	24.0	60.7
Did not attend school	0	2.8	18.1	75.6	76.0	39.3

$X^2 = 186.43$ df = 4 $p < 0.0001$ $V = 0.66$ $C = 0.55$ Gamma = 0.87

Source: U. Mehrländer, *Türkische Jugendliche – keine beruflichen Chancen in Deutschland?* (Neue Gesellschaft, Bonn, 1983), Table 111, p. 127.

school in Germany, Table 2.2 relates duration of school attendance to command of the German language. Table 2.3 looks at the type of school attended and relates this to age at the time of immigration.

The German educational system has to be regarded as an institution for the allocation of occupational positions. Those Turkish adolescents who did not go to school in Germany are thus disadvantaged with regard to their occupational status in their first job. My survey confirms that the Turks who arrived as adolescents were only employed as unskilled or semi-skilled labourers in the FRG.[5] Among those who had attended school in Germany, however, about 30 per cent filled positions as skilled workers on their first job.

Table 2.3 Final school examination in the FRG according to age at time of immigration (per cent), $N = 209$

Final school examination (FRG)	Age				
	Under 6	6–9	10–14	15–25	Total
Did not complete *Hauptschule*	*	45.3	72.6	73.9	62.7
Completed *Hauptschule* (grades 9 and/or 10)		48.4	25.5	4.3	30.1
Completed *Realschule, Gymnasium*		6.3	1.9	21.7	7.2

* Number of cases < 30
$X^2 = 36.81$ df = 6 $p < 0.0001$ $V = 0.30$ $C = 0.39$ Gamma = −0.36
Source: U. Mehrländer, op. cit. in Table 2.1, Table 116, p. 131

Table 2.2 Influence of duration of school attendance in the FRG* on command of the German language (per cent), $N = 202$

Command of the German language	Duration of school attendance in the FRG (years)											Total
	Men					Women						
	1-2	3-4	5-6	7-8	9+	1-2	3-4	5-6	7-8	9+		
Very high, high	46.7	53.1	73.7	85.7	93.3	52.0	73.3	78.9	85.7	94.7		69.3
Average	46.7	46.9	26.3	14.3	6.7	32.0	20.0	21.1	14.3	5.3		27.2
Low, very low	6.7	0	0	0	0	16.0	6.7	0	0	0		3.5

$X^2 = 43.09$ df $= 18$ $p = 0.0008$ $V = 0.33$ $C = 0.42$ Gamma $= 0.36$

* in regular classes, together with German classmates

Source: U. Mehrländer, op. cit. in Table 2.1, Table 114, p. 130.

Table 2.4   Occupational status in 1980, according to final school examination in the FRG (per cent), $N = 104$

Occupational status	Final school examination			
	Did not complete Hauptschule	Completed Hauptschule	Completed Realschule, Gymnasium	Total
Unskilled and semi-skilled workers (lower lower class)	81.8	61.3	*	71.2
Skilled workers, un-skilled clerical employees, apprentices (upper lower class)	16.7	38.7		26.0
Qualified industrial, clerical and technical employees (lower middle class)	1.5	0		2.9

* Number of cases < 30.

$X^2 = 28.75$ df $= 4$ $p < 0.001$ $V = 0.37$ $C = 0.47$ Gamma $= 0.62$

Source: U. Mehrländer, op. cit. in Table 2.1, Table 120, p. 135

Occupational status in the FRG depends on the final school exmination (see Table 2.4). The higher the age of migrants at entry into the German school system, the lower the chance of passing the German final examination. In this context not only the duration of school attendance in Germany but above all attendance in classes with German students and additional measures such as German lessons or tutoring were of great importance. I would emphasize, however, that 60 per cent of the Turkish adolescents who passed a German final examination worked as unskilled or semi-skilled workers on their first job as a result of the unfavourable economic situation in the FRG in recent years and the consequent lack of opportunities for occupational training.

Factors influencing Turkish adolescents' occupational status

An examination of Turkish adolescents' occupational status in

Germany in 1980 indicates that 74 per cent held unskilled or semi-skilled jobs (see Table 2.5). Less than one-fifth of Germans of the same age had a similar occupational status. These contrasting statistics demonstrate that Turkish adolescents form a new level below the various strata of the German occupational system. Their low ranking is attributable to their status as migrants, their social background and inadequate schooling, these three factors being interdependent.

Most of the Turkish adolescents come from working-class families. Their fathers' low educational achievement and occupational status in Turkey is a key determinant in the children's attending *Hauptschule* (grades 5 to 9 of elementary school) in the FRG rather than the German *Gymnasium* (grades 5 to 13, leading to further academic education) or similar schools. Moreover, the adolescents' age at the time of entry to the FRG renders the switch from the *Hauptschule* to *Gymnasium* difficult. Yet, for certain occupations the final *Gymnasium*

Table 2.5 Comparison of Turkish and German adolescents (aged 15–25) by occupational status (per cent)

Status group*	Turks (1980)	Germans (1979)
Professional managerial employees, self-employed, higher civil servants, academic liberal professionals (upper, upper middle class)	0	5
Higher sales or technical employees, middle and high civil servants, non-academic liberal professionals (middle middle class)	2	20
Qualified industrial, clerical and technical employees (lower middle class)		
Skilled workers, lower civil servants (upper lower class)	24	53
Unskilled and semi-skilled workers (lower middle class)	74	18
Unpaid family workers and no answer	0	4

* In the case of the Turkish workers, the category 'skilled workers' includes apprentices.
Source: U. Mehrländer, op. cit. in Table 2.1, Table 30, p. 51.

Examination is mandatory. The social background, school attended and passing of the final examination determine the Turkish adolescents' opportunities for occupational training and their future social status.

Interestingly, no significant correlation can be found between the fathers' occupational status in the FRG and the type of school attended by their children. One explanation perhaps lies in certain discrepancies between the fathers' occupational classifications in Turkey and those in the FRG. A father's higher occupational status in 1980, however, determined higher expectations for the child's social status in the FRG.

Most Turkish families are very interested in their children's admittance to the German school system and expect their children to enter well-regarded occupations. Turkish families, however, cannot help their children with the German language as their own command of it is generally worse than the children's. They cannot help them with their homework either because in most instances they themselves have had only five years of elementary schooling in Turkey. Migrant parents also usually have little information concerning the relationship between the type of school attended and the choice of occupation or the different occupational training alternatives available.

Unemployment among Turkish adolescents

It is important to emphasize that 40 per cent of Turkish adolescents in the FRG questioned in 1980 were unemployed. The majority of these unemployed migrated when they were between 15 and 25 years old and thus did not attend school in the FRG (see Table 2.6). Those who entered the FRG between 1977 and 1979 were also affected by legal regulations unfavourable to foreigners' taking jobs or receiving occupational training. In general these adolescents have the chance to obtain a work permit only after two years of residence in the FRG. Only if they succeed in participating in a job-training course of at least half a year's duration do they have a chance of obtaining a work permit earlier. For those who migrated before 1977, the lack of appropriate education and a generally insufficient command of the German language prove to be serious barriers (see Tabl2 2.7). Owing the current unfavourable situation in the German job market with its rising unemployment, these adolescents will have great difficulty

Table 2.6 Correlation of school attendance in the FRG and unemployment (per cent), $N = 351$

Unemployment	Attended school	Did not attend school	Total
Unemployed	22.0	36.5	26.8
Not unemployed	65.7	56.5	62.7
No answer	12.3	7.0	10.5

$X^2 = 9.18$ df = 2 $p = 0.0102$ $V = 0.16$ $C = 0.16$
Source: U. Mehrländer, op. cit. in Table 2.1, Table 129, p. 144

finding employment. They can be expected to gain admittance only to the lower occupational categories as unskilled and semi-skilled workers.

Upward mobility rates

Intra-generational mobility is influenced by societal structures (regulations concerning foreigners, changes in the economic structure, and unfavourable economic circumstances such as high unemployment) as well as personal, subjective variables (such as mobility expectations).[6] These influences frequently overlap. My study finds that only 3 per cent of Turkish adolescents were able to rise from an unskilled or semi-skilled to a skilled or white-collar position between their first job in the FRG and 1980 by changing their place of

Table 2.7 Correlation of German language command and unemployment (per cent) $N = 351$

Unemployment	Command of German			
	Very high, high	Average	Very low, low	Total
Unemployed	19.0	23.7	65.2	26.8
Not unemployed	67.8	68.7	26.1	62.7
No answer	13.2	7.6	8.7	10.5

$X^2 = 43.52$ df = 4 $p < 0.0001$ $V = 0.25$ $C = 0.33$ Gamma = 0.38
Source: U. Mehrländer, op. cit. in Table 2.1, Table 130, p. 144

Table 2.8 Subjective judgement of intra-generational mobility according to sex and school attendance in the FRG (percentages), $N = 129$)

Judgement of individual situation	Men		Women		
	Attended school	Did not attend school	Attended school	Did not attend school	Total
Current job situation better than situation at time of entry into the labour force	36.4	45.7	52.0	42.9	43.4
Current job situation the same as at time of entry into labour force	34.1	30.4	44.0	21.4	33.3
Current job situation worse than at time of entry into the labour force	20.5	10.9	0	0	10.9
Undecided	9.1	13.0	4.0	35.7	12.4

$X^2 = 18.49$ df $= 9$ $p = 0.0299$ $V = 0.22$ $C = 0.35$
Source: U. Mehrländer, op. cit. in Table 2.1, Table 79, p. 94

employment. In these cases, upward mobility was limited to movement from the lower lower to the upper lower social class. This mobility holds true only for males aged 15 to 25 at time of entry into the FRG who had concluded their schooling and job training in Turkey. At the time their status was examined they had been living in the FRG for at least five years. However, 17 per cent of the young Turks were able to rise in job status within the firm where they were first employed.

Among those surveyed, 43 per cent declared that their employment conditions had improved since their first job in the FRG (see Table 2.8). Only 11 per cent spoke of declining conditions. It is interesting to note that those Turkish adolescents who pointed to a worsening in their occupational status tended to be those who attended school in the FRG. An examination of the occupational positions actually held by this group indicates that they occupied higher positions than those Turkish adolescents who had not gone to school in Germany. This result, which is important in understanding intra-generational mobility from the adolescents' point of view, can be interpreted as follows: the expectations concerning upward mobility among those Turkish adolescents who attended school in the FRG and were influenced by the values and norms of German society were higher than those among adolescents who had not gone to school in Germany. Social contacts with German classmates probably led to an adoption of the German peer group's values.

This analysis implies that Turkish adolescents' expectations increased with their growing integration into German society. These workers were sceptical about their occupational positions because they compared them to those of their German peers.[7] A similar development was shown to prevail among Italian adolescents.[8]

Indicators of Turkish adolescents' integration process

Owing to the uncertainty caused by the Aliens Act (*Ausländergesetz*) of 1965, many Turkish families still do not know how long they will be allowed to stay in Germany, notwithstanding the improvements concerning the permanent residence permit (*Aufenthaltsberechtigung*) that were introduced in 1978. Although in 1981 about 4 per cent of the Turks had been in Germany for eight years or more and had therefore met one of the prerequisites for the issuance of this kind of residence permit, only 0.3 per cent had obtained this 'permanent' resident status.[9]

The federal government's declaration that Germany is 'no country of immigration' encourages Turkish families to cling to the illusory goal of returning to their country of origin. In fact, 40 per cent of the Turkish adolescents interviewed stated a desire to return. The number of parents holding this view is equally high. As a prerequisite for return migration, however, Turkish families demand guarantees of jobs in Turkey paying salaries equivalent to those they are now earning in Germany. The percentage of returnees also drops rapidly when other family members elect to stay in the FRG. In most cases, in fact, no date of return can be specified.[10]

The percentage of girls aspiring to return is higher than that of boys, possibly because of migrant girls' greater isolation in German society. Those Turkish adolescents who live in predominantly ethnic neighbourhoods are less motivated to return than those living in neighbourhoods with primarily German population, probably because those young Turks who live in less segregated residential areas are to a greater degree confronted with the German population's prejudices and discrimination. The growing hostility toward foreigners as well as the resolutions encouraging them to return issued by the CDU–FDP government in 1983 have greatly disconcerted Turkish families in planning for their futures and reinforced their illusions about returning to Turkey.

One should recognize that the majority of Turkish adolescents have made a considerable effort to integrate. One indication of this process is that 43 per cent have a good or very good knowledge of German, which, in turn, depends on their school attendance in Germany. There is a high correlation between working in the FRG and fluency in German. For example, economically non-active Turkish girls and women generally have a deficient knowledge of German. Turkish adolescents' friendships with their German peers can be taken as another measure of integration. Two out of five adolescents questioned have German as well as Turkish friends. This percentage is highest among migrants with a low age of entry and thus extensive school attendance in Germany. When age at time of entry is controlled, young Turkish males more often have German friends than young Turkish females. Turkish girls are restricted in their use of leisure time by their parents. School attendance in the FRG facilitates the forming of friendships between Turkish and German girls. Forming of friendships with German adolescents is also facilitated when the young Turks take up employment. The majority of Turkish adolescents (70 per cent) want social contacts with young Germans, and one-third of the Turkish adolescents who have a job are members of a German trade union. Only 6 per cent of the young Turks aspire to naturalization, and 11 per cent are uncertain. Twice as many men as women desire German citizenship, and, independent of sex, those employed are more likely to aspire to naturalization than those who are economically non-active.

The migrant workers and their families have not caused Germany's housing and school problems, but with their arrival these problems became more visible, especially in the big cities where ghettos have developed. In sixteen districts of Frankfurt am Main there are more six-year-old foreigners than Germans,[11] exacerbating a fear of foreignization among the local German population. In addition, German parents are worried because of the number of foreign children attending the same class. Half of the German population can be considered as latently xenophobic,[12] and hostility toward foreigners is growing.

Politicians, sociopolitical groups such as trade unions and churches, as well as the institutions for adult education should provide leadership and assistance to counter these trends. Encouragement to return should not be emphasized since there will not be much remigration as long as the social and economic conditions in the sending countries remain relatively poor. No more than 14,000 foreigners applied for a return-bonus (payment offered to certain workers to leave Germany) in 1984 and left the country. Thus there appears to be no alternative but to integrate the foreign population into German society. This process of integration can be successful only if the foreign adolescents' admission to all branches of the German school and occupational systems is secured and special support provided. In the long run, it cannot be tolerated that almost an entire generation of foreign adolescents should hold only the lowest positions in the occupational pyramid.

Notes

1. U. Mehrländer, *Türkische Jugendliche – keine beruflichen Chancen in Deutschland?*, Neue Gesellschaft, Bonn, 1983.
2. U. Mehrländer, 'Federal Republic of Germany' in D. Kubat *et al.* (eds), *The Politics of Migration Policies*, Center for Migration Studies, New York, 1979, pp. 145–62.
3. Statistisches Bundesamt, *Wirtschaft und Statistik*, vol. 2, W. Kohlhammer, Stuttgart and Mainz, 1984, pp. 98–101.
4. U. Mehrländer, 'The "Human Resource" Problem in Europe: Migrant Labor in the Federal Republic of Germany' in J.P. Roche and U. Ra'anan (eds), *Ethnic Resurgence in Modern Democratic States*, Pergamon Press, New York, 1980, pp. 77–100.
5. Merhrländer, *Türkische Jugendliche*.
6. K.M. Bolte and H. Recker, 'Vertikale Mobilität' in R. König (ed.), *Handbuch der empirischen Sozialforschung*, Enke, Stuttgart, 1976, pp. 40–103.
7. U. Merhrländer, 'Turkish Youth – Occupational Opportunities in the Federal Republic of Germany', *Environment and Planning C: Government and Policy*, vol. 2 (1984), pp. 375–81.
8. U. Mehrländer, 'Integration Process of Second Generation Migrants: Results of an Empirical Study on Italian Youths in the Federal Republic of Germany' in H. Korte (ed.), *Cultural Identity and Structural Marginalization*, European Science Foundation, Strasbourg, 1982, pp. 109–16; U. Mehrländer, 'Career Aspirations of Native and Foreign Born: Federal Republic of Germany', *International Migration Review*, vol. 15 (1981), pp. 522–8; U. Mehrländer, *Einflussfaktoren auf das Bildungsverhalten ausländischer Jugendlicher*, Neue Gesellschaft, Bonn, 1978.

24　*Ursula Mehrländer*

9. Deutscher Bundestag, Drucksache 2/1629, Heger, Bonn, 1982.
10. U. Mehrländer *et al., Situation der ausländischen Arbeitnehmer und ihrer Familienangehörigen in der Bundesrepublik Deutschland,* Bundes-ministerium für Arbeit und Sozialordnung, Bonn, 1981.
11. U. Helmert, 'Konzentrations– und Segregationsprozesse der ausländischen Bevölkerung in Frankfurt a.M.' in H.-J. Hoffmann-Nowotny and K.O. Hondrich (eds), *Ausländer in der Bundesrepublik Deutschland und in der Schweiz,* Campus, Frankfurt am Main and New York, 1982.
12. D. Just and P.C. Mülhens, 'Ausländerzunahme: objektives Problem oder Einstellungsfrage?', *Das Parlament* (26 June 1982), pp. 35–8.

3 LANGUAGE TRAINING AND SOCIAL INTEGRATION OF MIGRANTS IN THE FEDERAL REPUBLIC OF GERMANY

Antje-Katrin Menk

I. 'Language training' defined

Though the constitution of the Federal Republic of Germany (FRG) states that nobody is to be discriminated against because of language, religion, etc., the country's only officially recognized language is German. This policy has never been questioned despite the presence of 4.5 million migrants speaking a language other than German. As a consequence, 'language learning' as a vehicle for social integration into German society means at present that migrants must learn German while the majority of the German population remains monolingual.

The languages spoken by the migrant populations play a negligible role in the education and cultural life of most Germans. Italian and Spanish are taught as foreign languages in a few German high schools; additionally, a few teachers, social workers and medical personnel are learning Turkish in order to deal more effectively with the Turkish minority. For most migrants, however, the ability to use their mother tongue does not open up special opportunities.

Some migrant children receive formal instruction in their native language at school. Others — depending on the laws of the federal state (*Land*) in which they live, the availability of teachers, and the number of children sharing the same language — never have that opportunity. The education policies of the *Länder* concerning the mother tongue of migrant children are bewildering to non-experts. They reflect the contradictions of migration policies whose objectives range from assimilation to repatriation. In general, the migrants' native language is given more attention in those *Länder* which consider the migration temporary. These schools stress the necessity of migrant children preserving their mother tongue in anticipation of their eventual return home. On the other hand those *Länder* which favour permanent integration follow a more assimilative policy. Such conflicting policies have severely handicapped the efforts of national groups, experts and teachers who have been calling for bilingual education in Germany.[1]

It should be kept in mind that the legal position of migrants in the FRG is weaker than the position of minorities in many other countries. Many migrants in Germany can be sent back to their countries of origin.[2] There is, in fact, a growing tendency towards a 'policy of return' based on the argument that migrants are 'too different' (and too many) to become integrated into German society.[3] The counter-position has largely been defensive: given a safer residential status, migrants would become more and better assimilated into the majority.[4] There has been almost no serious discussion of the idea of a multi-cultural Germany granting permanent resident status to members of non-German ethnic groups or accepting the permanent existence of cultures and languages other than German within German society.

II. Teaching German to migrants

As late as the mid-1970s, instruction in German as a foreign language was restricted to learners with considerable formal education (foreign students at universities and students at Goethe Institutes, for example). Teachers were not specially trained for this task. Although they needed some kind of academic degree, they usually learned their 'trade' through experience, receiving varying amounts of in-service training according to the practices of the institution where they were employed. By the late 1970s, however, courses of study had been created, and school administrations started to provide in-service training on a large scale. Such training usually encompassed learning something about the countries of origin of migrant groups as well as language-teaching methodology, German linguistics, and basic language instruction in Turkish or the native language of the migrant group to be taught.[5]

The growing number of migrants living in Germany by the early 1970s, however, created the need for a different kind of approach to teaching German as a second language. In many ways, the changing characteristics of the migrant population were also reflected in the development of course organization and the debates over aims, methodology and materials.[6] Although, initially, foreign learners came from different countries (such as Italy, Spain and Yugoslavia), the word 'foreigner' increasingly became a synonym for 'Turk'. The age groups receiving the greatest attention, also changed. Up to 1973–4 the learning problems of the fathers predominated: adolescents were at the centre of the debate from 1978–82; recently the discussion has begun to focus on migrant women and their language problems.

Different age groups among the migrants learn German in different institutions. Adults attend courses organized by sponsored institutions (*Träger*), children up to age 15 study at school, and older adolescents may do either or both.

Language courses for adults

The average German course for adults consists of sixty to eighty lessons. These courses are organized by a variety of sponsored institutions for adult education or benevolent societies. Most of the organizations belong to the *Sprachverband*, an association of language-teaching institutions founded in 1974 in Mainz, which finances courses and offers in-service training for teachers and produces learning materials.

The teachers working at these institutions, many of whom are students, are paid honoraria and receive ten days of in-service training per year. The language they teach is supposed to be standard spoken German. Although they provide students with a basic set of rules for speech production, however, the pronunciation and fossilized rules of *Gastarbeiter-Deutsch* (foreign worker's pidgin) are hard to correct.

These courses are open only to migrants. Nevertheless, different native languages, varied lengths of residence, contrasting levels of German proficiency, and unequal educational backgrounds result in considerable heterogeneity among the students. In general, this kind of adult education programme enables those who successfully complete it to deal a bit more effectively with everyday situations ('At the doctor', 'In a restaurant', 'At the station'). The courses, however, are most profitable for those already in a relatively favourable situation and those with fairly broad social contacts. They rarely open up opportunities for more extensive communication for migrants living in ghetto-type environments.[7]

The situation of migrant women who attend German language courses differs slightly from that of migrant men. Many of these women are prompted to begin studying by the irritation they feel when their children begin speaking German to each other in their presence. Others are sent by their husbands who, though still very traditional in their ways, find the task of handling all the necessary contacts with German society by themselves too demanding. In addition to holding down a job, many of these men have been doing the shopping, dealing with the authorities, the bank, the post office, taking their wives and children to the doctor, and so on. They find it a great relief when their wives know enough German to be able to do many of these chores independently. For these women, even a little knowledge of German often opens up a range of new experiences and contacts.

Teaching German to migrant children

Migrant children between 6 and 15 years of age have to attend regular schools just as German chidren do. Since the *Länder* are responsible for school administration, there are twelve different state laws regulating educational policy. The result is a bewildering tangle of circumstances affecting the education of migrant children, including the number of German children in the area, the number of foreign children with the same mother tongue, how many foreign and German teachers are available, and political attitudes of the respective school administrations.

The results, as far as learning German is concerned, are uneven and often unsatisfactory:

1. There are a considerable number of migrant children in Germany who, during their schooling, have no contact at all with German children. They learn German as a foreign language and are exposed to it as a medium of instruction (depending on the teachers teaching them), but they do not use it as a means of communication.[8]
2. A significant number of migrant children live in areas where there are few migrants.[9] These children are typically placed in regular classes with German children and get little or no additional help. Theoretically speaking they have the opportunity to make friends with German children and learn the spoken language, but in practice this does not necessarily happen. In fact, these children rarely acquire written standard and academic German without additional help.

3. A third group consists of children assigned to special learning groups for a certain part of their schooling (usually two to three years) so they can receive more or less systematic and concentrated German instruction.

A migrant child under good circumstances gets a systematic German course of about 300–400 lessons. In addition he or she might receive remedial help in other subjects. The average result is a good knowledge of spoken German, depending, among other variables, on opportunities for communication with peers and the age at which the student begins the course.

The German thus learned can be characterized formally as comprising approximately 2,000 words and the basics for structuring simple German sentences. Many teachers, especially those with no experience in language teaching, would classify children at this level as fluent and not needing additional remedial help. The children rate themselves in the same way. They seem to feel that the ability to communicate with Germans in everyday situations satisfies their need to develop their German language skills.

The majority of migrant children, however, including those with a functional conversational knowledge of German, cannot understand or use the academic language that constitutes the medium of instruction in higher education. As long as the migrant child does not reach a higher level of secondary education (*Realschule* or *Gymnasium*) these deficits are likely to remain undiscovered. Expectations at the lowest level of schooling (*Hauptschule*) are so low that about 50 per cent of the migrant children pass the final examination. Students attending any other type of school will need further help (two or three years) in the language in order to deal with the various academic subjects. The estimated vocabulary necessary for the *Abitur* (final examination of the highest level of secondary education) is a passive command of 20–30,000 words plus the structures of written standard German.

Considering the difficulty adolescents have in securing apprenticeships in Germany, a diploma higher than *Hauptschulabschluss* is virtually a prerequisite for a migrant child seeking such a formation. The only alternative is placement through one of the few special programmes designed to give migrant children the necessary qualifications.

In short, the level of German migrant children are likely to acquire from the better schooling opportunities available to them suffices for a *Hauptschulabschluss* and is sufficient to deal with Germans in everyday situations. It does not suffice, however, to succeed in higher levels of secondary education (*Realschule* or *Gymnasium*) and very likely does not suffice to complete a qualified formation (if one is lucky enough to get a place as an apprentice).

Adolescents

The political situation in Turkey towards the end of the 1970s caused a large number of Turkish adolescents to migrate to the FRG.[10] They created new problems for schools and administrations still struggling with the question of what to do with the younger migrant children in their charge. The adolescents arriving between 1978 and 1980 we called *Seiteneinsteiger* (literally 'those boarding the train while it is on its way'). This term implied that they were disturbing the order of things and that the correct way to enter the German school system was to start with kindergarten or at least primary school.

The *Seiteneinsteiger* consist of two very different groups. There had always been poorly educated adolescents immigrating at an age when they were allowed to work. The new arrivals, however, had completed high school or had left Turkey shortly before graduation.

The appearance of these well-schooled migrant adolescents brought to light various deficiencies in the German school system:

1. The majority of migrant children were placed in *Hauptschule* (the lowest level of secondary education, terminating in most *Länder* at the age of 15). The higher levels of secondary education (*Realschule* or *Gymnasium*) had not managed to integrate migrant children with language difficulties. There was no place for *Seiteneinsteiger* who were 16 or older.
2. The vocational schools (*Berufsschulen*) were unable to integrate the *Seiteneinsteiger* except into those classes designed for weak learners, drop-outs, or adolescents with cognitive and/or emotional maladjustments. As a result, large numbers of *Seiteneinsteiger* ended up in special classes (*Berufsvorbereitungsjahr* or *Ausbildungsvorbereitungsjahr*, depending on the state) for German adolescents with learning difficulties. Students in these classes concentrate on practical subjects (such as metalwork and domestic science) and spend comparatively little time on academic subjects. At best 400 lessons of German as a foreign language are included for migrant students.

3. Sponsored institutions created a programme called MBSE (*Massnahme zur beruflichen und sozialen Eingliederung ausländischer Jugendlicher*) for migrant drop-outs. MBSE developed into a refuge for *Seiteneinsteiger*. Like the vocational school curriculum, this programme consists primarily of practical training with a small amount of general education. German instruction is limited to 200–250 lessons per year.

Critics argue that *Berufsvorbereitungsjahr* and MBSE are like schools for handicapped learners where German as a foreign language has taken the place of 'basket weaving'.[11] They imply that adolescents attending these types of school are treated as having deficits which render them incapable of learning a normal trade or rising above the status of unskilled worker. The language proficiency of those completing MBSE or *Berufsvorbereitungsjahr* is fairly low. Since apprenticeships are hard to find, only a few migrant adolescents get adequate vocational training (10 per cent of 15–20-year-olds in 1982). A small number of migrant adolescents (about 2,000) receive vocational training through special federal programmes (*Benachteiligtenprogramm* and *Modellversuche des Bundesinstituts für Berufsbildung*).

Those projects in which many *Seiteneinsteiger* take part have produced some interesting findings. Many *Seiteneinsteiger* suffer initially from language difficulties, but if they get continuous training they learn at a much faster rate than their peers who have been in the German school system for years. They acquire a more systematic command of German, they are more proficient in mathematics, and they develop better learning techniques. Though their migrant peers who entered German schools at an earlier age speak better conversational German, the *Seiteneinsteiger* have fewer reading problems and acquire a better knowledge of the academic language. In general, they are also more successful in the vocational training programmes.[12]

From the psycholinguistic point of view,[13] a foreign academic language is acquired more effectively by students who have mastered academic language skills in their mother tongue. Consequently the great number of migrant children in non-ghetto areas who do not receive adequate instruction in their own mother tongue have difficulties in expanding their German beyond a certain communicative level into what is called cognitive academic language proficiency.

Another possible explanation, however, is that migrant children in German schools simply have no access to teaching adequate to their capabilities. They are minority children thrown together with underprivileged or handicapped German children into learning situations where effective teaching is often impossible.

On the other hand those *Seiteneinsteiger* who attended school up to the point of migration may have had to learn under less favourable material conditions at home, but their cognitive capabilities could still develop better than under the learning conditions prevalent in the German *Hauptschule*. Thus they are generally able to compensate for initial language difficulties at the time of migration and are more successful during their vocational training than migrant children who finish the *Hauptschule* in Germany.

III.   The German majority and the German proficiency of migrants

Most migrants under present conditions can acquire only a very limited command of the German language. Yet a certain proficiency in German is necessary for integration into the neighbourhood, better schools, vocational training, and so on. Even those among the German majority who are well-disposed towards foreigners feel that the migrants must learn German in order to become integrated. Knowledge of German is used as a measuring stick to determine the degree to which migrants try to be 'like us' and whether they deserve further assistance.

Though I am convinced that proficiency in German is important in the integration of migrants, I cannot overlook the way in which judgements about supposed language proficiency are used to legitimate decisions which are actually taken for quite different reasons. The following examples illustrate how language issues are used to justify policies or practices based, in reality, on other considerations.

1. I participate in a project to prepare Turkish girls for apprenticeships as doctors', lawyers', or pharmacists' assistants. One of our tasks was to find placements as apprentices for twenty girls. Since the jobs in question demand considerable clerical skills, we made enormous efforts to improve their German as much as possible during the preparation year. When the time came for the girls to

apply for the jobs we selected them according to their German proficiency (especially their academic German) and sent them to prospective employers.

All the prospective employers had said they would only take a girl with fluent German. Having made a choice every employer justified it by saying 'her German was the best'. But the selections that were made were bewildering to both teachers and girls alike. Despite their claims, employers rarely chose 'the best according to language'. Instead they chose the most beautiful and charming girls and justified their choices with the language argument.

2. The Senate of Berlin decided that when migrant children with language problems account for 30 per cent or more of the students in an integrated class, an unacceptable situation is created. If the number of migrants reaches or exceeds this level, special classes are to be formed. To justify the necessary selection, a German language test (*projektives linguistisches Analyseverfahren*) has been devised.[14] This test, which has been criticized by many experts, is not based on the specific level of German proficiency a migrant child should reach in order to be integrated into regular classes. Rather it permits a flexible selection and placement process based on the particular situation in each district, thus revealing that the alleged interests of the German majority children are what matter most and not the German language proficiency of the migrant youngsters.

3. Judgements about language proficiency have been used since 1978 to decide whether an adult migrant who has fulfilled all other necessary conditions (proof of adequate housing, an employment contract, at least eight years' residence, and so on) should be granted a safer residence status (*Aufenthaltsberechtigung*). The applicant's proficiency in German, in this case, is judged by the employees of the local police administration. They rely heavily on dictations with varying criteria of evaluation. As the language courses offered to migrants centre on spoken language and many of the women taking these courses are illiterate, this method of examination is clearly inadequate. Furthermore, the evaluation of these dictations is subject to use by the authorities as an instrument for increasing or reducing the number of permits issued in accordance with the policy of the local government with respect to migrant settlement.

4. The Ministry of Interior plans to lower the maximum immigration age of migrant children from sixteen to six to enable them 'to make

full use of the German school system'. Schools, once again, are considered the main instruments of integration. An alternative being considered is that children may immigrate beyond that age if they already have adequate knowledge of German. Here the language argument is used to limit immigration. Previous experience with the *Seiteneinsteiger* shows that this restriction will force migrant children into the dead-end *Hauptschule* track or keep them out of Germany. The government, meanwhile, will continue to argue that these policies are being carried out in 'the best interest of the child'.[15]

In summary, judgements about language proficiency *can* be used as an effective instrument of discrimination. They help the German majority to allocate the inadequate opportunities for integration which are available without ever raising the question of whether the number should be increased. At the same time they maintain the illusion that it is possible for the individual migrant to do better, to improve, and finally to grab at a better chance for integration.

Notes

1. See Tove Skutnabb-Kangas, 'Gastarbeiter oder Immigrant — verschiedene Arten, eine Unterschicht zu reproduzieren', *Deutsch lernen*, no. 1 (1982), pp. 59–80.
2. From the legal point of view the residential status of about 1 million migrants is not 'safe' — see Gert Hammar, 'Handlungsspielraum deutscher Ausländerpolitik' in Heiner Geissler (ed.), *Ausländer in Deutschland — für eine gemeinsame Zukunft*, vol. 1. Munich, 1982, pp. 148–55.
3. See Georg Auernheimer, *Handwörterbuch Ausländerarbeit*, Weinheim, 1984, pp. 65–70.
4. Ibid., pp. 66, 67.
5. See Hans H. Reich, 'Deutschlehrer für Gastarbeiterkinder: Eine Übersicht über Ausbildungsmöglichkeiten in der Bundesrepublik', *Deutsch lernen*, no. 3 (1979), pp. 3–14.
6. See Chapter 2 of this book.
7. See Hans Barkowski *et al.*, *Handbuch für den Deutschunterricht mit ausländischen Arbeitern*, Königstein/Ts., 1980.
8. See Ursula Boos-Nünning, 'Muttersprachliche Klassen für ausländische Kinder: Eine kritische Diskussion des bayerischen "offenen Modells" ', *Deutsch lernen*, no. 2 (1981), pp. 40–70.
9. See Michael Damanakis, 'Ausländische Schüler in Streugebieten', *Deutsch lernen*, no. 1 (1984), pp. 47–9.

10. See Chapter 2 of this book.
11. See Rudolf Hoberg (ed.), *Sprachprobleme ausländischer Jugendlicher. Aufgaben der beruflichen Bildung*, Frankfurt, 1983.
12. See Gerda Krüger and Antje-Katrin Menk, 'Fachbericht 1983 über den Verlauf des Projektes. Ausbildung türkischer Mädchen zu Gehilfinnen in medizinischen und juristischen Berufen' (mimeo), Bremen, 1984.
13. See J. Cummins, *Cognitive/Academic Language Proficiency, Linguistic Interdependence, the Optimum Age Question and Some Other Matters*, Working Papers on Bilingualism no. 19, Toronto, 1979.
14. See Gisela Bruche-Schulz *et al.*, 'Sprachstandserhebungen im Grundschulalter' (mimeo), Der Senator für Schulwesen, Jugend und Sport, Berlin, 1983.
15. See Der Bundesminister des Innern, *Bericht der Kommission 'Ausländerpolitik'*, Bonn, 1983.

4 THE EDUCATION OF KOREAN CHILDREN IN JAPAN

Toru Umakoshi

Korean residents in Japan

Korean residents in Japan numbered 663,631 in 1980. This figure represents only 0.5 per cent of the total population of Japan but 86 per cent of all foreign residents. Korean residents live primarily in major (industrial) cities such as Tokyo, Osaka, Kyoto, Kobe, Nagoya and Fukuoka, with 28 per cent (186,000) concentrated in Osaka.

Over 90 per cent of all Korean residents originally came from the southern coastal areas of Korea. The great majority of them were brought to Japan between 1910 and 1945 as forced labourers during the Japanese occupation of Korea. Only a very small number of Koreans entered Japan after the Second World War. But this first generation now constitutes only 25 per cent of the total Korean resident population with the remainder being Japanese born. There is, in other words, a transition from the first to the second and third generations taking place in the composition of the Korean minority.

Several indications of generational change with respect to assimilation are worth noting. One of these is the increase in intermarriage between Korean residents and Japanese citizens, particularly Korean women and Japanese men. During the past twenty years (1960–80) the intermarriage rate for Koreans living in Japan increased from 34.7 per cent to 56.7 per cent.

The majority of Korean residents consider themselves permanent residents of Japan. They do not want to be repatriated. Moreover, as most of them have never lived in Korea, their ethnic values and identity are gradually weakening, and assimilation is taking place. Under these circumstances, the schools, both Japanese and Korean, will have a central role to play if this fading ethnicity is to be revived.

Ethnicity in the home

From the viewpoint of the maintenance and revival of Korean ethnicity, what happens in the home is in a sense much more important than what is taught at school. Home life is central to the preservation of ethnic identification through the maintenance of customs, language, eating habits and basic family values.

It is of interest to examine the kind of educational function the home is serving in this era of assimilation. In the case of language, a recent survey carried out in the Osaka area among Korean residents (Hong and Nakashima 1980) showed that 96 per cent of the families surveyed used Japanese exclusively, 5.3 per cent used both Korean and Japanese equally and only 0.4 per cent used exclusively Korean at home. In addition 77.3 per cent of the persons interviewed said that they could not understand Korean at all, 18.7 per cent responded that they could understand a little and only 2.6 per cent said that they were completely fluent.

Although the family normally has an important role in carrying on the language tradition, this role has been considerably weakened among Koreans in contemporary Japanese society. During a recent interview I learned that even the principal of the Hiroshima Chosoren Ethnic Korean School (North Korean affiliated) generally converses in his own home in Japanese. The only time Korean is spoken is on holidays such as New Year when the children give ceremonial greetings to their elderly relatives as part of the celebration.

Another significant change can be seen in the dress and eating habits of Korean residents. Young Koreans have come to prefer Japanese and Western dishes to the more traditional Korean foods, and while most women have a traditional *chogori-chima*, they very seldom wear it except on rare festive occasions. As for men, it would be almost impossible to find one who owns a *trumagi*. These trends are not so surprising since young Japanese have also come to prefer Western foods and very seldom wear such traditional garments as the *kimono* or *haori hakama*. Nevertheless, these changes are another indication that Korean ethnicity is gradually losing out to modernization and assimilation.

38   Toru Umakoshi

The role of schools

School-age children of Korean residents numbered approximately 130,000 in 1978. The schools they attend can be divided broadly into two categories. One includes public and private Japanese schools, where more than three-quarters of Korean children are enrolled. The other consists of Korean ethnic schools, which are operated with the support of Chosoren (Federation of Korean Residents in Japan, affiliated with the Democratic People's Republic of Korea) and Mindan (Association of Korean Residents in Japan, affiliated with the Republic of Korea). Thee Korean ethnic schools serve a significant but much smaller number of Korean children.

Chosoren has a unified school system of ethnic education, ranging from elementary to higher education. Its elementary and secondary schools have been established in twenty-nine prefectures. A great majority of the Korean ethnic schools are Chosoren-affiliated (eighty-six elementary schools, fifty-five junior high schools, eleven senior high schools and a university) and their students account for 21.8 per cent of all school-aged Korean children in Japan. Only a very small fraction (1 per cent or 1,361) of all school-aged Korean children in Japan belong to Mindan-affiliated schools (one kindergarten, three elementary schools, four junior high schools and four high schools). These schools are all located in Tokyo, Osaka and Kyoto.

Table 4.1   Enrolment in Korean ethnic schools (1960–78)

	Mindan-affiliated		Chosoren-affiliated	
	Schools	Students	Schools	Students
1960	11	1,806	371	46,294
1968	12*	2,139*	179	34,388
1978	12	1,361	153	28,298

* 1970 figures
Source: Zainichi Doho (Korean Residents in Japan), 2 (1980), pp. 51, 77.

As can be seen in Table 4.1, enrolment in both Chosoren- and Mindan-affiliated schools is decreasing year by year. Chosoren-affiliated schools have experienced a drastic decline in enrolment, from 46,294 in 1960 to 28,298 in 1978. Mindan-affiliated schools have failed to attract Korean students even though Mindan has had a political advantage over Chosoren due to the enactment of the Japan–Republic of Korea (ROK) Treaty in 1965. It is not likely that enrolment in Korean ethnic schools will increase in the future.

Ethnic education in Japanese schools

The Japanese Ministry of Education, Science and Culture has taken the position that educational opportunities for Korean children in Japan should be equal to those of Japanese children. This decree is based on the Japan–ROK Treaty of 1965. However, Chosoren and Mindan have criticized this principle of equality in education as an assimilation policy devoid of respect for Korean ethnicity. There are surely very few Japanese schools in either the public or private sector providing ethnic education for Korean children.

Regardless of this criticism, the proportion of Korean children attending Japanese schools — now 77.2 per cent — is constantly rising. A recent opinion survey attempted to find out the main reasons why Korean parents send their children to Japanese schools. Results of the survey (Hong and Nakashima 1980) are as follows:

Because we live in Japanese society 77.6%
Facilitates entering colleges and universities 32.6%
Dissatisfied with the curriculum of Korean ethnic school 31.4%
Advantages for employment 26.3%
Economical 22.1%
Ethnic identity has already been established 17.5%
No access to a Korean ethnic school 4.4%
Other 4.5%

The main reasons why Korean parents prefer Japanese schools are related to their understanding of the realities of being permanent residents in Japan. In the above-mentioned survey one-third of the Korean parents questioned expressed dissatisfaction with the curriculum of Korean ethnic schools exclusively devoted to Korean ethnicity and political identification.

Once Korean students enter Japanese schools, one of the big problems they face is whether or not to use their Korean names. In Yokohama only 10.7 per cent of the Korean junior high school students and 8.0 per cent of the elementary school pupils were reported to be using their Korean names in 1980 despite efforts of the board of education to encourage Korean parents to register their children under their Korean names as part of the ethnic education movement. Osaka showed a somewhat higher percentage (24.4 per cent) of students using Korean names than in neighbouring Toyonaka (7.7 per cent) and Amagasaki (4.4 per cent). Generally Korean parents who send their children to Japanese school attempt to hide their Korean ethnicity in order to avoid prejudice.

If Korean children do not use their Korean names, it is not possible to distinguish them from Japanese children, because the speech of Korean resident children is indistinguishable from that of Japanese children and there are very few physical differences between Koreans and Japanese.

During the past twenty years the public elementary schools in Osaka, Nagoya and Fukuoka — all cities with large Korean populations — have established supplementary 'ethnic education classes' (known as *minzoku gakkyu*) for Korean children. These ethnic education classes in twenty-eight public elementary schools in the three cities provide 1,317 Korean children two to four hours' instruction per week in Korean history and geography, an introductory course in the Korean language and traditional music. All the subjects are taught in Japanese by Korean teachers on a part-time basis with the cooperation of Japanese teachers. Although Korean parents are encouraged to enrol their children in the ethnic education programme, the attendance rate in Osaka and Fukuoka is not particularly high. As shown in Table 4.2, only half the Korean children are enrolled in the ethnic education classes in spite of the movement to promote ethnic education by the board of education and teachers concerned with ethnic education. One reason for this low attendance is teachers' insistence that children should use their Korean names in the class. A gap seems to exist between what teachers consider theoretically correct and the emotions of the parents of Korean children where ethnic education and their children's social identities are concerned.

At the secondary level, a majority of Korean students have no chance to participate in ethnic education classes. Even in Osaka there are no public junior high schools which provide ethnic classes. In senior high schools we can find a movement to create clubs for Korean students known as *chobunken* (Korean culture study clubs) as an extra-curricular activity after school. Usually club members meet once a week to study conversational Korean, Korean history and geography, and to discuss minority problems. It is reported that approximately 10 per cent of the 212 senior high schools in Hyogo

Table 4.2 Enrolment of Korean children in 'ethnic education classes' in public elementary schools (1977)

Area	Number of schools with ethnic classes	Total number of Korean pupils (A)	Number of Koreans attending ethnic class (B)	(B) (A) %
Osaka City	7	1,204	514	42.7
Fukuoka City	3	159	86	54.1

Source: Zainicho Doho (Korean Residents in Japan), 2 (1980), p. 58.

prefecture have such clubs. But senior high schools with these clubs tend to be mostly vocation-oriented and not ranked highly on the academic scale. In the academic-oriented senior high schools where concentration on preparation for university entrance examinations takes precedence over club activities, neither students nor teachers are particularly eager to engage in club activities for ethnic education.

Korean ethnic schools

Chosoren-affiliated schools
Because of the political split between South and North Korea, Korean residents in Japan have been divided into two groups, Chosoren and Mindan. Korean ethnic schools are also divided in this way, each group receiving subsidies from its respective sponsoring government. Unfortunately, very few politically non-aligned Korean ethnic schools have survived.

The Chosoren-affiliated schools, as a general rule, offer a systematic ethnic education from elementary to secondary school. There is even a Chosoren-affiliated university (Chosen University). These schools are explicitly designed to support North Korean government ideals and the goal of unification of Korea under northern leadership. They are located in all parts of Japan so that many Korean residents can send their children to them, and they receive an endowment of approximately 50 per cent from the North Korean government. Curricula and textbooks are closely patterned on North Korean educational principles.

Korean is the language of instruction for all subjects in the Chosoren-affiliated schools. Teachers are recruited mainly from graduates of Chosen University. In ethnic schools all students have to use Korean names, and female students must wear a *chogori-chima-* style uniform. The instruction, needles to say, emphasizes Korean ethnic subjects such as the Korean language, Korean geography and Korean history, which are taught in strict accordance with the political guidelines of North Korea (DPRK). The flag of the DPRK is prominently displayed, as are pictures of Kim Il-Song. These are important symbols of allegiance in the schools.

A great majority of the families of the students attending these schools belong to Chosoren. Korean parents who belong to Chosoren are strongly recommended to send their children to the Federation's ethnic schools. However, a decline in enrolment has recently been reported. One of the reasons why many parents have become reluctant to send their children to ethnic schools is that many of them are not interested in being repatriated and just want their children to grow up and make a good living in Japan. Second- and third-generation Korean residents want their children to improve their Japanese language ability and practical skills for working in Japan rather than follow a politically-oriented ethnic curriculum. They consider it a serious problem, for example, that Japanese language is taught only three hours a week as a foreign language (similar to instruction in English or Russian) at the ethnic secondary schools.

Another problem is the difficulty Korean ethnic school graduates experience when seeking to enter or transfer into Japanese higher educational institutions because their schools have not been accredited as 'legal school corporations' by the Japanese Ministry of Education, Science and Culture. The graduates of Chosoren-affiliated senior high schools can not apply for Japanese public and national university places unless they pass the qualification examination for entering a university in advance.

These restrictions should be eased after the standards of the Chosoren-affiliated schools have been fairly evaluated and consultations between Chosoren representatives and Japanese university authorities have taken place. Reportedly some private universities have already opened their doors to the graduates of Chosoren-affiliated senior high schools.

Mindan-affiliated schools

As previously noted, Mindan-affiliated schools are very limited in number. Enrolment in these schools accounts for only 1 per cent of all school-aged Korean children even though 60 per cent of the Korean residents of Japan have joined Mindan during the past fifteen years. Despite the rapid economic growth of South Korea (ROK), financial support for Mindan-affiliated schools from the South Korean government is very small compared to that received by the Chosoren-affiliated schools from the government of North Korea (DPRK).

Unlike the Chosoren-affiliated schools, Mindan schools use Japanese as the principal language of instruction, and their curriculum is based on guidelines from the Japanese Ministry of Education, Science and Culture. Only ethnic subjects such as Korean and Korean history and culture are taught using both Korean and Japanese. Textbooks in these ethnic subjects come directly from the Korean Ministry of Education. In comparison to the normal course load, these ethnic subjects represent a relatively small part of the curriculum, varying from 11.8 per cent to 23.7 per cent.

One of the problems the Mindan-affiliated schools face is a decline in enrolment. It is very hard to hold back this trend, however, because the parents of Mindan members are not under direct pressure to make their children attend Mindan-affiliated schools.

Under these circumstances the educational focus of Mindan has shifted from managing these full-time ethnic schools to providing a part-time ethnic education for adult residents. A programme called '50 Hours of Ethnic Education' started in the Nagoya branch of Mindan in 1975, has spread all over the country. This course provides lectures and workshops on the Korean language, Korean history, traditional culture and music in cooperation with a cultural attaché from the Republic of Korea. Approximately 9,000 Korean residents attended this course in 1979.

Barriers to employment

Young Koreans in Japan face bitter discrimination and resulting frustration upon graduation from school. Graduates of the ethnic Korean schools are not qualified to take entrance examinations for Japanese colleges and universities because their schools are not legally recognized as formal educational institutions as prescribed by the School Education Law. The Korean schools have been classified as 'miscellaneous schools' along with such institutions as barber and cookery schools. As a result of this policy, young Koreans are turning away from these schools and entering Japanese schools.

The educational achievement of Korean students has little bearing upon their success or failure in seeking employment. In contrast, the overall employment situation has great influence on their chances of being employed, with Koreans always given low priority in comparison to Japanese students. When these young Koreans become aware of the overt and covert discrimination against them in the working world, they lose their dreams and hopes for more distinguished careers. As a general rule many Japanese *zaibatsu* (large corporations or conglomerates) are not willing to recruit Korean graduates. Even if they are successful in getting entry-level positions in such companies, however, Koreans' chances for managerial posts or promotions are not very good.

The Hitachi case is one well-known example of job discrimination against Koreans in Japan. In 1974, a Korean youth (Park Jong Sok), using his Japanese name (Arai Shoji), was hired by Hitachi, a highly prestigious corporation, on the basis of high scores on his employment examination and good record. His employment was terminated, however, when personnel officials discovered that he was Korean on examining his family register. He prosecuted Hitachi and finally won the case. Since that time a number of Japanese companies, beginning with local banks, have begun to hire limited numbers of Korean graduates.

Even though the Constitution does not explicitly discriminate against foreign residents, Japanese law has been interpreted as prohibiting foreigners from taking positions in national and local governments, many public corporations, public schools and even national universities. In the case of schools and universities, foreigners have been hired but not on equal legal status with Japanese. The reason for this interpretation of the Constitution was linked with the definition of a civil servant (teachers in government-related schools are considered civil servants) as one who formulates and carries out national and local policy. Hence barriers to the employment of Korean residents have been erected and maintained by the government itself.

The professions of lawyer, patent attorney and pilot have also been exclusively held by Japanese nationals. An illustrative case is that of Kim Kyong Dok, who passed the bar exam for entrance to the Judicial Training Institute. He was not admitted due to his Korean resident status. He refused to change his citizenship to Japanese and openly criticized the system. Finally, under strong pressure from Korean and Japanese groups, the Supreme Court admitted him as an exception.

A few Korean residents who graduated from Japanese universities have recently taken teaching positions at elementary and junior high schools in the Osaka and Kanagawa areas. Due to variation in local and prefectural laws, however, there are still many prefectures which do not allow foreign residents to become teachers. Private schools and universities have had full-time tenured foreign faculty members on their staffs for many years, but national and public universities until 1982 did not give foreign staff equal treatment as government employees. In 1982 a law was passed stipulating that foreign persons could take equal government-employee status and from 1982 to February 1984 fifteen foreign scholars took full-time staff positions. Of these fifteen, four have been Korean residents. At the legal level, discrimination seems to be lessening, but in society deep-rooted prejudice still remains in the form of lack of promotion for Korean residents and the difficulty in getting supervisory or managerial posts.

Many Korean residents, despite being university graduates, face so many barriers that they eventually return to traditional family busineses, ending up as *packinko* hall owners, bar owners, restaurant managers, etc. Almost all of the ethnic school graduates, owing to difficulty in gaining employment outside the Korean resident world, remain within it or eventually return to it to help with family businesses.

Conclusion

The future of education for Korean children in Japan needs to be considered from two perspectives: one is the changing values of Korean residents, and the other is how to improve Japanese attitudes towards Korean residents.

First of all, in the Korean community some conflict and ambiguity exists between individual families and Korean organizations such as Mindan and Chosoren over how to handle the question of ethnicity. As a general rule, Korean residents are losing their ethnicity with regard to eating habits, dress and language. Leaders of the two groups stress a revival of ethnicity and insist on education as one way of promoting it, but this emphasis has a limited impact as only about 20 per cent of Korean youth atend Korean schools where their original language is taught.

Judging from the gradual loss of Korean ethnicity in clothing, food, traditional celebrations and a rise in the intermarriage rate, the process of assimilation can be expected to continue in the future. These assimilative tendencies can not be ignored by Korean organizations when they formulate future policies. To counteract the so-called 'trend away from Korean ethnic schools', Korean ethnic schools should upgrade their legal status from that of 'miscellaneous school' to 'juridical school corporation' in order to attract more young Koreans. Reorganization must also be accompanied by curriculum revision to enable the graduates of Korean schools to gain access to Japanese colleges and universities.

From the Japanese side of the issue, Japanese society should open the door to Koreans in terms of administrative rights, educational opportunities and employment. The Japanese public should realize that Japanese society itself will be enriched through the acceptance of its Korean residents. Ethnicity is becoming an increasingly important intellectual and symbolic commodity in the educational world. Gradual changes have begun to appear in Japanese attitudes towards Korean ethnicity. Indications of this more accepting attitude can be seen, for example, in the introduction of a Korean language course by NHK (Public Broadcasting Corporation of Japan) in 1984, the enactment of a new bill concerning foreign college teachers' employment in 1982, and the establishment of special ethnic courses in public elementary schools in local areas.

The Japanese public school systems, colleges and universities are particularly expected to play a central role in producing a rich multi-cultured environment in Japanese society.

Support should be given to Korean-resident movements to gain equal rights in Japan, and at the same time the importance of ethnicity and ethnic identification must be recognized.

Bibliography

Comprehensive Research Center of Kanagawa Prefecture, *Kanagawa no Kankoku-Chosenjin* (Koreans in Kanagawa Prefecture), Kojin Press, 1984, p. 202.

Hiroshima Shin Shi (New History of Hiroshima), 1983.

Hiroto, Miyata, *65 Mannin-Zainichi Chosenjin* (650 thousand Korean in Japan), 1977, Suzusawa Press.

Hong Sang-Jin and Tomoko Nakashima, 'Nihon no Gakko ni Kodomo wo Kayowaseteiru Zainichi Chosenjin Fubo no Kyoikukan ni kansuru Chosa' (A Survey of the Consciousness of Korean Parents on the

Education of their Children in Japanese Schools), *Zainichi Chosenjin shi Kenkyu (Study of the History of Korean Residents in Japan)*, no. 7 (1980), pp. 93–139.

Kengo, Mochida and Yoshio Gondo, 'Zainichi Kankokujin Shitei no Kyoiku Mondai ni Kansuru Hikaku Kyoikugaku teki Kenkyu' (Comparative Study of Educational Problems of Korean Children in Japan), Research Report to the Japanese Ministry of Education, Science and Culture, 1981.

Kim Chang Shik, 'Zainichi Doho no Minzoku Kyoiku' (Ethnic Education of Korean Residents in Japan), *Zainichi Doho* (Korean Residents in Japan), 2 (1980), pp. 49–80.

Lee Chang So and George De Vos, *Koreans in Japan*, University of California Press, 1981.

Mitchell, Richard Hanks, *The Korean Minority in Japan*, University of California Press, 1967.

Shin Hyeon-Ha and Yoshio Gondo, 'Zainichi Kankokujin Shitei no National Identity ni kansuru Chosa Kenkyu' (A Research on Identity of Korean Children in Japan), *Research Bulletin of the Research Institute of Comparative Education and Culture, Kyushu University*, no. 33 (1982), pp. 55–76.

Shin Hyeon-Ha, 'Zainichi Kankokujin no Ishiki no Henyo to Shijyo Kyoiku ni kansuru Kosatsu' (On the Transformation of Values and the Children's Education of Korean Minority in Japan), *Research Bulletin of the Research Institute of Comparative Education and Culture, Kyushu University*, no. 35 (1984), pp. 57–72.

5 CHINESE EDUCATION IN MALAYSIA AND INDONESIA

Mary F. Somers Heidhues

The Malay Peninsula and the Indonesian Archipelago in Southeast Asia have been areas of Chinese immigration and trading activity for centuries: as a result substantial communities of ethnic Chinese reside there today. Malaysia's Chinese minority of about 4.3 million persons forms 33 per cent of its total population of 13.1 million. The approximately 4 million ethnic Chinese in Indonesia are a comparatively insignificant 2.7 per cent of the total population of that nation. In the neighbouring country of Singapore, ethnic Chinese make up about 75 per cent of the population of 2.4 million.[1] Obviously, education for the Chinese in Singapore is not minority education, but it should be kept in mind that these three nations once formed a cultural area with many similarities of language, religion and political institutions before they were colonized by the British (Malaysia and Singapore) and the Dutch (Indonesia, formerly the Netherlands East Indies). Both the indigenous communities and the ethnic Chinese still maintain some links across national boundaries.

Like ethnic Chinese elsewhere in Southeast Asia — they are often called overseas Chinese or, in Chinese, *huaqiao* — persons of Chinese origin in Malaysia and Indonesia are more likely than the indigenous peoples to be (1) engaged in commerce (although significant numbers are also employed in agriculture, especially in Malaysia) (2) more urbanized (3) on average wealthier and, as we shall see (4) better educated. They are, in the eyes of many observers, privileged, in spite of their relative numbers.

The indigenous Malays, who make up nearly 50 per cent of Malaysia's population,[2] enjoy, together with other, smaller indigenous ethnic groups, constitutional protection as 'Bumiputra' or 'sons of the soil' in land tenure, the recognition of Islam (the religion of the Malays) as the state religion, of Malay as the national language (Bahasa Malaysia), and favoured access to both education and government employment. They also benefit from various kinds of assistance in economic activities and virtually an iron grip on political life, both through an electoral system which gives more weight to Malay than non-Malay voters and, quite visibly, through the retention of hereditary Malay Sultans as chiefs of nine of Malaysia's thirteen states, one of the Sultans being elected head of state or king. Both before and since independence in 1957, most of the political bargaining in the Federation has involved trade-offs affecting the diverging interests of the bare majority of Bumiputras and the so-called 'immigrant communities', the ethnic Chinese and Indians, who differ in mother tongue, religion (although some Indians are Muslims) and other cultural and physical attributes from the Malays. Many of these trade-offs have concerned education.

The legal distinction between indigenous, or 'Pribumi', Indonesians and Indonesian citizens who are ethnic Chinese (non-Pribumi) is less clearly drawn than that between Bumiputra and Chinese in Malaysia.[3] Nevertheless, Indonesian citizens of Chinese origin face a certain amount of legal, semi-legal and illegal discrimination, usually justified by the argument that the colonial system unduly favoured the non-Pribumis. Ethnic Chinese have difficulty obtaining title to agricultural land; there are quotas for admission to universities; and the government has tried repeatedly to foster the interests of Pribumi businessmen at the expense of non-Pribumis, apparently to little avail. Ethnic Chinese who are not citizens, perhaps as many as 1 million[4] of the total, are even more handicapped and face formidable barriers to obtaining citizenship, even if they are locally born.

Obviously an important influence on education in both Malaysia and Indonesia — indeed, the most important influence before the Second World War — was their status as colonies of Great Britain and the Netherlands, respectively. For example, colonial policies inhibited the assimilation of ethnic Chinese to the indigenous culture; elsewhere in Southeast Asia, intermarriage with and assimilation to the indigenous population were not uncommon.[5] Furthermore, in both Malaysia and Indonesia Western education for the Chinese in English or Dutch competed with education in Chinese and affected the relations of the ethnic Chinese minorities with the indigenous majorities as well.

Chinese-language education in the colonial period

The earliest schools for the Chinese in Southeast Asia were small, privately sponsored, and had curricula based on traditional education in China, at the core of which was the rote learning of classical texts. Schools in China, of course, existed to prepare students for the examinations for admission to the imperial Mandarin bureaucracy. Little boys (and sometimes girls) in Southeast Asia may have needed rudimentary literacy and some ability to keep accounts in order to enter trade, but a bureaucratic career was out of their reach. These old-fashioned schools, which used Southern Chinese dialects as the language of teaching since these dialects were spoken by ethnic Chinese in Southeast Asia, were not even self-perpetuating: teachers usually had to be imported from China.[6]

Influenced in part by the revolution in China, a surge in immigration, and colonial policies which affected the Chinese, Chinese education in Southeast Asia began to undergo revolutionary changes around the turn of this century:

- The numbers of pupils and schools increased dramatically, as schools began to be open to all, with fees which were modest or even non-existent.
- Private sponsorship of schools was replaced by school boards composed of well-to-do individuals, often formed by community organizations based on common place of origin, dialect/speech group or family name.
- The curriculum was reformed and modernized in accord with new trends in China and reinforced by the nationalist political ideas which were gaining ground there. Modernization gathered momentum after China's 1911 revolution and the May Fourth Movement of 1919. In Southeast Asia, new textbooks were imported and teachers were recruited from the mainland. The Chinese government soon asserted its authority over schools abroad, and in 1928 the Nationalists (Guomindang) set up an Overseas Chinese Education Committee, the first of several official agencies, to support and control Chinese schools in Southeast Asia and elsewhere.[7]
- Finally, and this point deserves special mention, the language of Chinese education changed. The national language of China, Mandarin, is not spoken natively in the southeastern provinces of China from which virtually all Chinese families in Southeast Asia originated. Instead, several mutually unintelligible dialects or languages are used. Some ethnic Chinese in Malaysia and Indonesia actually spoke only Malay. Mandarin was practically a

foreign language for Southeast Asia's Chinese, but the new modern schools made Mandarin a powerful integrating force.

Chinese education in Indonesia in colonial times

The Netherlands Indies had substantial numbers of domiciled Chinese long before the late nineteenth-century boom in immigration from China. They formed settled communities in the towns and cities of Java and in other parts of the archipelago as well. This group, many of whom used Malay or a regional language in daily communication, is usually called 'Peranakan' or 'Baba' Chinese. They were often literate in Malay, and in Java they produced their own Malay-language publications.[8] Some learned Malay or Dutch from tutors or in school; others attended old-fashioned Chinese-language schools, of which there were over 350, with more than 6,500 pupils, at the end of the nineteenth century.

At the turn of the century the first modern Chinese school opened in Batavia (Jakarta). How important the modernization movement was, and how rapidly it spread, can be seen from the growth of these schools: in 1908 there were already seventy-five modern schools with over 5,500 pupils. For the Dutch authorities, these new schools represented a challenge; in an attempt to woo the Chinese away from them, the colonial government authorized the opening of Dutch-Chinese schools (*Hollands-Chinese scholen (HCS)*).

These HCS followed the plan of education used in the Netherlands, and the language of instruction was Dutch. Many were run by Christian missionaries; a majority of the teachers were Europeans. The student body alone was Chinese. This was education for Chinese but not Chinese education. Statistics show, nevertheless, that the schools attracted a majority of the Peranakan children although children of Chinese immigrants probably continued to favour the Chinese schools.

There were few secondary schools among modern Chinese schools, however, and the only chance for higher education was to go to China. The HCS offered more promise, opening the way to higher education in the Netherlands and, later, in Indonesia. In fact, ethnic Chinese formed a comparatively large proportion of college and university students from the Indies up to the Second World War. The HCS clearly promoted Westernization under conditions of ethnic exclusivism. The system did not, however, encourage the formation of a national, Western-educated élite including representatives of the ethnic Chinese[9] because indigenous Indonesians, even those who attended Dutch-language schools, usually attended separate schools.

The Second World War and the early post-war years

During the Japanese occupation of Indonesia from 1942 to 1945, Western schools were closed, but Japanese policy encouraged ethnic Chinese to be more conscious of their Chinese identity and some Chinese-language schools were allowed to remain open. After the war, Western schools soon reopened, but Chinese schools grew, in Mao Zedong's phrase, like 'bamboo shoots after spring rain'. By 1948 there were an estimated 200,000 students in several hundred Chinese-language schools, and these schools continued to mushroom in the following years.

Pride in the Chinese homeland diminished somewhat as Chinese communities in Southeast Asia became aware of the civil war in China. Two Chinese governments soon competed for influence in these communities, the People's Republic of China and the Guomindang Nationalist government which had fled to Taiwan in 1949. Battle lines were drawn over teachers, textbooks and the control of school boards. The Chinese-language schools seemed to outsiders to be a law unto themselves, hotbeds of radical politics and Chinese chauvinism, their students politicized, undisciplined, and sometimes poorly educated.

The Indonesianization of the Chinese schools

By the mid-1950s an estimated 425,000 children were attending 'alien' (mostly Chinese) schools in Indonesia. Well over half of these pupils were Indonesian citizens. In 1957, the Indonesian goverment forbade Indonesian citizens to attend these schools; closure of all Chinese schools run by organizations sympathetic to the Guomindang followed. Alien schools, now open only to non-citizens, could exist only in about 150 of the larger towns and cities, and teachers and curriculum became subject to stricter controls. At about the same time, the remaining Dutch schools were closed and the teaching of Dutch curtailed.

A large-scale shift of Indonesian citizens of Chinese origin into

Indonesian-language national schools took place after 1957. Most of the 250,000 pupils affected moved to private schools, many operated by Chinese community organizations for Indonesian citizens. One highly influential organization of ethnic Chinese, Baperki, operated about 100 schools; in Jakarta alone they taught over 15,000 pupils. A few years later, Baperki also founded a private university.[10] These institutions were not openly ethnically exclusive, but obviously most of the students were ethnic Chinese and some were aliens as well. This system of national schools with a strong ethnic coloration ended soon after it had begun.

In the wake of the anti-communist and anti-Chinese violence following the abortive *coup d'état* of 30 September 1965, all remaining Chinese-language schools in Indonesia had to close. Baperki was dissolved, but most of its national schools, including the university, continued to operate under the sponsorship of other organizations. Because so many alien Chinese children who were permanent residents of Indonesia (some of whom had tried in vain to obtain Indonesian citizenship) were left without an opportunity to continue their schooling, the Indonesian government did make a brief attempt, beginning in 1972, to provide transitional instruction in Chinese. By 1976, however, these 'Special Project National Schools' had closed.[11]

Indonesian policy on Chinese-language education and on the education of ethnic Chinese has been, in a word, Indonesianization. Today neither Indonesian leaders nor the general public are prepared to recognize Chinese influences as part of Indonesian history and culture. Even the open use of Chinese characters, for example in shop signs, has been suppressed. In a way, the situation of the nineteenth century has returned in Chinese education: parents who wish their children to learn Chinese may hire tutors, find special courses in community centres, or send them abroad if they can afford it.

Although ethnic Chinese are expected to be Indonesianized, they do not compete on equal terms with other Indonesian citizens. The quota system limiting their admission to public universities is one reason why private universities continue to exist: they are open to ethnic Chinese (and others) who can pay the fees.

Being a small minority, the ethnic Chinese have had little political clout, especially since 1965, and they influence government policies, if at all, through personal alliances. That kind of influence, however, is usually reserved for personal interests, financial or business affairs, and not for matters affecting the minority as a whole.

Chinese education in British Malaya

English-language education in British Malaya was largely left to private initiative, and missionary groups usually took the lead in opening schools for the local population. The Malays avoided these Christian schools. Subsequently colonial authorities supported elementary education in Malay for village agriculturalists, training for Malay schoolteachers, and special English-language schools for administrators, most of whom were Malay aristocrats and their sons. In addition, plantations employing immigrant Indian labour had to provide schools for their children, usually offering instruction in Tamil. The Chinese were considered to be wealthy enough to support their own schools and, in any case, most of them were immigrant labourers who were expected to return to China.

Contrary to this assumption, however, these temporary 'sojourners' began to grow into a permanent community, especially after Chinese women began to come to Malaya in the late nineteenth century. When the influence of the modernization movement and of Chinese nationalism described above began to be felt in the Chinese schools of Malaya, colonial authorities abandoned their laissez-faire policy toward Chinese education. Chinese schoolchildren born in Malaya were, after all, British subjects, whatever claims China might make on them.

After 1920, the British intervened in Chinese schools: they conducted health inspections and began to control schoolteachers and the content of textbooks, some of which were blatantly anti-British and anti-imperialist. Chinese-language schools which met certain standards were entitled to small subsidies, but the schools, and especially the politically sensitive teachers, were wary of this policy.

On the other hand, the British were reluctant to offer subsidies for English-language education to ethnic Chinese, the only exception being a few grants for talented but needy youths wishing to attend English-language schools. In fact, although there were few secondary schools in the Chinese-language system, these schools were far more popular among the Chinese than English schools. Nevertheless, English-language schools attracted some of the 'cream' of the pupils, and they contributed to the creation of a multi-racial, Chinese–Malay–Indian, English-speaking elite in Malaya.[12]

Transitions in Chinese education after 1945

As in Indonesia, the Japanese occupation period which ended in 1945 had caused the ethnic Chinese of Malaya to draw closer together, particularly as a response to violence used against them. Before then, of course, some questions concerning Chinese education had been settled: inspections and control by the colonial government, the possibility of subsidies, and the use of Mandarin as the language of instruction. Other questions remained open: the adaptation of the curriculum and texts to Malayan conditions, the relative weight of instruction in English and later in the national language Bahasa Malaysia, examination requirements for admission to secondary school (grades seven to nine), and the continued existence of the English-language schools after independence in 1957. Significant changes were under way before 1957, and subsequently Malayanization has proceeded rapidly, although not without controversy. After 1970 the pace of transition to a 'Malaysian' system quickened, but it was still gradual compared to what happened in Indonesia.

The first post-war changes in Chinese education came shortly after the outbreak of guerrilla war in 1948, the so-called Emergency, at a time when the loyalty of the Chinese to Malaya was in question because of their support for terrorist activities and when Chinese schools were suspected, as was the case in Indonesia, of fostering racialism and chauvinism.[13] A report on Chinese education in Malaya in 1951, produced by two internationally-known educators of Chinese origin, proposed the development of a Malayan national consciousness in the Chinese-language schools, which at that time were completely oriented towards China. The colonial government, which had commissioned the report, in addition to introducing Malaya-oriented textbooks, took steps to eliminate left-wing influence in the schools, even deporting teachers who were suspected of being pro-Communist.[14]

Further reports and further changes followed, leading to a major turning point in the entire education system in 1962. From that year primary schools (grades one to six) could continue to teach in one of four languages (Malay, English, Chinese or Tamil), but instruction in Malay was required from the first year of school and proficiency in Malay became necessary for admission to secondary school. Government-supported secondary schools could instruct only in Malay or English, although courses in the Chinese language could be offered if enough parents wished. At this time, there were no Tamil secondary schools, but a number of Chinese-language secondary schools existed. Secondary education in Malay was relatively new, with most schools dating from 1957 or later. Many Chinese schools chose at this time to 'go private', doing without a subsidy and continuing to instruct their pupils in Chinese at the secondary level.

Chinese parents, however, began to show a strong preference for English-language secondary schools; they were also sending their children in increasing numbers to the English primary schools. After 1962, 'the vast majority of Chinese children were moving into the English schools',[15] which suggests that parents were less concerned with preserving Chinese culture and language — at least in school — than with offering their children the best possible chance for a modern education in a world language, one which was also important within Malaysia.

The English-speaking and English-educated multi-racial elite, composed of the Malay leadership of UMNO (United Malays National Organization), the Chinese of the Malayan Chinese Association, and the Indians of the Malayan Indian Congress, had hammered out the inter-communal agreements that made possible the independence of Malaya in 1957. This group continued to determine policies in Malaysia under the alliance of the three parties in the 1960s. The Chinese, or at least the MCA, had acquiesced in the expansion of English education, even at the expense of Chinese-language education. While both Chinese leaders and the public accepted the inevitability of learning Bahasa Malaysia, there seemed to be little urgency about it. What was acceptable to the ethnic Chinese, however, appeared to many Malays to be foot-dragging.

New goals in post-1969 educational policy

At the heart of educational policy, especially since 1969, has been the principle of a Malay Malaysia: the continued special position of the Malays, their religion, language, culture and economic interests (together with those of other Bumiputras) must be safeguarded. Non-Bumiputra minorities have a subordinate but officially recognized position and the constitution proclaims their right to preserve their own cultures and languages, although not for 'official' language purposes.[16]

A new generation of Malays, however, was gaining influence in

UMNO, and they did not belong to the English-educated elite. Their impatience with existing conditions became evident when, on 13 May 1969, racial violence lasting for several days broke out, clearly demonstrating the extent of inter-ethnic tension. Parliament was immediately suspended. Thereafter, by constitutional amendment, both the language issue and the special position of the Malays/ Bumiputras were removed, under penalty of law, from public debate. The government blamed the discrepancy in wealth and status between the immigrant communities and the disadvantaged Malays for the outbreaks and determined to improve the relative position of the Malays in education and business as rapidly as possible.

Malayanization of the schools and universities was one obvious way to put Malays on a more equal footing with the minority communities. Beginning in 1970, the government eliminated English-language primary and secondary education: year by year these schools were transformed into Malay-language schools. The university level, where Malay students had demonstrated for change in 1970, was particularly sensitive. In the early 1960s, when the language of instruction at the University of Malaya was English, a majority of the students had been Chinese. As of 1983–4, Bahasa Malaysia was to be the sole language of tertiary instruction in Malaysia. In the meantime, new universities had been opened, teaching in Malay, some with overwhelming Malay majorities. The net effect was a dramatic decline in the proportion of Chinese among all university students in Malaysia.[17]

Chinese leaders have had to retreat to a defence of the Chinese-language primary schools while accepting an important role for Bahasa Malaysia as the national language in all schools. There remain, however, about fifty to sixty private Chinese-language secondary schools which, of course, teach Bahasa Malaysia as a subject and also use it as a language of instruction in some other subjects.[18]

For pupils in the Malay-language schools, English is the first foreign language, beginning in the third year of primary school. Chinese and Tamil primary schools, which teach Malay from the first year, also begin instruction in English in the third year. Students from non-Malay primary schools attend one-year 'remove' classes to receive intensive instruction in Bahasa Malaysia before moving to an entirely Malay-language secondary school. Thus their schooling is one year longer than that of children who begin in the Malay schools.

The phasing out of English-language education since 1970 has resulted in a partial revival of Chinese education as larger numbers of Chinese children moved to the Chinese-language primary schools. That these schools could be secured as part of the Malaysian education system must give the ethnic Chinese of Malaysia a sense of satisfaction. Their success is, of course, partly attributable to the relatively large proportion of Chinese in the population and partly to the financial resources which the community has put into education.

Serious Malay political leaders have repeatedly offered guarantees to the ethnic Chinese that they may keep their own schools, not least the present Prime Minister, Dr Mahathir bin Mohamad, whose early political record led some observers to classify him as a Malay 'ultra' with little sympathy for the interests of the non-Bumiputra.

How the system looks in practice

At the grass-roots level, however, problems continue. Young Chinese children, virtually segregated in their primary school years, have little opportunity for interaction with those of other ethnic groups, although in the urban areas they may pick up a little Malay on the streets. Neighbourhoods, however, are often ethnically homogeneous, and several hundred thousand ethnic Chinese live in so-called 'new villages' in rural and semi-rural areas. These settlements, established during the years of guerrilla warfare (Emergency), are often exclusively Chinese. Only the policeman or the occasional government clerk are likely to be native speakers of Malay.

A study of one such village in the state of Perak has asserted that, for most village children, Chinese primary school is a dead end. Although admission to a secondary school in a nearby town is unrestricted and attendance free, children coming from Chinese schools must first pass through a year's 'remove' class before entering the Malay-language lower secondary school. Few succeed, having had little or no chance to use Malay outside the classroom. The ambitious, however, are prepared to travel an even greater distance to an independent Chinese secondary school supported by the Chinese community. There, although they also have to become proficient in Malay, they find teachers who understand Chinese, and they learn the national language better because the teachers understand their problems. Although the certificate from a Chinese independent school is not recognized for purposes of continuing education or for government employment, parents and children believe the education in the Chinese schools is better. Furthermore, they view the chances for an ethnic Chinese to compete against Malays in obtaining a place in government employment or in higher education as limited in any case.[19]

This leads to another problem: ethnic Chinese pupils are reported to feel pessimistic about their future prospects since in the public sector jobs are awarded preferentially to Malays and in the private sector, where Chinese have long had the upper hand, increasing pressures for the hiring and training of Malays or for the founding of new all-Malay business institutions may push the Chinese aside. At the village level, this may help explain the lack of motivation and the high failure and drop-out rates among Chinese pupils.[20]

A recent study of secondary schools in urban areas came to the conclusion that Chinese pupils in the Chinese schools actually had a greater sense of their national identity as Malaysians and more optimism about their chances of achieving their goals in life than did those in the ethnically mixed secondary schools. Although the latter interacted more with Malays, and thus could be considered more 'integrated', they were also more aware of inter-ethnic competition and tended to view policies in favour of Bumiputras as having potentially detrimental effects on their future prospects.[21]

Upper-class urban parents, some of whom attended English-language schools, are particularly eager to give their children the advantages of an adequate knowledge of English. They support early education in Chinese and accept that their children must know Bahasa Malaysia, but they may, if well-to-do, try to send their children abroad, even to secondary school, perhaps to Singapore, where English is a national language. Singapore, however, is reluctant to open its schools to a potential flood of pupils from neighbouring countries, and other English-language schools abroad are even more expensive.

University education for the Chinese

The fact that there was no tertiary education in Chinese in Malaya had been a selling point for the English-language schools. As the relative numbers of Malays in higher education increased, the ethnic Chinese began to feel that they were being discriminated against in Malaysian colleges and universities. Furthermore, study in the

English-speaking world has become prohibitively expensive. Attendance at Chinese universities in Taiwan or, in the past, the People's Republic of China, on the other hand, is fraught with political and other risks.

The Nanyang (South Seas, or Southeast Asia) University, established with private funds in Singapore in 1953, was meant to be a centre of Chinese culture, language and education for ethnic Chinese in Southeast Asia, but it quickly became the focus of political rivalries within the community. Financial difficulties forced the University to turn to the government of Singapore for support; in 1965 it ceased to be a private institution. The authorities purged radical elements, introduced more instruction in English and finally, in 1979–80, integrated students and faculties with the National University of Singapore, an English-language institution.[22] Singapore's government, although committed to the teaching of Mandarin in schools, insisted that only an English-trained and scientifically and technologically competent labour force would enable Singapore to compete internationally and develop economically.

Chinese community organizations in Malaysia also launched a plan for a Chinese-language university there in 1968. The project for Merdeka (Freedom) University had, however, to be put aside temporarily after the May 1969 riots, although some 4,000 groups had pledged funds for the new undertaking. When the idea was revived in 1971, the government took steps to block the establishment of any private university, and the Minister of Education turned down the proposal. Supporters of Merdeka University took their case to court, but in July 1982 the Federal Court finally decided against them.

The Court's arguments followed those used by the minister. There were practical objections: the experience of Nanyang University had shown, for example, that Merdeka University might eventually become dependent on government financial support. The Federal Court also agreed that the university would be too exclusive, being open essentially only to graduates of the Chinese independent secondary schools (the university's supporters did suggest at one point that it might offer courses taught in English or Malay as well). Most important, however, the judges insisted that the university would be undertaking an 'official' purpose, education, and the Constitution provides that, for official purposes, *only* Bahasa Malaysia may be used. The role of the national language foreseen in the Constitution is intended to forge a united Malaysian nation; the use of other languages, although constitutionally guaranteed for non-official, including educational, purposes, might be tolerated but would hardly be promoted.[23]

Conclusions

The year 1900 marked the beginning of modern Chinese education in Indonesia. The story reached a climax in the 1950s and came rapidly to a close with the phasing out of the Special Project National Schools in 1976. Modern Chinese education in Malaysia began at about the same time, grew rapidly, and, in a modified form, was able to withstand attempts to abolish it in favour of a more 'national' system. In both Indonesia and Malaysia, in colonial and early post-independence times, Western education demonstrated considerable appeal for ethnic Chinese, but nationalist currents have eliminated that alternative.

At the moment the prospect in Malaysia is for Chinese primary schools to continue on a private basis. Ethnic Chinese leaders in Malaysia are fully aware of what has happened to Chinese education in Indonesia, but those who wish to promote Chinese-language education in Malaysia have two advantages: the community itself has substantial financial resources and has proved that it can support a considerable number of non-government institutions, and the greater relative numbers of ethnic Chinese give them additional political leverage, either in the form of votes or, perhaps, through the threat of radicalization.

On the other hand, Malaysian politics has undergone considerable change since 1969, especially in terms of the political mobilization of the younger Malays. The kind of inter-ethnic bargaining among members of an English-educated elite which characterized the 'alliance system' (the coalition of UMNO, MCA and MIC) has given way to a Malay- and UMNO-dominated governing coalition, and the bargaining position of the representatives of the ethnic Chinese is correspondingly weaker. Should Malay 'ultras' gain political power, there would be no intrinsic, legal or constitutional barriers to further measures limiting Chinese-language education.

Notes

1.   For these figures, see Mary F. Somers Heidhues, *Politik in Südostasien: Grundlagen*

und Perspektiven (Hamburg: Mitteilungen des Instituts für Asienkunde, 1983), pp. 15 and 157. Malaysia and Singapore actually *count* ethnic Chinese; the figure for Indonesia is an educated guess.

2. The British colonies on the Malay Peninsula, including Singapore, were often referred to as British Malaya. In 1957, they formed the independent Federation of Malaya, without Singapore, which continued to be a British colony. In 1963, Malaysia was formed from the Federation of Malaya, Singapore, and two British colonies on the island of Borneo, Sabah and Sarawak. Singapore separated from Malaysia in 1965. This paper deals essentially with West Malaysia, that is the former Federation of Malaya. Chinese education in East Malaysia (Sabah and Sarawak) followed a similar pattern, but English remained an official language there until 1973. See Wolfgang Franke, 'Some Remarks on Chinese Education in Sarawak and Sabah', *Malaysian Journal of Education* 3:1 (June 1966), pp. 1–10.

3. For the origin of the words 'Pribumi' and Bumiputra', see Sharon Siddique and Leo Suryadinata, 'Bumiputra and Pribumi: Economic Nationalism (Indigenism) in Malaysia and Indonesia', *Pacific Affairs* 54:4 (Winter 1981–2), pp. 662–87.

4. A recent source is Charles A. Coppel, 'China and the Ethnic Chinese in Indonesia' in James J. Fox *et al.* (eds), *Indonesia: Australian Perspectives* (Canberra: Research School of Pacific Studies, The Australian National University, 1980), pp. 729–34.

5. The classic studies of assimilation of the Chinese in Thailand and the Philippines are G. William Skinner, *Chinese Society in Thailand: An Analytical History* (Ithaca, N.Y.: Cornell University Press, 1957) and Edgar Wickberg, *The Chinese in Philippine Life, 1850–1898* (New Haven: Yale University Press, 1965). In Vietnam and Cambodia there is also evidence of assimilation of Chinese, but it was rare in Indonesia and virtually unheard of in Malaysia.

6. Philip Loh Fook Seng, *Seeds of Separatism: Educational Policy in Malaya, 1874–1940* (Kuala Lumpur: Oxford University Press, 1975), pp. 36–9; Lea E. Williams, *Overseas Chinese Nationalism: The Genesis of the Pan-Chinese Movement in Indonesia, 1900–1916* (Glencoe, Ill.: The Free Press, 1960), pp. 66–8.

7. Loh, op. cit., p. 103.

8. Claudine Salmon, *Literature in Malay by the Chinese of Indonesia: A Provisional Annotated Bibliography* (Paris: Editions de la Maison des Sciences de l'Homme, 1981); Leo Suryadinata, *The Pre-World War II Peranakan Chinese Press of Java: A Preliminary Survey* (Athens, Ohio: Ohio University Center for International Studies, Southeast Asia Program, 1971).

9. The above discussion and figures are taken from Mary F. Somers Heidhues, 'Peranakan Chinese Politics in Indonesia' (unpublished PhD dissertation, Cornell University, 1965), pp. 48–63 and Leo Suryadinata, 'Indonesian Chinese Education: Past and Present', *Indonesia* 14 (1972), pp. 49–71.

10. Somers, op. cit., pp. 133, 162–9; figures based on official Indonesian sources.

11. Christine Inglis, 'Chinese Education in Southeast Asia' in Kenneth Orr (ed.), *Appetite for Education in Contemporary Asia* (Canberra: Australian National University, Development Studies Centre, 1977), pp. 126–8.
12. On modern Chinese education in Malaya, see Loh, op. cit., pp. 41–3, 92–100; Wolfgang Moese *et al.*, 'Chinese Regionalism in West Malaysia and Singapore', *Mitteilung der Gesellschaft für Natur-und Völkerkunde Ostasiens* 77 (1972), pp. 386–415; Victor Purcell, *The Chinese in Malaya* (London: Oxford University Press, 1948, repr. 1967), pp. 227–34.
13. On Malaya, for example, see Laurence K.L. Siaw, *Chinese Society in Rural Malaysia* (Kuala Lumpur: Oxford University Press for the Institute of Southeast Asian Studies, 1983), pp. 78–9, 154–8.
14. Chai Hon-chan, *Education and Nation-building in Plural Societies: The West Malaysian Experience* (Canberra: Australian National University, Development Studies Centre, 1977), pp. 20ff; Wolfgang Franke, 'Problems of Chinese Education in Singapore and Malaya', *Malaysian Journal of Education* 2:2 (December 1965), pp. 182–98.
15. Chai, op. cit., p. 32. This refers to the period 1957–67.
16. Ibid., pp. 15–18. On the Malaysian Constitution and politics in general, see R. S. Milne and Diane K. Mauzy, *Politics and Government in Malaysia* (Singapore: Federal Publications, 1977) and Stanley S. Bedlington, *Malaysia and Singapore: The Building of New States* (Ithaca, N.Y.: Cornell University Press, 1978).
17. Chai, op. cit., pp. 48–57. According to *Far Eastern Economic Review*, 16 July 1982, Bumiputras were about 44 per cent of university students in 1970 (as against 46 per cent Chinese), 54 per cent in 1972 (Chinese 38 per cent) and 68 per cent in 1977 (Chinese 26 per cent). In 1977, however, the figures for all students in tertiary education (including colleges as well as universities and perhaps also those studying abroad) probably reflected the ethnic composition of the entire population more clearly.
18. Volkmar Sturm, 'Der Fall der Merdeka-Universität', *Asien* 9 (October 1983), p. 73. According to information from Tan Liok Ee, only 34 of these schools are in West Malaysia, the rest in East Malaysia.
19. Loh, Francis Kok-Wah, 'Beyond the Tin Mines: The Political Economy of Chinese Squatter Farmers in the Kinta New Villages, Malaysia' (unpublished PhD dissertation, Cornell University, 1980), pp. 278–86.
20. Ibid.; Chai, op. cit., pp. 36ff.
21. Yew Yeok Kim, 'Education, National Identity, and National Integration: A Survey of Secondary School Students of Chinese Origin in Urban Peninsular Malaysia' (unpublished PhD dissertation, Stanford University, 1982), pp. 221–35, 255. At the time of Yew's study, both English-language secondary schools and former Chinese secondary schools which had switched to English existed, as well as the independent, private Chinese-language secondary schools. The first two were ethnically mixed, the independent Chinese schools were exclusively Chinese. Since then, the English-language secondary schools have become Malay-language schools.
22. Moese, op. cit., pp. 412–15.
23. Sturm, op. cit., pp. 70–7; K. Das, 'Requiem for a Dream', *Far Eastern Economic Review*, 7 July 1982.

6 ISRAELI EDUCATION ADDRESSING DILEMMAS CAUSED BY PLURALISM: A SOCIOLOGICAL PERSPECTIVE

Chaim Adler

I. Introduction*

Israeli society exhibits three main divisions which may be looked at as an expression of pluralism.[1] As in most similar situations these divisions are the result of demographic, religious and national differences or cleavages. More specifically:

(a) The Jewish majority of Israel includes in its composition the main subdivisions of the Jewish people as they existed in the Jewish communities all over the world from which the Jewish citizens of Israel (their parents or grandparents) emigrated. One such subdivision may be defined as 'ethnic' and traced to differences in religious practices, mores and traditions, or paths of the Jewish dispersion. Essentially it reflects the social and cultural context from which people (or communities) originated: those who immigrated to Israel *after* having assimilated the main elements of the Western industrial civilization (mostly of European and American background and those who immigrated to Israel after *partial* assimilation of such patterns or even *prior* to such processes of assimilation (mostly of Asian and African background). The dilemma which these differences pose for

* I wish to express my thanks to my colleagues, Mrs Lorraine Gastwirt, Assistant Director of the National Council of Jewish Women U.S.A. Research Institute for Innovation in Education and Dr Reuven Kahane of the Department of Sociology and the School of Education for suggesting alterations in the manuscript; to my colleague Mrs Ilana Felsenthal of the NCJW Research Institute and the School of Education for her careful reading of the manuscript and suggesting valuable changes and additions; to Dr Geulah Solomon of the Institute of Contemporary Jewry, and to Mrs Chaya Buckwold for her kind help and patience in typing and retyping the manuscript.

Israeli schools is how to contribute to equalization of opportunities and elimination of the educational and social gaps
resulting from this ethnic division while at the same time
preserving (and, perhaps, raising) standards of education.

(b) Another important subdivision of the Jewish majority of Israel is
along religious parameters, essentially setting apart those who
abide strictly by the faith and traditions from those who do not.
These differences in religious adherence and practice, for
reasons beyond the scope of this paper, have given rise to a quite
divided social system. Differences in attitude toward religion are
reflected in the structure of communities (housing and settlements), politics (parties) and even legal arrangements. Public
schools, too, are subdivided into 'state religious' and 'general'
schools.

The dilemma for the educational system results from its
having been conceived as one of the main tools for integrating a
new society born of immigration from eighty different countries.
Education was expected to strengthen the purpose and ideals
that constituted Israel's *raison d'être* as an independent contemporary state while simultaneously drawing on the age-old Jewish
heritage to create a stronger sense of shared cultural roots.

Will the identity of the Israeli-born younger generation be
shaped by the age-old Jewish religious tradition, or will there
emerge a modern adapted secular blend? And is there not the
looming danger that instead of treating such a modern Jewish
culture, Israel's educational system will unintentionally contribute to the blurring of the Jewish identity of its students (at least
of the majority who study in state secular schools)?

(c) A different kind of subdivision of Israeli society exists along the
lines of 'nationhood', that is, the Jewish majority and the Arab
minority. About 17 per cent of the 4,000,000 Israeli citizens are
Arabs. This division creates a particularly difficult dilemma for
the whole of Israeli society. On the one hand the social and
cultural revolution which gave rise to Israel was essentially a
Jewish one, resulting in the formation of an independent,
democratic, creative, modern society based on a vision of social
justice. On the other hand, however, the democratic and
egalitarian elements of this vision surely call for the incorporation
(at least in the realms of the polity and the economy) of any
minority living within its borders. The dilemma is sharpened by
the fact that while the Arabs of Israel are a minority among the

Jews, the Jews are a tiny minority in the Arab Middle and Near East. Unfortunately, moreover, the Jewish entity has so far been unwelcome in the Arab world, so much so that in thirty-five years of Israel's statehood five wars have erupted and a continuous state of war with at least part of the Arab world has persisted. The Arabs of Israel, consequently, while being Israeli citizens (by volition, in view of the option to emigrate), are also part of the Arab world (culturally, linguistically, religiously, and to an extent, politically). This feature makes for mutual ambivalences as to social incorporation on the part of both the Jewish majority (due to political and military sensitivities) and the Arab minority (due to their desire to keep their distinct and separate identity). Consequently, while schools are expected to play an integrative and equalizing role for the Jewish majority, the separateness of schools for Arabs and Jews may curtail their ability to provide equalization of social opportunities for Arab students.

II. Background

Although Israel's statehood is only about thirty-five years old, its educational system dates back about eighty years. When Israel gained independence in 1948, there already existed a fully-fledged educational system from kindergarten through university that included teacher training institutions, a curriculum, a school inspectorate, and a quite elaborate examination system. Perhaps most important, from the early 1920s there existed a language — Hebrew — which was universally used as the vehicle of instruction and served as a symbol of the emergence of a revived culture.

Three prominent features characterized the pre-independence educational system:

Uniformity. The educational system of the pre-statehood Jewish community in Palestine was essentially uniform in structure and content. This uniformity coincided with the social, cultural and demographic homogeneity of the Jewish population in Palestine during the 1930s and 1940s. A basically non-differentiated educational system could meet the educational needs of most children. However, with the foundation of the state in 1948, and the tremendous growth of the population due to mass immigration from four continents, the almost perfect fit between students' needs and the opportunities offered by this uniform educational system began to come apart.

At the same time, the educational system from the 1920s until the 1940s was not expected to be responsible for the preparation and promotion of sophisticated manpower as needed by industry, scientific endeavours or complex bureaucracy. Most of the positions which required highly trained manpower were occupied by people educated in Europe who immigrated as adults. Since independence, however, Israel's educational system has been increasingly vested with responsibility for the development of such sophisticated manpower. It remains to be seen whether the system inherited from the Jewish community in Palestine was sufficiently equipped to fulfil this function.

Partisan affiliation. Secondly, the educational system which was handed down from the Jewish community in Palestine to the state of Israel was politically subdivided along partisan lines. The absence of centralized state institutions meant there was no centralized public schooling. Instead the school system was owned, conducted and supervised by the main political parties. This resulted in three major trends of schooling — socialist, religious (essentially orthodox) and general.[2]

This political subdivision, which was essentially of an ideological nature, did not countervail the far-reaching curricular and structural uniformity. Although schools were run by three different political movements, they did not differ dramatically in their curricular emphases and certainly not in their general structure, educational approaches or academic standards. In 1953 the political 'trends' in education were abolished, and a bipartite state school system was established, introducing 'general' and 'religious' (orthodox) state schools. One problem that emerged has been the segregatedness of those two distinct educational subsystems (both, as mentioned, part of state-run education)[3] Perhaps an even more critical issue concerns the nature, contents and flavour of the Jewish identity to be nurtured in the general, non-religious sector of public school education, the segment that caters for about 75 per cent of the school population.

Separateness of Arab education. As indicated, the educational system of the Jewish community in Palestine was essentially directed towards the creation of an independent Jewish political entity.

Schools were seen as a major tool for the stimulation and acceleration of the social revolution that was put into motion by Zionism. It is, therefore, not surprising that the Jews of Palestine preferred their own school system from kindergarten (almost universally attended) to a Hebrew university (which, of course, only very few attended).

The state schools run by the British mandatory administration were unsatisfactory to the Jews in terms of duration of schooling (only six compulsory years), in terms of language (a mixture of English, Arabic and Hebrew), and most importantly in that they did not serve the national-revolutionary fervour of the society. The Arabs of Palestine, on the other hand, many of whom were still illiterate, perceived these government schools as serving their needs perfectly. For some of these Arabs, many of whom were peasants, it was conceived as even too much schooling, especially as far as their daughters were concerned.

The growing momentum of Zionism, peaking with the holocaust and the end of the Second World War, came into increasing conflict with the Palestinian Arab national movement. Separate school systems, one private (Hebrew) and one public (the government's, almost exclusively serving Arabs) contributed to the growing segregatedness of the Jewish and Arab social systems in Palestine.

Against this background three basic challenges have existed for Israel's educational system to this day:

(1) The recognition that an egalitarian ideology calls for a democratic education system providing equal educational opportunities despite serious social and economic inequalities, stimulated extensive policy and curriculum adaptations.[4] At the same time Israel has had to mobilize all its potential for human and intellectual excellence so as to secure its very survival and sustain its economic, technological, cultural and structural growth. Equalizing opportunities and nurturing excellence, however, are directions that usually lead to conflicting or even opposing policies.

(2) Israel's educational system has had to address itself to the fact that between two-thirds and three-quarters of the nation's children grow up in secular homes and study in the general sector of the public school system. They thus need to acquire motivation and sources of legitimation for their Jewishness other

than the traditional religious-based ones that had predominated. The general school is being torn between a non-orthodox though traditional orientations, and a modern-scientific though Judaic orientation.[5]

(3) The Israeli educational system's democratic structure and commitments call for the provision of equal opportunities. At the same time, however, the separateness of the Jewish and Arab school systems (in view of the desire to preserve independent cultural, social and political entities) casts a shadow over the chances of providing equal educational opportunities.

In line with the basic theme of this book, the paper will concentrate on the first and third challenges only.

III. Coping with the first challenge: bridging social gaps and coping with the manpower needs of an industrialized civilization

From the late nineteenth century until the establishment of the state of Israel in 1948, the Jewish settlers of modern Palestine were predominantly of European origin. In 1948 more than 90 per cent of Israeli Jewish inhabitants were of European background. Then mass immigration began, doubling the population in the first three years of statehood and trebling it over the first twelve years. It is the combination of the origin of the immigrants and their numbers which is of interest here. Since independence, only some 50 per cent of the new immigrants have been of European or American origin, the remainder coming from Near and Middle Eastern Jewish communities — mainly Iran, Iraq, Yemen, and North Africa. The chief ethnic division among Jews in Israel, therefore, is between citizens of European or Anglo-Saxon background and those of Asian or African origin.[6]

Because European cultural styles and institutional patterns prevail in modern Israel, immigration for many Asian and African Jews has meant an encounter with an unknown and basically different social system. Some characteristics of the Asian and African immigrant groups have constituted a priori obstacles to immediate social integration. For example, many Asian and African adults have enjoyed little or no formal schooling prior to immigration, and very few have undergone technological training congruent with the needs of a modern economy. In addition, many have arrived with very large families and often have been ignorant of, or opposed to, family planning. These characteristics have placed these immigrants in the lower socioeconomic strata of Israeli society. In consequence, a high correlation between socioeconomic status and ethnic origin has emerged, a correlation manifested in school performance as well as by other institutional indicators.[7]

At the same time the school system has been seen as one of the main agents of social integration.[8] Indeed, it was harnessed to that purpose from the early 1950s. The main strategies applied by the educational system to reducing the gap between ethnic groups may be subsumed under the following five categories:

(a) *Administrative measures.* In the first years, when mass failure showed up even in the low grades, the educational system was so overwhelmed by the growth in student numbers on the one hand and the wide gaps in achievement on the other that it could only respond administratively. For instance, the practice of holding over failing students was abolished. This measure indeed removed the obstacles faced by students of disadvantaged backgrounds from promotion to the following grade. It did not, however (like most other administrative measures), have any impact on the source of the problem.

(b) *Pedagogical measures.* Towards the end of the 1950s pedagogical intervention was initiated. Some of the measures introduced included:

  (i) early intervention, mainly through kindergartens and nurseries; home intervention programmes were introduced later;

  (ii) experimentation with didactic measures, remedial teaching methods, and curricular innovations;

  (iii) enrichment programmes aimed specifically at the upper achievement quartile of the disadvantaged.

(c) *Structural differentiating measures.* Schools faced with mounting numbers of 'underachievers' at the end of the 1960s, despite the pedagogic measures, applied instituted patterns of ability groupings. Even though such measures helped schools to overcome problems incurred by great gaps in achievement between students, they evidently contributed to the segregation of students by ethnic background without, at the same time, having any impact on their achievement levels.[9]

(d) *Structural integrative measures*. The continued existence of a social and economic division based on the ethnic origin of Jewish parents conflicted with the goal of a modern unified Jewish nation and the egalitarian principles on which it was founded. As structural differentiation seemed to perpetuate this division (although it did not grow larger), integrative measures were tried. Integrative efforts focused on enrichment, aiming at raising scholastic achievements and school retention rates of students of disadvantaged origin. At the same time these measures carried a symbolic message by offering all students in the integrated system, irrespective of their (or their parents') country of origin, shared school environments (the school building, the teachers, the curriculum). It thus symbolized structurally the commitment to national unity, social solidarity and equality.[10] In fact, as research shows, the quality of educational inputs into integrated schools is considerably better than that of the segregated ones.[11] A school reform, the core of which was the formation of integrated junior high schools, was introduced in 1968 as a result of a resolution of the Knesset.[12]

(e) *Intensive focusing on hard-core disadvantaged communities*. In the early 1970s, the Educational Welfare Programme singled out the most depressed and disadvantaged communities to receive intensive and concerted compensatory efforts (specifically decided upon by local steering committees). Secluded and mostly homogeneous cities or neighbourhoods, where integration is virtually impossible to achieve without massive bussing, became the target for this programme.[13]

Impact of these reforms

Although it is not possible to evaluate the total impact of these measures, perhaps the most impressive indicator is the expansion of the educational system.[14] Not only has school-leaving age been raised twice since 1948 — schooling is compulsory today between the ages of 5 and 16 — but all four-year-olds and almost all three-year-olds are in kindergartens or nurseries.[15] Ability grouping (from seventh grade) and tracking (from tenth or eleventh grade) result in school paths for students of Asian or African (AA) and European or Anglo-Saxon (EA) origin that are not necessarily identical, but 13 years of almost universal school attendance cannot but leave its imprint on students, even if differential school achievements persist.

With the abolition in 1978 of school fees up to age 18 and the essential success of many of the compensatory measures applied over more than a generation, almost two-thirds of seventeen-year-old Jews were completing twelfth grade! (It should be added, however, that about two-thirds of the AA students complete vocational, non-university directed, programmes while two-thirds of the EA students complete academic, university directed, programmes).[16] An additional 5–6 per cent combine study and work during their adolescent years.[17]

This expansion of the educational system can be viewed as a *policy* directed at creating opportunities for all young Israelis as well as equalizing opportunities for the disadvantaged. The dramatic diminution of drop-out rates in secondary schools during the 1970s, on the other hand, should be viewed as a *result* (at least in part) of educational policies (see Tables 6.1 and 6.2). Indeed, research clearly shows that length of participation in school is highly correlated with social mobility.[18]

Table 6.1   The development of transition rates from first to twelfth grade (two cohorts, commencing first grade in 1957–58 and 1967–68 respectively)

Year commenced			Percentage reaching				
1st grade	8th grade	12th grade	8th grade	9th grade	10th grade	11th grade	12th grade
1957–58	1964–65	1968–69	82.7	64.8	55.7	44.7	32.2
1967–68	1974–75	1978–79	95.5	91.2	77.9	64.6	55.9

Source: M. Egorzi and P. Bilezki, *The Educational System in the Mirror of Numbers,* Ministry of Education and Culture, Jerusalem, 1980, Table 11 (Hebrew, mimeo)

Another indicator of the impact of these democratizing educational measures is success of AA and EA candidates in the government-administered matriculation examinations. These examinations, taken mostly by the about-to-graduate students of academic high schools, are necessary for university admission. While in the late 1960s about 6 per cent of all the seventeen-year-olds of AA origin in Israeli society successfully passed these examinations (as compared with about 33 per cent of the EA seventeen-year-olds), this rate rose to about 15 per cent in the early 1980s while the percentage of EA seventeen-year-olds remained constant.[19]

Table 6.2 Transition rates from tenth to twelfth grade (per cent)

	Grade	Total	Israeli and European or American origin	Asian or African origin
		First cohort 1970–72		
		Secondary education – total		
1970	10th	100	100	100
1971	11th	78.5	84.8	72.8
1972	12th	59.6	68.4	48.2
		Second cohort 1975–77		
		Secondary education – total		
1975	10th	100	100	100
1976	11th	78.9	84.1	74.4
1977	12th	67.8	75.0	61.5
		Vocational and agriculture		
1975	10th	100	100	100
1976	11th	71.4	75.9	69.2
1977	12th	56.0	62.8	52.7
		Academic education		
1975	10th	100	100	100
1976	11th	88.7	89.4	87.4
1977	12th	83.1	83.0	83.3

Source: Egozi and Bilezki, *The Educational System in the Mirror of Numbers,* 1979, Table 16.

Table 6.3 The proportion of 14–17 year-old Asian and African adolescents in the population at large and in secondary education (per cent)

	Amongst 14–17 year olds	In secondary schools	9th grade	12th grade	Academic schools	Vocational schools	Agricultural schools
1966–67	49.9	35.6	45.3	18.9	25.4	47.0	52.4
1976–77	58.7	50.6	54.6	46.6	37.5	63.7	65.9
1977–78	58.4	51.3	55.0	47.5	38.4	64.1	65.3
1978–79	57.7	51.5	53.5	48.3	38.7	64.3	64.7
1979–80	57.3	51.9	54.9	49.6	39.9	64.4	64.6

Source: Egozi and Bilezki, *The Educational System in the Mirror of Numbers*, 1980, Table 25; and Bilezki and Ch. Turki, *The Educational System in the Mirror of Numbers*, 1982, Table 26.

Table 6.4 The participation of 14–17-year-old adolescents of Asian and African origin in academic secondary schools

	1966–67	*1973–74*	*1976–77*
The proportion of Asians and African adolescents among 14–17-year-olds	49.9	57.7	58.7
The proportion of Asian and African adolescents:			
Secondary schools – Total	35.6	46.6	50.6
Academic schools			
9th grade	33.9	37.2	39.7
12th grade	16.4	27.7	33.7

Source: Egozi and Bilezki, *The Educational System in the Mirror of Numbers*, 1978, adapted from Table 13.

As Table 6.3 clearly indicates, the rate of under-representation of AA adolescents (aged 14–17) in secondary schools changed from 14.3 per cent in 1966–7 to only 5.4 per cent in 1978–9. Table 6.4 shows that the underrepresentation of AA 14–17-year-olds in academic schools decreased from 24.5 per cent in 1966–7 to only 17.4 per cent twelve years later. Table 6.4 shows that in twelfth grade academic schools the rate of underrepresentation shrank from 33.5 per cent to 25 per cent over the same period. And Table 6.5 shows that the relative

Table 6.5 University attendance of 20–29-year-olds,* by continent of birth (rates per 10,000 in respective population groups)

	1964–65	*1974–75*
Israeli born – Total	893	951
Father Israeli born	524	997
Father Asian or African born	158	299
Father European or American born	1,074	1,405
Asian or African born	79	211
European or American born	535	842
Total	413	716

* In view of the universal military services of Israeli youth, freshmen at Israeli universities are 20–21 years old.

Source: Egozi and Bilezki, *The Educational System in the Mirror of Numbers*, 1979, Table 33.

participation of 20–29-year-olds of AA origin in higher education expanded between the years 1965–6 and 1974–5 much more than did the participation among their counterparts of EA origin. Indeed, the rate of increase was about 100 per cent for Israeli-born young adults of AA origin and about 200 per cent for AA-born as compared to about 30 per cent growth among Israeli-born of EA origin and about 50 per cent for EA-born young adults.

This progress may be cautiously related to the emergence of an AA Jewish middle class in Israel and to the beginning of a penetration of people of AA origin into élite positions in politics, the military, business, and to a lesser degree the professions.

Nevertheless, essentially all of Israel's lower class is composed of people of AA origin. The policies enacted during the past decade to diminish inequalities and prevent the perpetuation thereof into future generations (such as that of Project Renewal) are therefore to be welcomed because they are directed at ecological pockets of lower-income or lower-class groups in Israel's population which exhibit signs of a self-perpetuating 'culture of poverty' rather than at entire ethnic groups. This statement does not contradict the fact that in recent years 'ethnic-consciousness' of people of AA origin has risen and been partially translated into political power. The analysis thereof, however, is beyond the scope of this paper.

To sum up, even though gaps in school achievements and inequality in the opportunity to attend academic secondary schools and universities have not disappeared, they certainly have not deepened and have in some respects considerably decreased. Although whether this shrinkage is socially significant (considering the very short time in which these developments took place and the circumstances under which they occurred) or not is a matter of value judgement, I strongly lean towards the opinion that it is.

Equal opportunity or selective excellence

Educational systems virtually everywhere are subject to opposing demands: one calls for efforts to democratize the system, offer mass education and equalize opportunities (which might lead to compromising standards); the other emphasizes maintaining high academic standards (and tends to be selective and even elitist). In the second case as few students will complete a fully-fledged academic course of study, fewer of them will have access to opportunities that require academic certification.

Israel was forced in its short history to try and satisfy both demands simultaneously. It undertook to reduce the serious social and economic gaps between groups of different ethnic origins and, at the same time, it also launched a rapid process of industrialization. Industrialization was complicated by the need to replace a generation of skilled manpower trained in Europe and America prior to their immigration by locally educated and trained workers. It is very hard to judge so far whether the results were merely a compromise between those essentially conflicting goals or constitute a development in which they successfully complement each other. As the following analysis will indicate, I tend to lean towards the latter conclusion.

Expansion of educational opportunity led to both the inclusion of the very young (three- to four-year-olds) in the system and the opening up of secondary education to all adolescents — clear strategies of democratization. Table 6.6 shows an annual growth rate of participation in education between 1970 and 1981 exceeding the population growth rates for respective age groups between 1970 and 1981, particularly in post-secondary and academic higher education institutions. At the same time, however, the educational system did not abandon the quite selective track of senior academic high schools. Only about 25 per cent of each year's age cohort successfully complete the course in those schools and thereby constitute the main pool of candidates for university admission. With the abolition of school fees in 1978, acceptance into this track has become almost

Table 6.6 Number of students by school rank (Jewish education) (thousands)

	1970–71	1975–76	1980–81	1981–82	Average annual growth rate 1970–81 (per cent)
Kindergartens	107.6	180.6	211.9	208.8	6.2
Elementary schools	409.8	441.7	509.6	523.0	2.2
Secondary schools	155.7	177.8	195.9	199.9	2.3
Post-secondary schools	18.3	31.6	34.9	36.7	6.5
Academic higher education	39.5	51.3	57.0	57.9	3.5
Total	730.9	883.0	1,009.3	1,026.2	3.1

Source: Bilezki and Turki, *The Educational System in the Mirror of Numbers*, 1982, Table 2.

Table 6.7 Numbers of 17-year-olds in the population and in the graduating class (12th grade) of academic high schools (1975, 1981)

	1975–76	1981–82
Numbers in population	about 52,000	about 55,000*
Numbers in graduating class of academic high schools	about 14,900	about 19,800**
Numbers of matriculated graduates	about 12,690 (24%)	about 16,800*** (30%)

* Table 23 reports that the number of 14–17-year-olds in those years was 209,000 and 215,000 respectively. We assumed that each age cohort comprised about 25%.
** Table 12 reports that the number of students in 12th grade in 1975 was about 27,500 and that about 55% of those studied in academic high schools; similarly in 1981 about 36,000 studied in 12th grades and 53% of them in academic high schools.
*** Based on the assumption that about 85% of the graduating class successfully pass the matriculation examination.

Source: Bilezki and Turki. *The Educational Systems in the Mirror of Numbers*, 1982.

solely dependent upon academic performance. Assuming that about 85 per cent of the graduating academic class successfully took the matriculation examination in 1975–6, this group would have included — according to Table 6.7 — about 2,700 students or about 24 per cent of that year's age cohort of seventeen-year-olds. In 1980–81 this number rose to about 16,800 or 30.5 per cent. Vocational education also contributes graduates who successfully pass the matriculation examination and thus increase the pool of university candidates (see Table 6.7).

Israel's system of higher education has dramatically expanded over the past thirty years from one university (the Hebrew University of Jerusalem) and one technological institute (the Technion) — both founded about twenty years prior to the establishment of the state — to include four additional universities, (Tel-Aviv, Bar-Ilan, Ben Gurion in Beer-Sheeva, and Haifa).

Many of the academic positions in these institutions are held by scholars and researchers who are products of Israeli secondary schools and undergraduate education. A growing number of the young faculty have even acquired their PhDs in Israel. At the same time, the rate of Israeli scholars' publications and their participation in international research teams, symposia or conferences is steadily rising. Thus, for instance, there were about 450 publications by Israeli

Table 6.8   Numbers of students in institutions of higher learning, by degree

	1948–49	1959–60	1969–70	1978–79	1980–81	1982–83
First degree	1,549	8,348	28,053	39,010	40,910	43,380
Second degree	*	*	5,156	2,370	13,550	11,155
Third degree	86	927	1,346	2,970	3,070	3,000
Diploma	—	—	819	1,390	4,390	4,830
Special programme	—	—	865	3,050	—	—
Total	1,635	9,275	36,239	55,790	58,970	63,365

* Included among those studying for degrees
Source: Statistical Abstract of Israel, 1980, Table XXII/26; *Statistical Abstract of Israel, 1983,* Table XXII/36; and Bilezki and Turki, *The Educational System in the Mirror of Numbers,* 1982, Table 21.

scholars until 1959, while in 1967 alone there were about 2,000 publications in the natural sciences.[20] The number of students in the Israeli institutions of higher education rose from about 200 in 1929 and 1,700 in 1949 to more than 63,000 in 1982–3 (see Table 6.8). This growth rate (almost thirty-five times) far transcends that of the population growth over the respective years (about six times). The growth rate of degree recipients is even more dramatic (see Table 6.9). In addition, the number of Israeli applications entered for registration of patents rose from 638 in 1949 to 2,917 in 1982.[21]

Parallel with this development an 'explosion' of technological and vocational training took place. These tracks became — certainly in the earlier years — the main avenue for educational promotion and mobility for adolescents of AA origin. Indeed, today about two-thirds of this student body comes from AA backgrounds. One could

Table 6.9   Recipients of university degrees, by degrees

	1948–49	1959–60	1969–70	1978–79	1981–82
First degree	135	779	4,064	6,602	7,396
Second degree	48	337	807	1,767	1,754
Third degree	10	81	238	401	353
Diploma	—	—	457	786	585
Total	193	1,237	5,566	9,556	10,088

Source: Statistical Abstract of Israel, 1980, Table XXII/32; and *Statistical Abstract of Israel, 1983,* Table XXII/42.

certainly argue that these statistics suggest a discriminatory selection procedure. However, we have already noted the growing penetration of young women and men of AA origin into post-secondary training and studies (alas, even if not rapidly enough), which suggests a general trend of upward mobility.[22]

The development of skilled, locally trained manpower has great social, economic and even military importance for Israeli society. Within that context the growing percentage of skilled blue-collar workers, foremen in industry, and technicians of AA origin is highly significant. Even if top management and most senior staff of Israel's industry are still of EA origin, Israel's emergence into modern industrial civilization cannot be explained without recognizing the impact of the massive expansion of vocational training and technological education and the critical role played by many young women and men whose families originated in North Africa and the Middle East. The importance of vocational education can be seen in the rise between 1970–71 and 1981–2 of the percentage of vocational school students from 29 per cent to almost 47 per cent of the total twelfth grade student population.[23] Moreover, in 1981–2 about 25 per cent of twelfth grade vocational students studied in the vocational academic stream, and of those, about 65 per cent (about 6,000 students) took a full matriculation examination.[24] Since the total number of students who took the matriculation exam in 1981–2 was about 16,000, the vocational track contributed about 38 per cent.[25] In many respects, Israel's internationally recognized success in science-based endeavours such as medicine, high technology or agriculture, not to mention the military, can be attributed to a secondary school system which has emphasized quality of education and standards of achievement in spite of understandable and surely legitimate efforts in the opposite direction.

In conclusion, Israel's massive investment in the expansion of public education and in making it available and accessible to all, as well as the deep commitment to education and willingness to share in the burden (through taxes or fees) of its maintenance and extension to growing parts of the population, may be a partial explanation for the relative openness and democratization of the educational system being able to coexist with its relatively high educational standards.

IV.   Coping with the third challenge: providing equal educational opportunities for Israel's Arab population

To understand the development of Arab education in Israel, some background information seems to be called for.

During the year-long Israeli War of Independence (in 1948–9) there was an exodus of about 750,000 Palestinian Arabs who feared being crushed by the combating forces (some, perhaps, hoping to return upon the victory of the four invading armies). The tendency of the educated Arab middle class (and other urban inhabitants) to leave the country was significantly higher than that of the rural and lower-class population. In consequence, the 250,000 Arabs who remained in the newly established state of Israel were bereft of their intelligentsia in general and teachers in particular. Consequently most of the teachers in Arab schools were unqualified during the first fifteen or twenty years of Israel's statehood. Indeed, many Arabic-speaking Jews were recruited so as to fill some of the vacancies. This situation has changed dramatically in recent years so that, by 1981–2, 72.5 per cent of Arab elementary school teachers, 91.7 per cent of Arab intermediate school teachers and 88.7 per cent of Arab secondary school teachers were graduates of either teachers' colleges or universities.[26]

Among the Arabs who chose to remain in Israel many were peasants. To this day Arabs tend to occupy lower socioeconomic positions in Israel to a greater degree than Jews. Although in 1982, for example, 24.5 per cent of the Jewish labour force (aged 14 and over) had only eight years' education or less, the corresponding figure for Israeli Arabs was 59.2 per cent.[27] This situation contributes to a vicious circle of low education of adults, leading to low socioeconomic employment opportunities, and again to relatively low achievements by the next generation in schools.

The language issue also needs to be discussed. As one of the two official languages of Israel, Arabic is the language of instruction for Arab students from kindergarten to twelfth grade. This policy is consistent with the existing situation in which neither the majority nor the minority wishes to lose its identity or to integrate socially or culturally with the other. Hebrew is taught as the main foreign language starting in the fourth grade and English in the sixth.

The Arab student is thus at a distinct disadvantage with respect to higher education. The language of instruction in all institutions of higher education in Israel is Hebrew. There are still far too few qualified Arab candidates to justify the opening of an Arabic teaching university. Both in competing for admission and, once admitted, in the university classroom, most Jewish students (except for recent immigrants) hold an edge not only in their command of Hebrew, which the Arabs learn as a foreign language, but in their ability to use English, which is essential to higher learning due to the almost complete lack of translated texts and scientific literature in either Hebrew or Arabic.

Additionally, the political situation and its social and cultural ramifications have influenced Arab education. On the one hand, the Arabs of Israel were almost entirely cut off from social, cultural, linguistic and ideological developments in the rest of the Arab world for nineteen years until the Six Day War of 1967 by the ongoing state of belligerence to which Israel was subjected by all its surrounding Arab neighbours. During that time the Arab minority in Israel also suffered from severe suspicion from the Jewish majority and even surveillance by the security forces. The relatively limited success of Arab children and youth in secondary and higher education in Israel's early years needs to be viewed against this background.

As of 1967, the state of the Arab minority in Israel changed dramatically. Israel's conquest of the West Bank of the Jordan and the Gaza strip opened up opportunities for contact between the 400,000 Arabs of Israel and the 1 million or so Arabs of the West Bank and Gaza. Moreover, the 'open bridges' policy of Israel *vis-à-vis* Jordan allowed for the emergence of a dialogue between the Arabs of Israel and the rest of the Arab world. These events did not, however, create a state of integration or mutual acceptance. The Arabs of Israel, with very few exceptions, decided to remain Israeli citizens. The Israeli Arabs' growing rate of modernization, rising standards of living and partial (perhaps, selective) absorption of Israeli lifestyle (as expressed in housing, dress, interpersonal behaviour and the like) were responsible for a growing ambivalence on the part of much of the rest of the Arab world and a reluctance to embrace them fully into their fold. In an almost tragic way the Arabs of Israel are regarded by many Jews of Israel as being hostile to Israel's independent statehood but are also regarded as alienated from Arab culture and the 'Arab nation' by major sectors of the Arab world.

The nationalistic extremism of certain Israeli Arabs does not, of course, increase chances for mutual Jewish–Arab acceptance. This growing militancy accounts for the continuous cautiousness of Israeli authorities toward the incorporation of Arabs into senior government positions. Furthermore, the exclusion of Arabs from the otherwise universal obligation to do military service — welcomed by them for obvious reasons — deepens the estrangement between the Arab and Jewish communities within Israel. It follows, therefore, that the growing participation of Israeli Arabs in education and their relative growing success in it is being frustrated by the limited available options for mobility into jobs congruent with that education.

The complete legal equality which the Arabs of Israel enjoy — exclusion from military service is the only exception — covers education as well. Thus, 94 per cent of Arab children aged 5–13 attended schools in 1980, as compared with 98 per cent among the Jews; even in the 14–17 age group there was an increase in attendance from 294 per 1,000 in 1970 to 573 per 1,000 in 1980.[28] Since the foundation of the state of Israel, elementary school attendance among Israeli Arabs has increased thirteen-fold or more than three times their rate of population growth.[29]

As in the Jewish sector, teachers' salaries are covered by the Ministry of Education; maintenance of schools and construction of new schools are paid for by local authorities. Among the Christian Arabs (who constitute about 10 per cent of all Arab children), there is a tendency to attend private schools (sponsored by the Church). Those, too, enjoy government support. In fact, 7 per cent of all Arab students attend private schools. The language of instruction is Arabic, and cultural studies are a basic component of the curriculum (literature, history and above all, the Koran).[30] Otherwise, the curriculum in Arab schools is identical to that in the Jewish sector. Indeed, in the early 1970s many critics complained about the heavy emphasis on Jewish studies in the curriculum of Arab schools.[31] As a result far-reaching revisions were implemented.

Arab education, nevertheless, suffers from certain structural disadvantages. First, Arab schools in Israel enjoy fewer educational support services than do Jewish schools, such as psychological counselling, special education and the like. Secondly, Arab secondary education is still much less diversified than Jewish education; specifically, vocational education — which caters among Jews for more than 60 per cent of all secondary school students — is still in the early development stage among the Arabs. The relatively lower rate of Arab participation in post-elementary education is certainly a consequence of this state of affairs. And thirdly, since most Arab local authorities are rural (or small towns), the financial means at their disposal are limited. Consequently, until about ten years ago, Arab communities had distinctly worse school buildings available for their students.[32] This situation has improved significantly over the past ten years.

Are these differences between the Arab and the Jewish sector in the quality of the educational inputs a function of deliberate discrimination? It is the author's conviction, shared by numerous observers, that they are not. The Arabs of Israel have been the victims of seriously disadvantageous conditions. Educational literature has documented that this explains much of the relative school failure of Arab children. Furthermore, some of the educational innovations aimed at the promotion and development of the underachieving segments of the Jewish sector have not been (or have only partially been) introduced in the Arab sector.[33] Teaching patterns in the Arab sector are, consequently, conservative to a large extent, featuring authoritative teachers, emphasis on discipline, frontal teaching, and repetitive daily routines.

Bashi, Cahan and Davis have performed the most comprehensive study of schooling in the Arab sector to date. One of the most interesting findings of their study was that the schools in Arab communities were homogeneous in terms of parents' education (which was medium to poor), and family size (six or more children per family on average, as compared to only 2.7 children on average in the Jewish sector). In consequence, very low correlations were found between students' socioeconomic background and their scholastic achievements. This finding differed dramatically from parallel findings in the Jewish sector. In Arab communities significant differences in scholastic achievement are to be found *within* and not *between* schools. A very important policy implication seems to be that compensatory or enrichment tactics ought to be directed at subgroups within each school class rather than at total classes or entire schools (as is the case in the Jewish sector).[34]

A contemporary study of Arab students' attitudes towards their schools[35] emphasizes the importance of expectations, which were found to be essentially instrumental. Unlike the prevailing sentiment among their Jewish peers, Arab students' sentiments were predominantly negative. They did not identify with their schools since their chances of successfully passing the matriculation examination were meagre.[36] It is interesting to note that, despite these low rates of success, Arab students tend to develop very high expectations. In view of their very limited chances of social mobility in Israeli society, these high expectations reflect the great prestige value that education carries within the Arab village or small town. University students displayed high expectations identical to those of school children, but comparisons between freshmen and seniors in college showed that confidence in fulfilling those expectations had shrunk as the students neared graduation.[37]

It is, therefore, not surprising that many of the approximately 50 per cent of the 14–17-year-old Israeli Arabs who are not in school are very critically oriented towards their environment. On the one hand, they have enjoyed nine to ten years of schooling (unlike most of the elders in their home communities) and are ambivalent towards their traditional setting; on the other hand, they cannot complete a full cycle of secondary education (or do not feel motivated to do so) and consequently do not foresee real chances for social participation congruent with education. It is likely that this conflict contributes to the relatively high (and rising) rates of juvenile delinquency in the Arab settlements.

Interestingly, Arab university graduates tend to face a similar though even more severe conflict. They have undergone an experience of modernization and consequently withdrawn from their traditional environment and find themselves to a degree in conflict with it. Yet they have only meagre opportunities for mobility within the broader Israeli society.[38]

In conclusion, Israel can legitimately claim that very significant improvements have taken place in the rates of Arab participation in the educational system. Table 6.10 clearly shows that in the twenty

Table 6.10 The educational achievements of adults (over 14 years), by national identity and number of years of schooling

| | | | Number of years of schooling | | | | |
		Total	0–4	5–8	9–12	13–13	16+
Jews	1961	100	20.1	35.4	34.6	9.9	
	1972	100	13.6	29.3	42.6	9.1	5.4
	1980	100	10.3	21.3	47.6	12.3	8.5
Arabs	1961	100	63.3	27.5	7.6	1.5	
	1972	100	48.0	35.7	13.9	1.9	0.4
	1980	100	28.9	33.9	29.5	5.5	2.2

Source: Bilezki and Turki, *Education in the Mirror of Numbers,* The Ministry of Education and Culture, Jerusalem, 1982, Table 34 (Hebrew, mimeo).

years between 1961 and 1980, the percentage of uneducated Arab adults has more than halved; similarly, between 1970 and 1980 the percentage of adults who completed thirteen or more years of education has more than tripled. The respective rate of growth among the Jews in those ten years was about 30 per cent. It is, of course, true that the absolute rates of Arab participation in the educational system are, in spite of the mentioned dramatic trend, still significantly lower than those of the Jews.

Parallel with this expansion of educational services (and the concomitant processes of modernization), we witness — in both Jews and Arabs — heightened nationalism attended by ethnocentrism.[39] This polarization may well be explained against the social and political background briefly described in this paper. The Ministry of Education's recently proposed educational interventions, in and of themselves most welcome developments, may contribute, even if only moderately, to the emergence of a more or less satisfying mode of coexistence, despite the continuing difficulties.[40]

Notes

1. This discussion follows the model described and analysed by S. Smooha, *Israel — Pluralism and Conflict*, Routledge & Kegan Paul, 1978. To what extent and in which respect Isreal indeed is a pluralistic society is beyond the scope of this paper.
2. E. Rieger, *Hebrew Education in Palestine*, Dvir Publishing Co., Tel Aviv, 1940 (Hebrew), pp. 1–95; J. Bentwich, *Education in Israel*, Routledge & Kegan Paul, London, 1965; R. Elboim-Dror, 'Israel's Educational Policies' in W. Ackerman *et al.* (eds), *Education in Israel*, Klett-Cotta, Stuttgart, Germany, 1982 (German), pp. 54–74.
3. R. Elboim-Dror, 'Israel's Educational Policies', pp. 74–81.
4. Ibid.
5. R. Kahane, 'Patterns of National Identity in Israel' in S.N. Eisenstadt *et al.* (eds), *Education and Society in Israel*, Academon, Jerusalem, 1968 (Hebrew).
6. Central Bureau of Statistics, *Statistical Abstract of Israel, 1980*, Jerusalem, 1981 (Hebrew and English), Table V/2, p. 134.
7. See for instance: C. Adler, 'The Place of Education in the Integration of Ethnic Communities in Israel', in S.N. Eisenstadt and A. Zloczower (eds), *Ingathering of Exiles*, The Magnes Press, Jerusalem, 1969 (Hebrew).
8. See for instance: C. Frankenstein (ed.), *Teaching as a Social Challenge*, School of Education, The Hebrew University of Jerusalem, and the Ministry of Education and Culture, Jerusalem, 1976 (in memory of Z. Aranne, late Minister of Education and Culture).

9. Y. Dar in collaboration with N. Resh. *Homogeneity and Heterogeneity in Education*, The NCJW Research Institute for Innovation in Education, School of Education, The Hebrew University of Jerusalem, 1981 (mimeo).

10. Z. Klein and Y. Eshel, *Integrating Jerusalem Schools*, Academic Press Inc., 1980. See also *Megamot: Behavioral Science Quarterly*, special edition, **XXIII**, nos. 3–4 (1977) (Hebrew, English Abstracts).

11. D. Davis, D. Sprinzak, and R. Osizon, *Who Benefits from Educational Resources: Allocation of Resources in Years 1973, 1978, 1981*, The Ministry of Education and Culture, Jerusalem, 1982 (Hebrew).

12. C. Adler, 'The Evaluation of the Israeli School Reform' in S. Goldstein (ed.), *Law and Equality in Education*, The Van Leer Jerusalem Foundation, 1980, pp. 53–9; E. Peled, 'The Educational Reform in Israel — The Political Aspect' in E. Ben-Baruch and Y. Newmann (eds), *Educational Policy and Policy Making*, Vinpress, Herzlia, Israel, 1982, pp. 85–109.

13. C. Adler and P. Melzer-Druker, *A Survey of Evaluations of Educational Intervention Programs Sponsored by Project Renewal*, The NCJW Research Institute for Innovation in Education, School of Education, The Hebrew University of Jerusalem, 1983 (mimeo).

14. Central Bureau of Statistics, op. cit., Table XXII/9, p. 586.

15. P. Bilezki and Ch. Turki, *The Educational System in the Mirror of Numbers, 1982*, Jerusalem, 1982, Table 7, p. 7 (mimeo, Hebrew).

16. Central Bureau of Statistics, op. cit., Table XXII/12.

17. Bilezki and Turki, op. cit., Table 17, p. 17.

18. See, for example, F. Musgrove, *School and the Social Order*, John Wiley & Sons, New York, 1979.

19. The relevant statistics have never been officially published. This statement is thus my own approximated calculation, based on unpublished reports, as well as on growth rates in university attendance (see, for example, Central Bureau of Statistics, *Statistical Abstracts of Israel, 1982*, Jerusalem, 1983, Table XXII/39).

20. R. Kahane, 'Preliminary Reflections on the University in Israel: A Sociological Perspective' (mimeo, presented at the Symposium on the International Issues in University Administration, Ankara University, March 1979).

21. See Central Bureau of Statistics, *Statistical Abstracts of Israel, 1983*, Jerusalem, 1983, Table XXIII/9.

22. R. Kahane and L. Starr, *Education and Work: Vocational Socialization Processes in Israel*, The Magnes Press, Jerusalem, 1984 (Hebrew).

23. See Bilezki and Turki, op. cit., Table 12.

24. Central Bureau of Statistics, *Statistical Abstracts of Israel, 1982*, Table XXII/28.

25. Ibid., Table XXII/27.

26. Bilezki and Turki, op. cit., Table 33.

27. Central Bureau of Statistics, *Statistical Abstracts of Israel, 1982*, Tables XII/5 and XII/8.

28. In 1970 the minimum school-leaving age was still 15. It was raised to 16 in 1978. See Bilezki and Turki, op. cit., Table 19.

29. J. Bashi, S. Cahan, D. Davis, *Educational Achievements of the Arab*

Elementary School in Israel, The Hebrew University of Jerusalem, 1981 (Hebrew).
30. As Arab students study two foreign languages (Hebrew and English), about 50 per cent of teaching time is devoted to language instruction (compared with only about 35 per cent in the Jewish sector).
31. Y. Perez, 'National Education for Arab Youth in Israel: A Comparative Analysis of Curricula', *The Jewish Journal of Sociology*, **12**, no. 2 (1970); and Sami Mar'i Khalil, *Arab Education in Israel*, Syracuse University Press, New York, 1978.
32. A.F. Kleinberger, op. cit., Pergamon Press, Oxford, 1969, Ch. VII.
33. Ibid.
34. Bashi *et al.*, op. cit.
35. Azis Haider, 'Determinants of Identification with and Alienation from School of Arab High-School Pupils in Israel', thesis submitted for the MA degree, The Hebrew University of Jerusalem, 1981 (Hebrew).
36. In 1980, 21 per cent of all Jewish adults (over fourteen years of age) had enjoyed more than twelve years' of education, while only about 8 per cent of all adults in the Arab sector had.
37. R. Peleg and A. Benjamin, *Higher Education and the Israeli Arabs*, Am-Oved, 1977 (Hebrew).
38. Peleg and Benjamin, op. cit.
39. Lazarovitz-Herz, 'Identity and Educational Environment', *BaShaar*, vol. 2 (June–September 1981) (Hebrew).
40. *Guidelines for Educational Intervention on the Subject of Education for Jewish Arab Coexistence*, Pedagogical Secretariat, Ministry of Education and Culture, September 1983 (Hebrew).

7 FEDERAL CHARACTER AND THE EDUCATIONAL SYSTEM IN NIGERIA

Uma O. Eleazu

Federal character

To understand the politics of education in Nigeria, one must examine the history of the development of Western education there. Western education was introduced and established by the work of missionaries who operated primarily in the southern part of the country. As a matter of fact, missionary work in education antedated outright colonialism by almost fifty years. By the time Nigeria came into being in 1900, the southern colonies and protectorate had a head start over the northern protectorate, a largely Muslim territory where Arabic learning predominated.

Colonial education policy did not help matters. For the first thirty years (that is, until the 1930s) a *laissez-faire* type of policy existed. Missionaries were left alone to carry on their educational work with minimal interference from the colonial administration. In the North it was also colonial policy not to interfere with Islamic religion and education. In fact, there was a conscious effort to discourage Christian evangelical missions in the North as part of the policy of not disturbing existing religious institutions. This policy had the effect of widening the gap in educational development between the two parts of Nigeria. Such Western education as was eventually to develop in the North was kept under the strict and watchful eye of the native authorities, overseen by the colonial master.

By the time of independence the wide gap in Western educational attainment between the North and South of Nigeria had become a major problem. However, Western education was seen as the key to modernity. Through Western educational institutions manpower was developed to run the various modern structures in the economy. Without that education, a Nigerian was unlikely to be able to compete with his fellow citizens on equal terms. Education, it was also believed, provided the means by which this imbalance could be redressed. As a result access to educational opportunity became a prized value in the political system.

Each succeeding government recognized the cleavage created by educational imbalance and the need to do something about it because of education's centrality in dealing with other cleavages in the society. Against this backdrop I propose to examine how the 'federal character principle' designed to cope with ethnic and other kinds of pluralism in Nigerian society was applied in education.

The idea of 'federal character'

The idea of 'federal character' was in the air when the Constitution of the Second Republic was drafted. The concept was developed as a way to recognize and accommodate the unmeltable core of ethnicity that made federalism necessary. It was as if we were saying to ourselves, 'We recognize that we are made up of various ethnic groups, we are not all equally endowed, but we all have to make it together as a nation, so in all our dealings we have to take into account that these differences exist and order our governance in a way that will be just and equitable in view of the said differences.'[1] The notion of federal character called for the adoption of various distributive techniques to ensure equitable treatment. The purpose of this paper is to assess how this concept has been applied to the all-important area of education.

The constitutional basis of the term 'federal character' has been discussed by many. Suffice it to summarize as follows.

The Constitution of the Second Republic provided that:

> The composition of the Federal Government or any of its agencies and the conduct of their affairs shall be carried out in such manner as to recognize the Federal character of Nigeria and the need to promote national unity and to command national loyalty.[2]

The Educational objectives and objective principles of educational policy also provided that:

> The Government shall endeavour to ensure that there are equal and adequate educational opportunities available at all levels to the people within the area of its authority.
>
> The Federal Government shall take all possible steps to ensure that the educational opportunities available at all levels to persons in any area or part of the Federation are equal to those in any other area or part of the Federation.[3]

It is important to note that both sections are merely directive principles of national policy. They are not justiciable. But the various levels of government are expected to adhere to the 'spirit of the Constitution' as much as possible.

Primary-level education is entirely an affair of state and local government with support given by the federal government. Although state governments are expected to respect the federal character principle as it applies to disparities which might exist within their areas of authority, I will not deal with state-run educational institutions in this paper. Instead, I will focus on those areas where most or all the ethnic groups are in competition for scarce opportunities and discuss three subsystems of the educational system in Nigeria: (1) federal government secondary schools; (2) federal polytechnics; and (3) federal universities.

Following the above constitutional guiding principle, the *National Policy on Education (Revised), 1981* stated that the philosophy of Nigerian education will be based 'on the integration of the individual into a sound and effective citizen and equal educational opportunities for all citizens . . .'[4] Thus, the aims and objectives of educational policy were spelled out to include:

> the inculcation of national consciousness and national unity;
> the inculcation of the right type of values and attitudes for the survival of the individual and the Nigerian Society . . .
> Furthermore, to foster the much needed unity of Nigeria, imbalances in inter-state and intra-state development have to be corrected. Not only is education the greatest force that can be used to bring about redress, it is also the greatest investment that the nation can make for the quick development of its economic, political, sociological and human resources.[5]

Here we find unambiguous expression of the hope and the belief that social engineering can correct certain imbalances while giving everybody equal opportunity and equal access to education. It is interesting to note that the importance of language as a means of preserving culture was recognized in the *National Policy on Education*:

> [It was therefore provided that] each child should be encouraged to learn one of the three major languages other than his own mother-tongue. In this connection, the Government considers the three major languages to be Hausa, Ibo and Yoruba.[6]

The educational system in Nigeria

As in most countries, formal education is structured in three tiers —
primary, secondary, and higher (tertiary) education including
professional education. In addition, there are continuing education
facilities provided by either employers or state institutions and
parastatals. Primary education covers the ages 5+ to 11+, secondary
education starts at 11+ to 17, while higher education can be
embarked upon at any time after the secondary stage.

Secondary education, which is of six years' duration, is designed to
take place in two stages — junior secondary school and senior
secondary school — each lasting three years. The national education
policy as revised in 1981 aimed at a 100 per cent transition from
primary to junior secondary including craft schools and other
vocational schools, the idea being to keep students in school until the
age of 15, after which those unable to cope with work in the senior
secondary school could leave the system for the job market with an
employable skill.

Higher education is defined as the post-secondary education
offered in universities, polytechnics, colleges of education or colleges
of technology. There is a National Universities Commission (NUC)
through which the federal government channels finances to the
various universities. The NUC also plays an important role in the
organization and administration of the universities. A similar body,
the National Board for Technical Education, also exists for the
polytechnics but has not developed the power and prestige of the
NUC.

Constitutionally, both the federal and state governments have
concurrent powers of legislation over education. Thus each can make
laws concerning education and can also establish educational
institutions. In practice, the federal government has left the field of
primary and pre-primary education to the states. The original idea of
the Constitution drafting committee was that the federal government
should be responsible for higher education while setting standards
through appropriate legislation for the lower levels. This provision
was not accepted by the Constituent Assembly, however, so state
governments can establish and run institutions of higher education
including universities, and the federal government can theoretically
establish and run primary schools. In fact there are federal primary
schools on military bases, but they constitute a special case and will
not be further discussed in this paper.

Control structure of secondary and higher education

Given the importance of education, each level of government (especially the states) wants to ensure access to education for its 'indigenes'. In so doing, each authority is expected to recognize the ethnic diversity existing in its territory. The greatest conflicts, however, usually arise not within the states or municipalities but over the educational opportunities available at the federal level.

Although the federal government dominates university education, some states have found it necessary to establish universities to provide more places for their own students for whom there are not sufficient places in the federal institutions. Table 7.1 shows the situation in 1982.

Table 7.1   Control/ownership structure

Level	Federal	State
Universities*	20	7
Polytechnics†	17	27
Secondary schools	39	1,691
Trade/vocational schools	—	109

* Includes Universities of Technology
† Includes Advanced Teachers' College and Schools of Agriculture

Application of the federal character in federal secondary schools

There are thirty-nine federal secondary schools. The idea that they should serve as a kind of 'melting pot' for the boys and girls who pass through them pre-dates the 1979 Constitution. The federal secondary schools were sometimes referred to as 'unity' schools with a uniform motto '*pro unitate*'. The National Policy on Education (Revised) 1981 reinforced this idea by stating categorically:

> Government believes that education should help develop in our youths a sense of unity, patriotism and love of country . . . Every secondary school should therefore function as a unity school by enrolling students belonging to other areas or states.

This turned out to be easier said than done as an examination of the admission practices of the federal secondary schools shows. Each year the West African Examinations Council sets a common entrance examination which is open to all boys and girls in the final class of primary school in all the states. Based on the examination results, the Council determines a qualifying score for applicants.

The maximum score in any year is 350 points. In 1984, for example, the highest score was 328, and the cut-off point was set at 297. Those who scored 297 points and above were then called up for another examination and an oral interview. The federal schools use the results of this second examination and interview to determine whom to admit. The guidelines from the Ministry of Education require each school to admit 20 per cent on merit, 50 per cent on the basis of equality of states and 30 per cent on 'environmental factors'. Thus for an intake of 120 pupils into class I, for example, the first 24 would be taken on merit, and the next 60 places would be shared equally among the 19 states, that is, roughly 3 from each state.

In selecting the state candidates, the schools take the four from each state with the highest test scores. Often the first four in one state will bunch between 80 and 90 per cent while in another the first four may spread from 40 to 90 per cent. As a result, one candidate may score 78 per cent and not be taken whereas another may score 39 per cent and gain admission via the state quota.

The remaining places reserved for 'environmental factors' are used to redress imbalances among the states. All the northern states plus Rivers State (a total of eleven) are considered 'disadvantaged' and must be given preference in the allocation of the remaining places. The 'disadvantaged' designation indicates that the number of school-age children actually enrolled in schools in those states is low in relation to the total that could be enrolled. This in itself raises a number of questions. How low is 'low' in a situation where no one really knows what the total population is? How will increased admission into federal secondary schools improve enrolment at the primary level? Is any progress being made towards making them less disadvantaged? Whether or not they are really disadvantaged is sometimes even disputed in government circles. As a result this 30 per cent quota, in practice, has gone largely to the indigenes of the state in which the school is situated and, to a lesser extent, and at the discretion of the principal, to children of federal officers serving in the state.

Some believe that if a state is 'disadvantaged' its students are handicapped to the extent that they cannot compete effectively with those from so-called 'advantaged' states. Unless special allocations or quotas are mandated, they argue, such states will not be able to produce students for the federal secondary schools. This is not necessarily true, since ability to compete is more a function of the quality of teaching and learning than of one's state of origin. Others have recognized that the quota system tends to sacrifice merit for mediocrity. They argue that the way to correct imbalances between the states is not by applying a quota system to the few federal secondary schools but by increasing the number and improving the quality of primary schools in the disadvantaged states. Still others argue that it is unfair to punish children from one state because of a presumed deficit in another state for which those children have no responsibility. After all, who comes from which state is an accident of birth.

The federal secondary schools' ability to mobilize young people to promote national unity should not be exaggerated. The number of children attending federal secondary schools is at best only 2 per cent of the total secondary school enrolment. To produce a significant impact on national unity, all secondary schools would have to be 'unity schools'. Some have argued, however, that any nation needs a core of people with specialized education and upbringing to form a ruling elite and that the federal secondary schools provide the first stage of this elitist upbringing. According to this theory 'unity schools' should be model secondary schools recruiting the best students and preparing them for the best places in the university system. From the university they emerge as future leaders whose ethnicity and parochial attachments will have rubbed off by contact with boys and girls from other ethnic groups and backgrounds.

Such elitist philosophy is not only anathema to a society that espouses equal opportunity for all as a national credo but the facts do not support its claims. While it may be true that federal secondary schools have the annual opportunity to cream off the 'best and the brightest' from each crop of primary school leavers, results of the West African School Certificate do not support the claim that these students are necessarily the best achievers at the secondary school level. Besides, some of the best teachers are in the state school systems rather than the federal. In spite of their relatively poorer financial endowment, some of the states do a comparatively better job of preparing the pupils for university work. Although there is some validity to the claim of positive socialization resulting from the mixing of children from various backgrounds, its impact on the population is minimal because it only applies to the limited number of children attending federal schools.

Application of federal character in federal polytechnics

There are ten federal polytechnics in the country, six in the northern states and four in the southern. Most of them are located in very awkward, out-of-the-way places. It is not exactly clear why the authorities chose the particular towns where these institutions have been established. However, the decision is usually influenced by a number of political factors including personal interests.

Unlike the federal secondary schools, admission into the federal polytechnics is not centralized. Each institution is allowed to recruit its own students. There are, however, a few guidelines such as the one calling on school authorities to ensure that 20 per cent of their intake is on merit and 80 per cent on the basis of equality among the states — which means that if a polytechnic admits ten applicants from one state, then each state must be given ten places. In point of fact, most northern states find it difficult to fill their quotas because their secondary school systems cannot produce enough candidates with the requisite qualifications.

A number of federal polytechnics have, therefore, established remedial courses to teach mathematics and science subjects up to O level (high school) standard to enable students from disadvantaged states to cope with various technical subjects. Yet even when the entry requirements are lowered and students are offered remedial courses, some states still find it difficult to fill all their places in the remedial classes. In some cases students who had no science subjects at all at secondary school and therefore could not profit from the remedial courses, which assume a certain level of preparation, have presented themselves at the start of the academic year. In cases where a student has taken, for example, mathematics at the school certificate examination and has not obtained a credit grade for it, remedial courses may help. For those students who have never taken mathematics at all, on the other hand, there is nothing to remedy.

Staffing

As in student admissions, each polytechnic is independent and can advertise for and recruit its own staff. The general guideline is that the lower-level, unskilled and semi-skilled jobs should go to indigenes of the states in which the institutions are located. But for the more academic or professional jobs, competence should take priority over federal character. However, in many of the polytechnics there have been persistent accusations and counter-accusations of favouritism and nepotism. Since 1979, each federal agency has been expected to reflect federal character, and most polytechnics have loosely applied the principle to the selection of senior staff.

Certain practical difficulties render the federal character role virtually unenforceable. Most northerners are in very high demand in services in their own states, where they usually get the cream of the jobs. There is no incentive for them to join the overcrowded federal services where advancement opportunities are generally few and highly competitive. Southern lecturers are reluctant to take up jobs in the north and vice versa because of family problems having to do with the inability of their wives to find alternative employment or the difficulty of finding suitable schools for their children owing to differences in state requirements and standards.

Since the advent of the present military administration, the government has sought to trim overstaffed federal agencies as a means of reducing government spending. This policy has not materially affected teachers and lecturers in federal schools or polytechnics. However, there has been a shift towards removing southern principals and teachers from their posts in other schools in the north and replacing them with northerners. This shift can be said to conflict with the spirit of the federal character principle.

University admissions and federal character

University admissions are complicated and evoke a lot of interest. Universities' positive contribution to the development of high-level manpower — indeed, manpower for the 'ruling class' — is reason enough for admissions to have become politicized. No state, section or ethnic group wants to be left out. After 1970, all universities in the country were taken over by the federal government; recently, however, some states and even private individuals and organizations have attempted to establish universities. In order to ensure even-handed development, universities are treated as another level of 'unity' institution and given more elaborate guidelines for admissions.

Joint Admissions and Matriculation Board

The Joint Admissions and Matriculation Board (JAMB) is an examination body whose major functions are:

> To organise, administer and conduct matriculation examinations for undergraduate admission into all universities and degree awarding institutions in Nigeria. . . .
> To place in Nigerian Universities candidates who satisfy matriculation requirements through a pass at the matriculation examination or at other recognised examinations like the G.C.E. (Advanced Level) and H.S.C. examinations . . .

Each year the JAMB sets examinations which are open to all who have completed secondary education or are in the final class of secondary school. In addition to passing the Joint Admission and Matriculation Examination, a candidate is also expected to have passed the West African School Certificate (WASC) with credit rating in English, mathematics and three other subjects relevant to the discipline he/she wishes to pursue.

People who enter through the JAM Examination usually take four years to complete a university degree course. Certain professional degrees (such as medicine) take up to six years. A second avenue for entry is to obtain passes at Advanced Level in the General Certificate of Education (GCE A level) in three relevant subjects in one sitting or four in two sittings. Candidates who enter by this so-called 'direct entry' do not sit the JAM Examination but proceed to a three-year course for the basic degree (except for the professional courses). These are the objective criteria for deciding who gets a place at university.

Universities are also given very detailed guidelines by the National Universities Commission on how to comply with federal character and other principles. For example, they are expected to reserve a certain percentage of places to be awarded on merit, a certain percentage in the various disciplines for students from each state, a certain percentage to applicants from their catchment area, and only 5 per cent of the places are left to be allocated at the discretion of the university administrators. The problem of availability of candidates from all the states is even more acute at this level than at the secondary or polytechnics levels. Yet each year there is a scramble for university places because the total demand is more than the universities can accommodate.

The NUC uses its power of the purse to reward universities that are faithful to its guidelines and punish those which do not keep them. But sometimes strict adherence to their guidelines can produce results counter to the real objective of the federal character principle. As in the case of polytechnics, many people feel that 'political' interference in admissions policy is costing the nation a lot in terms of potential manpower lost to the system.

Federal character in staffing

Universities, like the polytechnics, are free to recruit professional and senior staff from anywhere. Because of the paucity of scholars in the various disciplines, it has not been possible (nor is it practical) to insist on each university reflecting federal character among its staff. In fact most university staffs take on an international rather than national character. At the lower level of non-academic staff, the tendency has been to employ people primarily from the catchment area of each particular university.

After the 1978 crisis in which several students were killed, leading to the dismissal of a number of vice-chancellors and registrars, the federal government took greater interest in the composition of the various university councils. The government decided to appoint well-known Nigerians or traditional rulers as chancellors with other council members drawn from other parts of the country. This move was designed to promote increased understanding among the managers of higher education institutions. It has, however, not stopped occasional bickering and quarrelling over who is favouring whom in admissions and employment.

Analysis and evaluation of data

After five years of systematic application of the principle of federal character, it is important to evaluate its prospects and problems. It is also important to look at the assumptions underlying some policy measures.

Historically some states of the federation appear to be more aware of the importance of Western education than others, partly because of the differential impact of the trappings of colonialism on the various peoples of Nigeria, partly because of cultural and religious structures existing at the time of colonial impact, and partly due to

Table 7.2 Population and primary school enrolment

State	LGA No. 1	1963 Population census	Projected Population for 1979	Enrolment in 1978–79	Enrolment as percentage of population	Transition rate to post-primary education
Anambra	23	3,596,618	5,321,000	903,019	16.97	9.86
Bauchi	16	2,431,296	3,596,900	357,212	9.93	2.75
Bendel	19	2,460,962	3,640,800	792,921	21.77	13.40
Benue	13	2,427,017	3,590,600	838,723	23.35	4.36
Borno	18	2,997,498	4,434,600	529,620	11.94	1.40
Cross River	17	3,478,131	5,145,700	863,700	16.78	11.20
Gongola	17	2,605,263	3,854,300	397,705	10.31	2.52
Imo	21	3,672,654	5,433,500	1,014,467	18.67	10.78
Kaduna	14	4,098,306	6,063,200	747,125	12.32	4.24
Kano	20	5,774,840	8,543,500	667,998	7.81	2.10
Kwara	12	1,714,485	2,536,500	493,241	19.44	10.82
Lagos	8	1,443,568	2,396,400	443,057	18.48	17.99
Niger	9	1,194,508	1,767,200	277,495	15.70	1.98
Ogun	10	1,550,966	2,294,600	345,393	15.05	10.96
Ondo	17	2,729,690	4,038,400	464,395	11.49	13.83
Oyo	24	5,208,884	7,706,200	996,362	12.92	8.54
Plateau	14	2,026,657	2,998,300	455,500	15.19	3.69
Rivers	9	1,719,925	2,544,500	470,438	18.48	3.91
Sokoto	19	4,538,787	6,714,800	397,401	5.91	1.92
Total all Nigeria	300	55,670,055	82,621,000	11,457,772	13.86* 14.86†	7.17†

* Percentage enrolment based on projected population for 1979.
† Unweighted mean of the percentages for 19 states.

conscious policy adopted by successive governments and variations in application.

Table 7.2 shows primary school enrolment in relation to population. The first problem is that the Census figure used is an extrapolation from 1963 Census figures. Since then no reliable Census has been taken. We do not know how many school-age children are in each state. The next best thing is to use the proportion of enrolment to total population. This gives an aggregate 11.4 million enrolment out of a total population of 82.62 million or 13.86 per cent. National average enrolment is 14.86. With this figure, the 'disadvantaged states' whose ratio of primary school enrolment to total population falls below the national average would appear to be Bauchi, Borno, Gongola, Kaduna, Kano, Ondo, Oyo and Sokoto.

Table 7.3 Enrolment in post-primary institutions, 1980–81

States	State schools						Federal schools		
	Male	Female	Mixed	Other	Total no. of schools	Total enrolment	No. of schools	Enrolment	
Anambra	101	64	17	3	185	89,137	2	1,100	
Bauchi	19	6	—	—	25	9,832	2	288	
Bendel	47	25	96	—	168	106,280	2	1,361	Fed. Sch. of A. & Sc. (496)
Benue	13	8	49	5	75	36,595	2	486	
Borno	1	1	15	—	17	7,662	2	939	Fed. Sch. of A. & Sc. (396)
Cross River	7	15	152	4	178	96,916	2	970	
Gongola	5	2	20	—	27	10,025	2	129	
Imo	55	36	55	1	147	109,455	2	933	Fed. Sch. of A. & Sc. (230)
Kaduna	Unspecified				49	31,715	2	927	
Kano	24	4	1	1	79	14,056	2	1,257	
Kwara	11	9	59	—	30	53,411	2	1,082	Fed. Sch. of A. & Sc. (1,374)
Lagos	13	12	31	15	71	79,744	3	2,018	
Niger	11	5	—	—	16	5,514	2	473	
Ogun	6	5	69	—	80	37,888	2	1,218	
Ondo	20	11	71	51	153	64,256	2	364	Fed. Sch. of A. & Sc. (412)
Oyo	12	16	174	31	233	85,093	2	878	
Plateau	7	6	30	6	49	16,810	2	550	
Rivers	32	16	36	3	87	18,441	2	946	
Sokoto	17	4	—	1	22	7,641	2	611	Fed. Sch. of A. & Sc. (230)
Total					1,691	880,471	39	17,592	Abuja F.C.T. (2) (New)

Table 7.3 shows the number and enrolment of secondary schools in each state. The states with low primary school enrolment also have low secondary school enrolment with the exception of Ondo and Oyo, which are 'advantaged states' with respect to secondary education. However, if one compares the secondary and primary school enrolment by taking the former as a proportion of the latter shown as the transition rate in Table 7.2 to measure opportunity and access to post primary education, another picture emerges. The mean national transition rate is 7.17 per cent, and using this figure as a basis for differentiation Oyo and Ondo drop out of the ranks of disadvantaged states, but Benue and Niger take their places.

The problem is not one of integrating an ethnic group or minority into a mainstream but rather one of welding everybody into a national unity out of the hodgepodge of nationalities that make up Nigeria. (Figures given above are for state schools.)

Column 7 of Table 7.3 shows that there are 39 federal secondary schools compared to a total of 1,691 state secondary schools. It is these 39 'unity' schools that are practising 'federal character'. Total 1980–81 enrolment in the federal 'unity' schools was 17,592 as against 880,471 for state schools. The state-by-state breakdown of enrolment in these federal secondary schools was unobtainable.

Federal polytechnics

We were unable to obtain the data for any federal polytechnic except the one located in Idah. One wonders how the Ministry of Education can monitor and evaluate whether its regulations are being followed and whether the policy is moving the nation towards its objectives when these figures are not systematically collected.

Federal universities

Table 7.4 is a breakdown of the number of requests for places in universities in 1982–3. Notice the close correlation between enrolment in secondary schools (Table 7.3) and applications to sit the JAM Examination. Table 7.5, on the other hand, details provisional admissions through the JAM Examination for the same academic session.

The effect of the quota system is seen in the proportion of those admitted as a percentage of those who applied, state by state. This raises the issue of whether the principle of federal character does not

Table 7.4 JAMB summary of applications for first degree courses, by faculties and states, for 1982–83 academic session, from students taking JAM examination

	Unspecified	Anambra	Bauchi	Bendel	Benue	Borno	Cross River	Gongola	Imo	Kaduna	Kano
Agriculture	2	675	93	784	182	28	296	41	1,219	30	22
Arts	6	2,958	273	3,295	474	60	1,085	63	4,110	66	29
Business Administration	1	2,957	111	3,186	351	58	613	67	4,292	60	49
Education	1	2,506	91	2,014	211	27	689	28	2,779	17	12
Engineering technology and environmental studies	7	2,635	185	2,721	533	92	911	122	3,623	123	100
Law	6	4,274	208	5,785	882	98	2,004	123	7,006	103	43
Medicine	2	3,082	132	3,295	500	65	1,261	101	4,361	88	57
Science	–	970	71	1,274	134	30	481	39	1,744	27	21
Social science	4	4,558	205	5,208	807	82	1,787	93	6,248	66	41
State total	29	24,615	1,369	27,562	4,074	540	9,127	677	35,382	580	374
Percentage of national total	0.0	14.2	0.8	15.9	2.4	0.3	5.3	0.4	20.4	0.3	0.2

Table 7.4 (continued)

	Kwara	Lagos	Niger	Ogun	Ondo	Oyo	Plateau	Rivers	Sokoto	Foreign	Faculty Total
Agriculture	217	130	39	692	838	1,225	75	71	6	6	6,671
Arts	600	311	42	1,181	1,934	2,570	189	729	25	33	20,033
Business Administration	1,005	474	33	1,802	2,376	3,426	116	404	13	18	21,112
Education	376	215	17	850	1,785	2,577	100	525	8	17	14,845
Engineering technology and environmental studies	697	415	79	1,686	1,870	2,780	268	514	32	102	19,495
Law	863	594	60	2,021	2,296	2,736	324	1,079	18	44	30,567
Medicine	838	512	64	2,008	2,028	3,064	166	828	23	207	22,682
Science	341	111	19	490	674	833	70	481	12	25	7,847
Social Science	750	447	56	1,596	2,653	2,794	231	1,805	23	21	29,475
State total	5,687	3,209	409	12,326	16,454	22,005	1,539	6,436	160	473	173,027
Percentage of national total	3.3	1.9	0.2	7.1	9.5	12.7	0.9	8.7	0.1	0.3	

Table 7.5 Joint Admissions and Matriculation Board summary of provisional admissions for first degree courses by states and universities for 1982/83 session

University	Anambra	Bauchi	Bendel	Benue	Borno	Cross River	Gongola	Imo	Kaduna	Kano
Ibadan	107	3	415	48	3	122	10	170	6	10
Lagos	113	3	359	15	2	124	2	202	12	5
Nsukka	1,341	9	194	47	8	68	13	984	4	4
Zaria	33	91	42	197	84	37	139	43	300	122
Ife	46	22	126	17	—	37	2	50	3	1
Benin	167	12	1,078	25	2	44	1	154	4	1
Jos	111	49	89	202	14	74	34	121	25	7
Calabar	109	5	86	26	1	453	2	233	2	—
Kano	4	24	7	20	12	13	5	6	89	168
Maidguri	10	42	9	24	91	12	55	8	11	10
Sokoto	10	7	16	14	3	25	6	10	30	15
Ilorin	38	3	97	37	1	45	8	48	5	3
Port Harcourt	42	1	72	5	—	34	—	69	—	—
Bauchi	17	14	10	6	2	12	9	13	13	10
Makurdi	16	10	24	51	2	10	5	18	5	3
Owerri	40	6	27	10	1	22	1	110	1	3
Akure	11	1	26	3	—	10	—	11	—	—
Yola	12	—	19	13	—	1	31	33	3	—
Total	2,227	282	2,696	760	226	1,143	323	2,283	513	362
% Distribution by state	10.8	1.4	13.0	3.7	1.1	5.5	1.6	11.0	2.5	1.8

Table 7.5 (*continued*)

University	Kwara	Lagos	Niger	Ogun	Ondo	Oyo	Plateau	Rivers	Sokoto	Non-Nigerian	Total
Ibadan	201	92	6	397	474	760	10	37	5	58	2,934
Lagos	58	215	1	535	434	506	1	37	1	32	2,657
Nsukka	46	16	4	24	56	71	13	41	—	22	2,965
Zaria	174	14	109	18	20	34	132	15	90	27	1,721
Ife	43	76	2	306	424	684	5	22	2	8	1,856
Benin	33	43	1	43	154	74	3	47	—	18	1,904
Jos	41	22	14	23	56	51	176	32	11	29	1,181
Calabar	11	14	—	10	28	24	2	34	—	6	1,046
Kano	15	2	41	2	6	6	5	3	21	2	451
Maidguri	12	2	14	7	6	5	16	6	4	1	345
Sokoto	20	3	51	3	3	10	13	6	134	8	387
Ilorin	723	49	13	79	254	310	4	8	5	10	1,740
Port Harcourt	2	5	—	5	6	8	3	163	—	1	416
Bauchi	10	8	7	9	7	22	15	6	—	6	196
Makurdi	6	9	6	10	12	11	13	14	3	7	235
Owerri	6	3	4	13	12	18	8	14	—	2	301
Akure	3	11	—	9	85	23	—	6	—	—	199
Yola	6	—	1	—	3	1	2	1	—	1	127
Total	1,410	584	274	1,493	2,040	2,618	421	492	276	238	20,661
% Distribution by state	6.8	2.8	1.3	7.2	9.9	12.7	2.0	2.4	1.3	1.2	100.0

Source: Cued from Joint Admissions and Matriculation Board (JAMB) papers.

negate the principle of equal opportunity and equal access to education which the Constitution seems to uphold.

The problem of displaced objectives

Many people have seen application of the federal principle as a way to correct the imbalance between the so-called educationally disadvantaged states and the others.

One would have thought that efforts to improve equality of educational opportunity should focus on getting more children of school age into primary schools in disadvantaged states and on achieving a higher rate of transition from primary to secondary school through the creation of more secondary schools in relation to primary schools. Such steps would then enable schools to produce more qualified candidates for the federal polytechnics and universities. One of the difficulties encountered at Idah Polytechnic was the inability of some northern states to fill their quotas, largely because qualified students simply did not exist. But these states would rather the places remained vacant than allow the authorities to fill them with candidates from the educationally advanced states. This situation results in wastage and underutilisation of capacity.

There is no doubt that a certain national consciousness rubs off on pupils who study in an environment made up of pupils from all parts of Nigeria, but this tendency in itself is hardly sufficient to have a significant impact on national unity, especially in the presence of countersocializing forces and structures within the institutions. The number of family, clan, divisional or state student unions and clubs on university campuses reinforcing attachment to primordial values and sentiments attests to the ineffectiveness of mere agglomeration without mixing. It would be very interesting to see a study of the sociometry of student relationships in a number of schools.

Notes

1.   For a more detailed discussion of the development of education in Nigeria, see Uma O. Eleazu, *Federalism and Nation-Building in Nigeria, 1946–1966*, Arthur Stockwell, London, 1977. On the idea of 'federal character' see also Uma O. Eleazu, 'Constitutional Structure and Development of Nigeria' in R.B. Goldmann and A.J. Wilson (eds). *From Independence to Statehood*, Frances Pinter, London, 1984.

2. *Constitution of the Federal Republic of Nigeria*, 1979, Chapter I, Article 10.
3. Ibid.
4. *National Policy on Education (Revised) 1981*, Government Printer, Lagos, p. 5.
5. Ibid., p. 20.
6. Ibid.

8 POSITIVE DISCRIMINATION: THE EDUCATIONAL ADVANCEMENT OF THE SCHEDULED CASTES IN INDIA

Suma Chitnis

Around the world today, governments and other bodies working towards equality and national integration are struggling to absorb into the mainstream of society, as equals, groups suffering social and cultural isolation and/or inferior status. The sources of these groups' isolation and inferiority range from ethnic discrimination or political subordination to geographical disadvantages or migrant status. On the surface, the specific task involved in remedying these situations seems to differ enormously from one country to another and according to the sources of the differences. However, the ethico-moral dilemmas and the political tensions involved present roughly similar challenges in different settings. Consequently, it is increasingly relevant to compare the strategies being used as instruments for equality and integration in different parts of the world, to share experiences, identify similarities and thus gain some insight into the larger issues involved.

This chapter describes some Indian efforts to achieve, through education, equality and integration of those who suffered social, political and economic discrimination for centuries because of their low rank in the Hindu religious hierarchy. Consisting of the untouchables[1] and members of a few other low castes, the recipients of these special educational benefits have been known since independence as the scheduled castes because they are listed in a presidential schedule for special benefits and protective discrimination.

The Indian policy of providing special facilities for the education of disadvantaged groups and reserving quotas for them in employment is perhaps one of the earliest efforts at positive discrimination in the modern world. As early as 1918 in Mysore, one of the princely states in British India, the Maharaja broke the Brahmin monopoly over government employment in his state by declaring all communities other than the Brahmins 'backward classes' and making available to them reserved employment quotas and reserved university admissions. The British government soon afterwards in the Government of India Act of 1918 accorded all 'backward classes' special political representation. Reforms in 1919 provided them with nominated seats in the Central Legislative Council. In addition, the government undertook in a scattered fashion to provide land, housing, education and government jobs to the 'depressed classes'.[2] Thus, the principle of special protection for the disadvantaged was firmly established in the country by the second decade of this century.

Although humanitarian sentiments certainly motivated this intervention on behalf of the backward groups, it is important to recognize that political considerations also contributed.[3] In fact the mix of philanthrophy and politics involved in policies of positive discrimination continues to play a critical role in shaping the outcomes of these policies in India — as perhaps in other parts of the world.

The scheduled castes and the issue of equality

The scheduled castes constitute 15 per cent or about 80 million of India's total population of about 700 million. In a country where official estimates place well above 40 per cent of the population below the poverty line, they constitute the poorest of the poor. Whatever the measures used — literacy, school and university enrolment, occupational placement, or holding of public office — they trail the rest of the population despite nearly six decades of action aimed at improving their situation.[4]

The source of the inferior status of the scheduled castes

To understand the source of the backwardness of the scheduled castes it is necessary to be acquainted with the unique caste system by which Hindu society has been stratified and integrated for centuries. This tiered system consists of strata known as 'jati', which are hierarchically organized according to the purity of their ritual status. Individuals belong to the jati of the family into which they are born. Birth into a particular family is explained in terms of 'karma' or 'doings' or 'action' in the previous incarnation. Thus the system is firmly anchored in the Hindu philosophy of karma and the transmigration of souls.[5]

There are four categories of caste: the Brahmins at the top, followed by the Kshatriyas, Vaishyas and Shudras. The divine origin of this hierarchy is symbolically explained in the Vedas by the sacred hymn of the Purusha Sukta. It says that the Brahmins are born of the head of the Purusha, the Kshatriyas born of the limbs, the Vaishyas of the torso and the Shudras of the feet. Apart from defining social positions, this symbolism indicates priesthood and scholarship as the occupational sphere of the Brahmins; statecraft, warfare and administration as that of the Kshatriyas; commerce and craft as that of the Vaishyas; and service as the sphere of the Shudras. The sub-castes (jatis) are accordingly ascribed specific occupations within the sphere appropriate to their caste category. Agriculture is the only occupation open to all.

Not only ritual status and occupation divide the castes. A series of rigid prescriptions concerning endogamy and exogamy and a complex system of rules and regulations concerning matters of daily behaviour, particularly personal interaction within and outside caste boundaries, maintain social distances among the jatis. Conformity to these rules is obtained by the unique Hindu concept of 'pollution', the notion that transgression of the regulations makes for ritual pollution. Jatis are also distinguishable from each other by a multitude of small indicators, such as dress, food habits, hairstyle and dialect. Though difficult for the outsider to identify, Hindus living in the same region can easily discern these differences.

In terms of their ritual status, most of the Shudra castes are ranked so low that their touch, and in some cases even their shadow, defiles high-caste Hindus. While Shudras generally constitute the lowest caste category, in some parts of the country other untouchable castes are considered to be even lower — so low that they lie beyond the pale of the fourfold division. Believed to be 'low-born', all these untouchable castes are confined to occupations such as carrying and disposing of night soil, cleaning gutters and latrines, carrying carcasses and curing hides. They are compelled by ritual obligation to live on the peripheries of their villages and towns. They are denied sacred rites, forbidden to enter temples, not allowed to draw water from wells used by caste Hindus, and generally prevented from using facilities and services in common with others.

Traditionally, access to education was strictly defined by caste status. Knowledge of the Vedas and of other sacred texts was considered to be a sacrament available only to Brahmins. The Kshatriyas were allowed knowledge relating to statecraft, administration and warfare. The Vaishyas were permitted knowledge relevant to trade and the crafts. But the Shudras were considered to be so low in ritual status that they were categorically excluded from learning. Since religious and ritualistic grounds were used to justify caste discrimination up to independence, it was easy for the upper castes to render the lower castes politically powerless and to exploit them economically. Consequently political and economic structures in the country have grown to be highly exploitative of the lower castes, particularly of the untouchable castes.

Breakthrough under British rule

The advent of British rule rendered the first major blow to the caste system. The British did not make any conscious effort to abolish caste. In fact they carefully steered clear of any administrative measures that would offend the religious sentiments of the Indians and disturb the security of their own position as rulers. But because they did not themselves practice caste discrimination, their behaviour helped set new norms. The British freely employed untouchables as domestic servants or as menials in their administrative services, enlisted them in military service and employed them on their railways. In these services untouchables often worked alongside caste Hindus.

Thus, the British regime provided occupational mobility for the untouchables and disrupted age-old practices confining them to occupations that were considered to be too lowly for their caste superiors. Furthermore, it dislocated the traditional mechanism for the segregation of the untouchables. The British railways, schools, hospitals and other services did not shut out or even segregate the untouchables.

Liberalism and social reform

Above all, the liberal philosophy educated Indians imbibed from the West generated a new moral consciousness and stimulated influential currents of thought and sentiment. By the second decade of the nineteenth century educated Indians were critically questioning traditional customs and beliefs, particularly such religiously sanctioned practices as the burning of widows and female infanticide. By the third decade of that century public movements for social reform were beginning to gather strength, especially in such regions as

Maharashtra and Bengal.[6] Though quick to recognize the importance
of voluntary action unaided by government support, the reformers
strongly criticized the British government for its 'apathy' towards the
Indian situation. They demanded that the British government
abandon its neutrality and take a more positive and active role in
reform. The British were initially hesitant to respond to this demand
lest their actions should jeopardize their rule. But public sentiment,
or at least the sentiment of the Indian elite who mattered to the
British rulers, so strongly favoured reform that they yielded. By the
middle (and certainly towards the end) of the nineteenth century the
British government was firmly committed to social reform including
action towards the welfare of the 'depressed classes', as the
untouchables and other lower castes were then called.

Liberalism and the awakening of new political consciousness

By the end of the nineteenth century liberalism among the Indian
elite was no longer confined to a commitment to social reform. It had
matured into a political consciousness wherein liberal ideals of
equality and personal freedom found expression in the political goal
of self-rule and the political commitment to a democratic, egalitarian
nation. The dream of a casteless, secular society, a brotherhood of
free individuals unfettered by slavery and servitude, was integral to
the concept of self-rule. Organization for freedom from domination
by and servitude to the British demanded first the abolition of
domination and servitude within the fabric of Indian life. This vision
of the political future of the country required, morally as well as
strategically, the abolition of untouchability and the integration of
low-caste Hindus as equals in Indian society.

Moral armament versus political pressure

It is always difficult to distinguish between purely moral or
humanitarian considerations and political ones in the struggle to
achieve equality for groups that have been historically discriminated
against. In India the issue was further complicated by the unusual
character of the political philosophy that guided the struggle for
independence from the last few decades of the nineteenth century
onwards. Gandhi, whose thinking primarily defined this philosophy,
and Tilak who preceded Gandhi and may be considered to have
founded the movement, saw self-rule as a basic human right. Tilak's

famous statement 'Swaraj [self-rule] is my birthright, and I shall have it', set the tone of the Indian demand for freedom.

Both Tilak and Gandhi believed that if the British were to be true to the values that they professed, they were morally bound to grant Indians self-rule. Whereas Tilak favoured a militant protest, however, Gandhi chose passive resistance and moral pressure as his weapons. To sharpen these weapons, he called for a moral armament he believed could only be achieved by discarding aggression and cultivating humanism at both the personal and societal levels. He believed removal of untouchability and acceptance of low-caste persons as equals was one of the corner-stones of this process.

Gandhi subjected the caste system to careful scrutiny and came to the conclusion, consistent with the spirit of the time, that it was essentially a sound arrangement for the division of labour and social integration but had become distorted by vested interests over a period of time. He declared that the system could be restored to its original functions if middle- and upper-caste Hindus learned to recognize the dignity of all labour and particularly to appreciate the lower castes who did the most disagreeable tasks for them. He demonstrated his convictions by cleaning his own latrines and expected everyone in his 'ashram' as well as others who accepted him as their political and moral 'guru' to do the same. He symbolically referred to the untouchables as 'harijans' — people of God. On his political pilgrimages, he made it a point to set up his own residence, as well as that of his entourage in the harijan quarters of the towns and cities that he visited. These were radical gestures. One cannot really appreciate their impact without having witnessed the degrading segregation of the untouchables and the distance that persons in the upper castes maintain from them under the supercilious notion that low caste persons are 'unclean'.

Liberalism found a totally different expression in Ambedkar, the leader of the untouchables. He believed that those who suffered inequality and oppression should strive for political equality with whatever leverage they could command. Himself an untouchable, Ambedkar had experienced directly the marginality of the lowest castes within Hinduism. He had also observed the British policy of communal consideration in their allocation of political rights and privileges and come to the conclusion that, since the untouchables were beyond the pale of the Hindu caste hierarchy, they should be considered non-Hindus and, following the practice adopted for Muslims and Christians, given separate representation in the legislative bodies appointed by the British.

Ambedkar's arguments were powerful and gained considerable sympathy with the British. But they disturbed nationalists such as Gandhi who considered the demand to be a threat to the cohesiveness of Indian society, already rendered unstable by the separatism of the Muslims. Gandhi, struggling towards unification of the country as a prerequisite for establishing a national liberation movement, pleaded with Ambedkar to halt his separatist activities. But Ambedkar was too committed to his convictions. He stepped out of Hinduism by conversion to Buddhism and called upon all others belonging to the several untouchable castes to follow his example.

Ambedkar's call for conversion had only limited success but a startling impact. It shook middle- and upper-caste Hindus into recognizing that secession of the untouchables would deplete their numbers and weaken their political power, as population size was critical for communities in the British system of communal awards. Inevitably, even those who had been cool towards Gandhi's moral plea for acceptance of the untouchables became anxious to appease and contain the scheduled castes. Thus, political expediency succeeded where moral armament had failed.[7]

In a sense, this duality of moral and political pressure combined to create a strong commitment to raising the social standing of the untouchables. This commitment inspired the far-reaching constitutional provisions and massive financial allocation with which independent India launched its effort on behalf of the untouchables.[8]

The advance of the scheduled castes

The provisions made

Untouchability was abolished by law as soon as independence was achieved, and the terms 'untouchable' and 'depressed' were dropped from official usage. The former untouchable and some other low castes were listed in a special presidential schedule as eligible for positive discrimination. Article 16 of the Constitution articulated the state's obligation to improve the situation of the scheduled castes and other weak sections of society as follows:

> The State shall promote with special care the educational and economic interests of the weaker sections of the people, and in particular, of the scheduled castes and the scheduled tribes, and shall protect them from social injustice and all forms of exploitation.

A series of other constitutional provisions guaranteed the advance of the scheduled castes and scheduled tribes. In each of the Five Year Plans substantial funds were earmarked for the purpose, and a series of programmes was launched for their welfare.[9]

Investment in education

Education accounts for the major share of funds allocated for the welfare of the scheduled castes.[10] The educational opportunities provided thereby have largely been designed to overcome the economic disadvantages suffered by the scheduled castes. They include free studentships and scholarships for study in India and abroad; grants for the purchase of books and clothes, for the payment of examination fees, excursion fees and other such expenditure as may be required by students; provision of hostel facilities; and special training cells to prepare scheduled caste students for the competitive examinations that are held for recruitment to high-level positions in government and public-sector undertakings.[11] One can better appreciate the value of these provisions after realizing that comparable opportunities are not available to others who live way below the poverty line and are economically as disadvantaged as the scheduled castes.

The policy of reservations

To ensure that traditional prejudices do not obstruct the admission of scheduled caste students to institutions of higher education, the government has introduced the policy of 'reservations'. This policy makes it obligatory for all educational institutions receiving government funds or grants of any kind to reserve 15 per cent of their places for the scheduled castes. Since most institutions of higher education in the country are at least partly funded by the goverment, this is a powerful measure.

Further, the policy stipulates that the scheduled castes are to be granted 'other' special concessions at the time of admission. For instance, where admissions are made on the basis of candidates' obtaining a minimum grade on some qualifying examination, the qualifying grade for scheduled caste applicants is 5 per cent lower. Where there is a maximum age limit, it has to be raised three years for the benefit of applicants from these castes.

Finally, to ensure that education functions as a mechanism for occupational mobility and to accelerate this mobility, the government has established a policy of 'reserving' 15 per cent positions in all central government services and in all public-sector undertakings for the scheduled castes. State governments are expected to follow suit.

The outcomes of education

Several indicators can help us assess the outcome of these provisions. Today, scheduled caste youths attend schools and universities in substantial numbers. This was impossible only a few decades ago. Because they speak the same language, wear the same clothes, play the same games and sing the same songs as all the others, they cannot be identified as former untouchables. Advance is also evident in the growing representation of the scheduled castes in employment. Data for the private sector, where the policy of reservations does not apply, are unavailable, but figures for employment in government indicate visible advancement (Table 8.1).

Table 8.1 Scheduled caste employment in central government service, 1953 and 1979

	Class I (Higher administrative) %	Class II (Lower administrative) %	Class III (Clerical) %	Class IV (Menial) %
1953	0.35	1.29	4.52	20.52
1979	4.75	7.37	12.55	19.32

Source: Report of the Commissioner for Scheduled Castes and Scheduled Tribes, Government of India, 1981

Table 8.1 could be used to argue that occupational mobility among the scheduled castes has been extremely limited. It is evident that employment of scheduled castes in Classes I, II and III is far below the 15 per cent reserved. 'Discrimination' is seldom blamed for this gap between positions reserved and positions actually filled. Instead, 'slack' and 'indifferent' administration of the policy and faulty phrasing of directives have often been singled out as responsible. However, it is important from the point of view of our focus on education to note that government records and documents repeatedly indicate that the policy of reservations fails to be fully effective because 'suitable' candidates are no ıvailable. A study undertaken by the Director General of Training and Employment of the Government of India, at the request of the Department of Social Welfare (quoted in the latest report by the Commissioner of Scheduled Castes and Scheduled Tribes) emphasizes this point. Its findings are as follows:

a) The proportion of filled vacancies to those notified is highest in the case of illiterates. As the educational requirements of reserved vacancies increase, the proportion of vacancies filled goes on declining.
b) The availability of candidates for vacancies requiring professional and technical qualifications is limited.
c) Employers report that the main factors which have hampered the filling of reserved vacancies are:
    i)   failure on the part of candidates to reach prescribed standards in the written and oral tests;
    ii) non-availability of qualified candidates;
    iii) lack of response from candidates with requisite qualifications;
    iv) lack of mobility (willingness to move out of the place in which they reside) among selected candidates; and
    v)   medical unfitness.

These findings indicate that in spite of the educational facilities available, members of the scheduled castes are not even adequately equipped for the jobs that are reserved for them. The scheduled castes' 'unsuitability' for the jobs reserved for them seems to stem from their failure to come up to the level of education required.

The scheduled castes and the education system

Available data indicate serious inadequacies in the education of the scheduled castes. In most of the twenty-two states and nine union territories in the country, the proportion of scheduled caste enrolment at secondary schools and universities is substantially smaller than the proportion of scheduled castes in the population. In some states it is smaller at the primary and middle school levels as well. Table 8.2 gives a rough idea of the situation for the country up to the middle school level.

The educational backwardness of the scheduled castes also takes several other forms. For instance, the rate at which they drop out of the school is very high, much higher than for the rest of the

Table 8.2   Enrolment percentages of students to population in the corresponding age group

	Standards I–V		Standards VI–VIII	
	General population	*Scheduled castes*	*General population*	*Scheduled castes*
1977–78	82.8	68.9	37.9	25.5

population. At university level they cluster into inferior institutions and in courses leading to relatively low-status, low-income occupations. Admitted to reserved quotas in prestigious institutions of higher education, they rarely survive.

School drop-out and poverty

In the country as a whole, the proportion of drop-outs at primary school is very high. Roughly 60 per cent of the children enrolled in standard I drop out before they complete the four standards of primary school. The rate of 'stagnation', as repeated failure and repetition of classes is called, is also very high. In this generally dismal picture of primary school education, the situation of the scheduled castes stands out as singularly bleak. Their drop-out and stagnation rates are 10–20 per cent higher than the figures for their non-scheduled cohorts — regardless of whether the context for comparison is the school, the district or the state.[12] The same holds true for secondary school and university education.

One of the most striking features of polarization in Indian society is the social class segregation in schooling.[13] Studies clearly indicate that the phenomenon of school drop-outs is confined to schools for the poor. It is conspicuously absent in middle and upper-class schools.[14] The drop-out rate is also distinctly higher in rural than urban areas. To some extent, the scheduled castes' higher drop-out rate may be explained both by their higher concentration in rural areas and by the greater depth and extensiveness of their poverty.

Contrary to the stereotype that blames school absenteeism on the 'apathy' of the poor, however, studies indicate that neither the urban nor the rural poor in India are apathetic to education. The problem is a far more serious one of their inability to bear the opportunity costs of schooling. It is significant that children drop out most frequently at about 8–9 years of age — just the age when they become old enough to work or look after younger siblings while their parents are at work. Furthermore, school leaving is noticeably higher during the part of the year when agricultural activity in rural areas and opportunities for employment in the cities are highest.

The dilemmas of distribution

Since India is constitutionally committed to universal primary school education, one would expect the government to 'compensate' the poor adequately and attempt to forestall early school leaving. But the country's poverty is so extensive that at least 40 per cent of the population would have to be compensated for significant gains to be achieved. Less extensive incentives would not solve the problem. The cost of primary school education in the country would more than double if this were done, and the country is in no position to bear this kind of expenditure. In view of the special constitutional commitment to the education of the scheduled castes, it could be argued that compensation should at least be provided to children from poor scheduled caste homes. However, this would not be politically feasible.

The government is at present engaged in seeking other ways to deal with the problem. Rescheduling the school year so that long vacations would coincide with periods in which children are required for agricultural work is one of the solutions being considered. The organization of gainful employment for school children is also being discussed in some quarters. In any case, as matters stand, officials acknowledge that the country is not likely to achieve universal primary school education even by the year 2000. Scheduled caste children will perhaps be the last to catch up when universalization is finally achieved.

Pedagogic problems

School drop-out and stagnation among the masses in India are also aggravated by the large proportion of the school population consisting of first-generation learners.[15] The economically disadvantaged among them suffer further because, as in other countries where formal education has historically been confined to the élite, the culture of the education system is heavily middle and upper class in its orientations. For the scheduled castes there is yet another disadvantage, namely the culture of formal education is also heavily upper caste in its orientations. Thus scheduled caste children suffer a double or triple disadvantage: as first-generation learners, through class differences in culture, and because of caste differences in culture.

As a result, the contents, modes and materials of schooling are often totally out of tune with the experiences, images and concepts of the world to which scheduled caste children belong. The norms for behaviour at school are alien and often opposite to the norms by which they live in their homes and their neighbourhoods. Even the language used in the school system is essentially middle and upper middle class in intonation, accent and vocabulary and distinctly different from the lower-caste dialects. Experimental efforts to enable scheduled caste children to overcome these shortcomings have had phenomenal success, thus proving that it is possible to bridge the gap.[16] But, once again the country does not have the financial resources or, more importantly, the dedication required to extend these efforts.

University education and poverty

Apart from 'reserved' admissions for university courses, scholarships are the principal instruments for advancing higher education opportunities for the scheduled castes. All scheduled caste students whose parents earn less than 700 rupees per month are eligible for scholarships. A scholarship is withdrawn only if a student fails a course of study twice.

Considering the income group for which scholarships are provided, one may assume that a scholarship is not merely an incentive but a living allowance which is expected to cover the student's needs adequately. However, studies consistently reveal that the amount (75–100 rupees) available for the purpose is far from adequate to cover the cost of living. Students either have to earn extra money to sustain themselves or depend on the bounty of some relative or philanthropist. Such supplementary support is not easily forthcoming.

While studies clearly indicate that regardless of their own poverty most scheduled caste families do all they can to support their children through college, they also show that many students have to use their meagre scholarship awards to meet the basic needs of their families. The studies poignantly reveal how students deny themselves and stretch their small scholarship amounts in different directions as they attempt to walk the tightrope through poverty. That many of them aim, nevertheless, for a good university education and survive the ordeal to achieve distinctly successful futures is one of the most encouraging features of the scholarship scheme.[17]

On the other hand, the same studies reveal that some scholarship holders accept their scholarships without any real intention of completing their courses. Having calculated employment opportunities after completing high school, they have concluded they can gain more by entering a 'reserved' slot in clerical employment and getting a head start over the others who will take the same kind of job after graduation from college. Nevertheless, they enter college — largely in order to benefit from scholarship support — while doing part-time work and job-hunting. This misuse of scholarship funds and the ease with which it is accomplished offer some different insights into how the scheduled castes make use of the special resources provided for their higher education.

Competition in higher education

In addition to having to struggle with poverty, scheduled caste students in higher education have other serious problems: for instance, diffidence in enrolling in prestigious courses and difficulty in surviving if they do sign up for them. Although higher education has expanded phenomenally since independence,[18] admission to colleges is highly competitive. Competition is basically among courses of study. For example, professional courses such as engineering, technology, medicine, management and, more recently, commerce attract the best talent. Students with relatively lower performance levels have to satisfy themselves with other courses. Competition is also sharp for the 'more prestigious' institutions. For instance, in engineering and technology the five national institutes of technology are at the top, followed by the regional colleges of engineering, and then by the several engineering colleges affiliated with various universities. Similar hierarchies prevail in management, medicine and even in arts and science courses. Students from upper-class homes and/or with high performance levels invariably enroll in the prestigious institutions.

Inability to cope with the demands of prestigious courses

The educational backwardness of the scheduled castes is most conspicuously reflected in their underrepresentation in prestigious courses such as engineering and medicine. In fact, until about 1970, their representation in these fields was extremely poor. The situation has improved considerably since, firstly because the second generation of scheduled castes to be college educated is now beginning to gain admission to these courses, and secondly because the requirements have been further relaxed to facilitate the admission of scheduled caste students. Efforts to force the issue, however, have not really succeeded. For instance, data on one of the five prestigious institutes of technology reveal that in spite of the heavy concessions offered, very few scheduled caste students qualified for admission up to as recently as 1973. Subsequently, requirements were further relaxed and a concerted effort made to fill the reserved quota. But only five of the fifteen scheduled caste students who were admitted to the institute in response to this effort had survived the year 1978. The others had dropped out. None of the five who survived had made it to the fifth or final year of the course. They were stagnating in the third or fourth year. Efforts to improve their performance by providing them with special instruction had also failed. The pattern for successive student generations is similar.

The rival claims of social justice and excellence

In the face of situations such as the one described above there are serious problems in giving scheduled caste students continued 'protection'. The policy of reservations conflicts with the obligation to maintain the high academic standards crucial to the professional and technological manpower needs of the nation. Even those who are otherwise committed to the welfare of the scheduled castes have seriously questioned the practice of reservations on the grounds of educational standards and efficiency.

At the same time, some of the 'achieving elite' who are unwilling to forfeit their traditional advantages and make room for the former untouchables have misused and exploited the issue of standards. Their agitations have often been violent. What is worse, they have directed the violence at the weakest of the scheduled caste population — the urban poor and the village masses. The violence that swept across the state of Gujarat a few years ago over the issue of the reservation of admissions for scheduled caste students to postgraduate courses in medicine is a prime example.[19]

Vested political interests in reservations

The resolution of the issue is further complicated by the fact that the scheduled castes have come to look upon reservations as a right, a sort of compensation for what they suffered through the ages. This creates a serious problem. The policy was initially promulgated for a period of only ten years with the faith that the scheduled castes would advance far enough to make such intervention unnecessary afterwards. However, the resolution has had to be extended for three successive ten-year periods — in 1961, 1971 and 1981 — in response to strong political pressures. The extensions are justifiable on the grounds that the scheduled castes continue to lag behind in education, but the visibility of the vested political interests that guide the political struggle for extension leads to strong resentments.

New inequalities and vested interests

Several other disconcerting features regarding the politics of inequality are beginning to surface in the course of implementing positive discrimination for the scheduled castes. One of the most serious is that the policy has inadvertently generated sharp inequalities among the scheduled castes. In each state, one or two castes use most of the educational opportunities and facilities to advance past the others.[20] For instance, the Mahars in the state of Maharashtra, who constitute about 32 per cent of the scheduled caste population of the state, use 80 per cent of the facilities, whereas figures for the Mangs are 30 per cent and a negligible 10 per cent respectively. A similar situation exists with respect to the Chamars in Uttar Pradesh, Bihar or Rajasthan.

It has been observed that urban location, a traditional caste occupation that is viable in a modern economy (such as tanning or leather work, the traditional occupation of the Chamars), or a head start in terms of employment in the British army or railways (as was the case for the Mahars of Maharashtra) correlate with such advancement. One explanation is that both urban location and proximity to the modern economy are conducive to utilization of the opportunities and facilities provided. Perhaps surprisingly, castes that have advanced because of such advantages reject the suggestion that they opt out of the benefits of reservation and make room for those who are more disadvantaged.[21]

The clamour to assert low-caste status

Another unexpected phenomenon is that several lower castes are today clamouring for inclusion in the presidential schedule. This is a startling regression. For centuries, throughout the history of caste in India, most castes had struggled to establish that their status was in fact higher than the one actually accorded to them in the ritual hierarchy.

Finally, another important observation is that well-placed people no longer hesitate to declare their low caste status if they can stand to benefit by such a declaration. This would not have happened a decade or two ago, when lower-caste persons who achieved occupational and economic mobility were eager to mask their scheduled caste origins and merge with the rest of the population.

Tensions, dilemmas and implications for the future

The foregoing discussion makes clear that the policy of positive discrimination for education of the scheduled castes in India is riddled with problems. It conflicts with the principle of secularism, overshadows problems of poverty, and legitimizes compromise with standards in higher education. In addition to generating resentment because it runs counter to established interests, it poses serious ethical and moral dilemmas for conscientious Indians. While some of the dilemmas are strictly contextual, there are at least three or four generic issues the Indian experience highlights for cross-cultural comparisons.

Nurturing of ethnicity through positive discrimination

The Indian policy aimed at the abolition of caste discrimination had in fact accentuated caste consciousness. Evidence of this renewed caste awareness exists in:

(a) the unwillingness of the scheduled castes to give up their caste identities and merge their cause with that of others who are socially and economically disadvantaged;
(b) the clamouring to be included in the presidential schedule by castes that would earlier have done anything to step out of the stigma of low-caste status; and

(c) the gradual assertion by other 'communities' of their communal identities in the wake of the successful utilization of the communal principle for political leverage by the scheduled castes — recent ethnic conflicts in Assam and the ongoing religious conflicts in Punjab also illustrate this phenomenon.

Consequently one is forced to question whether policies of positive discrimination can ever function without accentuating ethnicism.

Dilemma regarding the 'fairest' utilization of resources

In a poor country such as India with highly limited resources, one must further question whether positive discrimination in favour of a selected few is justifiable at all.

Scheduled caste students at school and college clearly need much more intensive help for a significant percentage of them to measure up to the standards required. However, the financial resources necessary for the purpose are not available. The government could, of course, reallocate existing resources to provide adequate help to a part of the scheduled caste population. But then it would have to decide whether to select those with superior capacity and guarantee some success, or to select the weakest and guarantee that help reaches where it is most needed. This decision would be difficult.

At present the government has chosen a third alternative, namely, that of spreading the benefits as widely as possible, but in the process the benefits are being spread too thin.

Ethnicity versus poverty

A related problem and one which many other countries must share is that of choosing between competing causes for help. In India today, opportunities of the kind available to the scheduled castes are not available to others who are economically disadvantaged, causing considerable resentment. The question that repeatedly arises is whether concern for social justice or political expediency motivates government action on behalf of the scheduled castes.

Moral commitment and political will

Unfortunately, I have not been able to address adequately in this discussion the most important lesson that emerges from the Indian attempts at social reform: the limits of bureaucratic action. Earlier, I pointed out that, whereas Gandhi believed the uplift of the scheduled castes could be obtained through a moral regeneration of the Indian consciousness, Ambedkar believed in political pressures alone. Prior to independence both forces were strong and generated highly effective voluntary action on behalf of the scheduled castes.

Today, the public's sense of responsibility for the scheduled castes seems to have dwindled to a minimum. So, in fact, has voluntary public activity on behalf of other disadvantaged groups. Everything seems to be left to bureaucratic action. In fact some observers have wryly remarked that in the earlier era when Indians freely accepted inequalities in their social structure but were committed to the conscientious fulfilment of obligations between unequals, they did much more for the downtrodden than they do today under their country's constitutional commitment to equality. The comment is not altogether fair, but it does raise some fundamental questions about the relationship between the traditional and the modern ethical orders.

Somehow one feels that the liberalism that flourished in the country in the nineteenth and early twentieth centuries was stifled before it grew into full stature as democratic egalitarianism. The moral regeneration that Gandhi tried to nurture has not matured effectively either. Perhaps it is too early to tell. There certainly is ample evidence of mounting political consciousness among the people. But whether this consciousness will take the shape of a Gandhian model or find expression as Ambedkar expected it would remains to be seen — and therein lies the destiny of the Indian policy of positive discrimination and India's scheduled caste people.

Notes

1. Since independence in 1947, untouchability has been declared an offence. The term 'untouchable', which was freely used earlier, is no longer permitted.
2. The 'depressed classes' roughly corresponded to the sector of the population known as the scheduled castes today. The 'backward classes' was a larger grouping that included the 'depressed classes'.
3. Marc Galanter, *Competing Equalities*, Oxford University Press, Delhi, 1984, Chapter 2.

4. The following data for 1981 illustrate the point:

Education	Scheduled castes %	Total population %
Literacy	21.38	36.17
School education		
Children enrolled in Standards I–V as percentage of relevant age group (6–11 years)	86.00	83.00
Children enrolled in Standards VI–VIII as percentage of relevant age group (11–14 years)	32.60	41.90
Children enrolled in Standards IX+ as percentage of children in relevant age groups (15+ years)	11.00	21.20
Enrolment in higher education as percentage of the relevant age group	0.15	1.00

Land holding	Percentage of total number of scheduled castes	Percentage of total number of other land holders
Persons holding more than:		
1 acre	29.29	11.00
1–2.4 acres	30.89	23.50
2.5–4.9 acres	22.89	22.80
5–9.9 acres	15.82	21.00
10–14.9 acres	4.82	8.00
More than 15 acres	5.29	12.80

5. M.N. Srinivas, 'Caste' in *Encyclopaedia Britannica*, **4**, Encyclopaedia Britannica Ltd, London pp. 977–986.
6. Gail Omvedt, *Cultural Revolt in a Colonial Society*, Scientific Socialist Education Trust, 1976, Chapters 1–4.
7. Eleanor Zelliot, 'Dr. Ambedkar and the Mahar Movement', unpublished Ph.D. Dissertation, University of Pennsylvania, 1969, p. 141.
8. Articles 14, 15, 16, 29, 32, 37, 226, 325, 342 and 346 of the Constitution of India assert and affirm in different ways the equality of all citizens. Article 17 forbids the practice of untouchability and Articles 15(4), 46, 330, 332, 334, 335, 338, 339, 340, 341 and 366 focus on the provision of compensatory discrimination for the scheduled castes.
9. Plan outlays for the welfare of the backward classes (scheduled castes, scheduled tribes and other backward classes) have been as follows: First Plan: Rs 390 million; Second Plan: Rs 900 million; Third Plan: Rs 1,140 million; Fourth Plan: Rs 1,1710.29 million; Fifth Plan: Rs 2,270.89 million. Source: *Sixth Five Year Plan 1980–85*, Government of India, Planning Commission.
10. In each Plan period, roughly between 65 and 80 per cent of the total

expenditure on the welfare of the scheduled castes has been spent on their education.

11. See the *Annual Reports* of the Commissioner of Scheduled Castes and Scheduled Tribes. Government of India. New Delhi. 1951 onwards.

12. See Suma Chitnis. '*Dropouts and Low Pupil Achievement among the Urban Poor in Bombay*'. Tate Institute of Social Sciences. Bombay. 1982 (mimeograph); S.L. Gupta. *Selected Bibliography on Educational Wastage and Stagnation*. NIE. NCERT. New Delhi. 1978. *Primary Education in Rural India: Participation and Wastage*. Agricultural Economics Research Centre. University of Delhi. 1968 (mimeograph); *A Wasted Asset. A Survey of Rural Youth in Two Indian Districts*. Report prepared for UNICEF by Indian Institute of Public Opinion. New Delhi. 1973.

13. See Suma Chitnis. op. cit. Also Suma Chitnis and C. Suvannathat. 'Schooling for Children of the Urban Poor' in P.J. Richards and A.M. Thomson. *Basic Needs and the Urban Poor*. Croom Helm. London. 1984.

14. See Suma Chitnis and C. Suvannathat op. cit.

15. This is inevitable in a country in which only 50 per cent of the adult population is literate.

16. See V.G. Kulkarni and S.C. Agarkar. 'Talent Search and Nurture among the Underprivileged: Interim Report 1980-81'. Homi Bhabha Centre for Science Education. Tate Institute of Fundamental Research. Bombay (Mimeograph).

17. V.P. Shah and T. Patel. *Who goes to College?: Scheduled Caste/Tribe post Matric Scholars in Gujarat*. (Ahmedabad. Rachana Prakashan) 1977; K.S. Mandal. *The Post Matric Scholarship Scheme for the SC/ST Students of Maharashtra: An Evaluation*. Tate Institute of Social Sciences. Bombay. 1985.

18. For instance the total enrolment in university education increased from 1,155,380 in 1961-62 to 3,375,409 (an increase of 192.15 per cent) in 1975-76 but enrolments in engineering, technology and medicine — the three most prestigious fields in the country — increased only from 97,797 to 210,629 (an increase of 115.37 per cent) during the same period.

19. A. Yagnik. 'Spectre of Caste War'. *Economic and Political Weekly*. XVI. no.13 (1981). pp. 553-5.

20. See Suma Chitnis. *A Long Way to Go*. Allied Pub.. New Delhi 1981. pp. 16-20.

21. See L. Dushkin. 'Scheduled Caste Politics' in M. Mahar (ed.). *The Untouchables in Contemporary India*. The University of Arizona Press. Tuscon. USA. 1972. pp. 220-224.

9 EDUCATIONAL STANDARDS AND SOCIAL DISTANCE: TWO TAMIL MINORITIES IN SRI LANKA

Dagmar Hellmann-Rajanayagam

Introduction

The integration of ethnic minorities is increasingly being discussed in many countries, mainly because ethnic conflicts are, in the words of Dietmar Rothermund, 'some of the most explosive issues in our world today'.[1] As Horowicz has shown, the term 'integration' can include quite a few different concepts,[2] depending on the types of majority and minority involved and the dynamics of the relationship between or among them.

The question arises as to whether integration is at all desirable for the minority in question. The answer depends as much on the situation and wishes of the majority as on those of the minority. First we must determine if the minority is a privileged or underprivileged one. This important distinction is disregarded in many cases, as a result of modern American sociology's[3] tendency to make 'minority' nearly synonymous with 'suppressed', thereby replacing a quantitative definition with a qualitative one. This equation, however, does not hold true in many cases. India, Malaysia and Sri Lanka offer examples of the opposite: societies in which an entrenched, dominant or at least privileged minority has become a 'persecuted' minority. The problems of these minorities become particularly visible with regard to the 'filter function' of education.[4]

Attitudes towards minorities differ from society to society. In some instances integration, in the sense of assimilation, is demanded by

This article is an enlarged and revised version of a paper read at the ICES workshop 'Education and the Integration of Minorities' in Bad Homburg, FRG, 5–8 June 1984, funded by the Stiftung Volkswagenwerk, whose help is herewith gratefully acknowledged. I also want to thank my colleagues and participants in the workshop for their helpful comments, criticisms and suggestions regarding this article, particularly Professor K.M. de Silva, Dr Neelan Tiruchelvam, Dr S.W. R.de A. Samarasinghe and Radhika Coomaraswamy.

the majority and desired by the minorities. The United States might be taken as a representative example (although all sorts of lively ethnic and other sub-cultures are present and active at the same time). There are also enough instances, however, of assimilation being demanded by the majority and opposed tooth and nail by minorities as, for example, in Malaysia. In addition, there is the model of unity in diversity, exemplified in quite different ways by India and Singapore. This model seems to work reasonably well under the circumstances (until very recently, at least, in India), largely because strict limitations and controls have been imposed to guarantee its not getting out of hand.

The question of whether integration is desirable and, if it is, what form it should take, is obviously a difficult one. When assimilation is demanded by the majority, the accusation of suppression of the minority is never far behind, and efforts arise to retain the minority's ethnic culture and identity. When, on the other hand, a minority succeeds in maintaining its ethnic culture, its links with the mainstream of the host country's economic, political and social life are often broken.

Within the context of this problem, education plays a crucial role. Depending on how the function of education is defined,[5] quite different systems are chosen with different consequences for the integration of minorities. An educational system geared to create a comprehensively educated elite has other programmes and consequences for integration than one that is only intended to supply suitable labour for a modern economy and thereby create career possibilities. Moreover, formal education is essentially an institution for the self-recruitment of the educated and, as such, its potential as an agent for integration in general and for the integration of minorities in particular is limited.[6] And especially in societies with highly visible minorities or in so-called plural societies, the question arises: is the education being offered conducive to integration — and if so, to what type of integration — or to segregation? In many cases, ethnic education designed to retain the identity of a minority other than a privileged minority produces the undesirable effect of handicapping the minority and limiting its progress.[7]

The case of Sri Lanka

If we take a look at Sri Lanka, the dilemma of integration vs.

segregation is compounded by a familiar paradox. The educational system ostensibly creates a labour force and career opportunities for a modern economy, but, in reality, it does no such thing — as testified to both by the contents of the syllabus and the huge army of unemployed educated youth. Education ceases to function as a filter, which, in Sri Lanka, it was not really intended to do anyway. On the contrary, the extension of educational opportunities to ever wider circles of the population has been the policy of successive governments in Sri Lanka. Unfortunately this policy has been maintained without regard to the capacity of the economy to absorb these graduates. Consequently, the net effect has been to aggravate one of the country's most persistent social problems.[8]

Moreover, Sri Lankan education is intended to foster patriotism and Sri Lankan nationalism.[9] But, one must ask, what kind of 'Sri Lanka' is being propagated and how does it serve integration — or does it do this at all? We shall examine this question in some detail later in this paper.

Sri Lanka's Tamils are a particularly interesting case study of an educational system's integrative capacities with regard to minorities. The Tamil minority actually consists of two ethnically and linguistically closely related groups, which are, however, far apart in social, economic and educational status: the Jaffna Tamils and the Indian Tamils. These two communities, with identical ethnic backgrounds, constitute, in the case of the Jaffna Tamils, a privileged and, in the case of the Indian Tamils, a distinctly underprivileged minority. Together they make up a little less than 20 per cent of the population of Sri Lanka: Jaffna Tamils constitute about 12.6 per cent, Indian Tamils 5.6 per cent.[10] The Jaffna Tamils have a secure territorial base of long standing in the Jaffna peninsula, where they have been domiciled for centuries as high-caste, powerful farmer-landowners. They are, in addition, a distinctly achievement-orientated minority. The Indian Tamils, on the other hand, only migrated to the country during the last century as low-caste, cheap labour for the rubber, coffee and tea plantations of the British colonial overlords.[11] These differences influence the type and content of education each group receives and further complicate a relationship between them that is already difficult in other respects.

Education in Sri Lanka

The British, during the colonial period, created a formally educated Ceylonese elite that was literate in English. The English educational system has often been termed integrative because the elite it produced certainly gave the appearance of one integrated whole, an impression which was kept up until after independence.[12] Rapidly, however, this unity showed its underlying weakness when other and younger forces, i.e. the Sinhala-educated elite below the English-educated one, started to claim their share of power in the country.[13] This Sinhala-educated group consisted of members of the Sinhalese middle class, the majority nationality of the island. They were educated in the Sinhala language in the primary and secondary schools. Their Tamil counterparts were, as will be shown, bilingual, i.e. they were educated in English and Tamil, whereas the Sinhalese group were often monolingual and did not know English at all or only very rudimentarily. The seeming unity of the elite proved to be a mere thin varnish which the continuation of education in English was not strong enough to maintain.

To create national unity, education in the country's 'national language', Sinhala, was demanded and finally granted in the 1950s. Yet this turned out to be the first visible step to distintegration because it left the Tamil minority out of the picture. Despite later regulations to give the Tamil language its 'reasonable' place in the country's administrative and educational system[14] (e.g. through permission for Tamils to use their language in dealings with government agencies and to receive instruction in their mother tongue), the Tamils never felt treated as equals. Their alienation was exacerbated by the explicit aim of the 'Sinhala-only' policy of successive governments to give the Sinhalese their rightful share in the country's educational, economic and political system, which they claimed they lacked up to then, owing to the constraints of the English-dominated educational system. This aim was the justification for making Sinhala the official and administrative language instead of English (in which the Tamils were particularly proficient).[15]

It is interesting to note that, in 1911, the English-educated elite had vehemently rejected plans to introduce education in the 'vernacular' in higher education as 'imperialistic prevention of progress'![16] The reasoning by which 'Sinhala only' was introduced opened the road up to segregation and disintegration.[17] From then onwards, the two educational systems, Sinhala and Tamil, went their different ways.

starting with Sinhala education for the whole country and Tamil education in the Tamil majority districts and ending up with a Sinhala-based standardization of grading to favour the 'under-privileged' Sinhalese young in the 1970s. Instead of creating a bilingual, integrated population, the *'swabhasha'** policy (as the Tamils prefer to call it) served to widen the gap between the two communities. The real or assumed predominance of the Jaffna Tamil minority in certain areas of occupation — such as highly visible government service — led to policies which not only did not redress this alleged wrong but embittered both sides to the point of no return. This policy could not even guarantee jobs for those Sinhalese youth who graduated from school and college into unemployment, and this was one of the major reasons for the 1971 uprising.[18]

Different educational systems for different groups of Tamils

In the case of the Tamils, the problem of education is exacerbated by the existence of two very different groups of Tamils with differing educational systems and achievements. The Sinhalese-dominated government has taken notice of this division only in so far as the schools and educational efforts of the plantation Tamils (also called estate or Indian Tamils) get virtually no attention whatever, while education in Jaffna at least theoretically comes under the purview of the Ministry of Education.

Jaffna

Jaffna Tamils have traditionally put a high premium on secular education for both males and females.[19] Praise of education in preference to material wealth can already be found in the Tirukkuṟaḷ, the holy book of aphorisms of the Tamils.[20] Jaffna Tamils were the first to avail themselves of the opportunities offered by English education both through mission and government institutions, in the early nineteenth century,[21] although the low-country Sinhalese, in contrast to the Kandyan Sinhalese, did not lag far behind. For the Tamils, education was the only means of enhancing their status or to

---

* Mother tongue.

maintain it and still move with the times. The Sinhalese, in contrast, often turned to trade and economic enterprise instead of government service, where an English education was imperative.[22]

So-called 'vernacular' education in the Tamil language always had its place beside English and was particularly fostered by missionaries who hoped to gain converts more easily by this device. Although there were considerable ups and downs in the intensity and reputation of education in the vernacular, it never ceased to be the medium of instruction, at least in primary education. Thus, a continuous tradition was maintained[23] and a foundation laid for education in the regional language.

At the same time, an English education gave Tamils a competitive edge in the scramble for jobs in government and civil service. As they had grasped the educational opportunities offered by the British much earlier than many Sinhalese and without prejudice against its being offered by proponents of another religion, they were able to gain a disproportionate number of posts in the administrative service, which the British gladly granted them. The reasons for this differential development are manifold. Among the Buddhist Sinhalese there existed an elaborate and entrenched — though at the time of British rule it was already becoming obsolete — system of formal education in the form of Buddhist temple schools where monks taught the pupils in Sinhala. There were no comparable institutions in Jaffna where traditional education was much more informal and personalized in the form of single teacher–pupil relationships or of instruction from father to son or to neighbours' children in so-called 'veranda schools'.[24] Tamil education and its content, moreover, were not exclusively linked with religion. Consequently, there was less resistance to its being imparted by people not of the same faith.

In Jaffna, the English and American missions stepped into a vacuum, both with regard to English and to vernacular education. In the Sinhalese areas, they encountered stiff resistance — often politically motivated — in the beginning. For both groups, however, English education frequently meant conversion to Christianity.[25] The Hindu revival movement in the middle of the nineteenth century, led by Ārumuka Nāvalar, though resenting this type of education, did not lead to an abandonment of education, the advantages of which were only too clear, but to the establishment of Hindu educational institutions set up as counterweights to the English and missionary ones. Among the Sinhalese, this resentment manifested itself rather later in the person of the Anāgarika

Dharmapāla, but also much more virulently and implicitly political at the same time. By that time, the Tamils had also gone ahead in the sphere of vernacular education. Their new schools taught both English and Tamil, a trend that continued until after independence.

Another reason for the success of English education in Jaffna can be found in the arid and infertile character of the soil, which yielded satisfactory crops only with an immense amount of diligent and painstaking work. The industriousness of the Jaffna Tamils had succeeded in making the land fertile and covering it with orchards and vegetable gardens, but economic and social changes in the wake of colonial occupation had, nevertheless, made it necessary to look for means to earn one's livelihood elsewhere. Government service was a welcome outlet.

The Jaffna Tamils thus gained a twofold advantage: their knowledge of English enabled them to secure jobs in the government service and, thereby, establish a link with modern development; at the same time they retained a stable and secure identity as Jaffna Tamils, thanks to their education in and knowledge of Tamil. At present, Tamil is the medium of instruction in all primary schools in Jaffna as well as in most secondary schools and most faculties in the colleges and the University of Jaffna. The literary development of the 1950s, which tried to define 'Sri Lanka Tamil nationalism' as distinct from both Tamil nationalism in Indian Tamilnadu and from 'Sinhalese nationalism' in Sri Lanka,[26] further supported the creation and maintenance of a stable ethnic identity. Although Jaffna Tamils had long been domiciled in Sri Lanka and felt themselves to be Ceylonese, they always regarded Tamilnadu as their country of origin and source of inspiration where religious, cultural and literary issues were concerned: Tamilnadu's was the 'mother literature', Jaffna's the 'child literature'.[27] This concept, which had long been overtaken by reality, was finally and radically challenged by the young authors of the 1950s who postulated a genuine and distinctive Jaffna Tamil literature, which by then had become a reality, and a Ceylonese Tamil identity and nationalism.

The policy of 'Sinhala only' and the equation of 'Sri Lanka nationalism' with 'Sinhala-Buddhist nationalism'[28] created a threat to education in both English and Tamil in Jaffna and also did much to ruin and destroy the integrative impact of the concept of 'Sri Lanka Tamil nationalism'. The abandonment of English threatened to cost the Tamils their government jobs because they were not prepared to learn Sinhala one-sidedly without securing a place for Tamil as well.

The demand for 'Sinhala only' also threatened their Tamil education and, thereby, their ethnic integration and identity. Feeling the basis of their identity as 'citizens of Ceylon' was jeopardized, quite apart from their identity as Tamils, they objected vehemently to this policy.

Since arid Jaffna has never created enough work for the growing population, many young people depended on job opportunities in the civil and administrative services, and these opportunities were undermined by the 'Sinhala only' policy. The protests of the Tamils succeeded in so far as Tamil was permitted to remain the medium of instruction in Tamil-majority districts and in schools with a majority of Tamil children, and (later) exam papers could be written in either language. As this bilingual examining process necessitated two sets of examiners, and as the Tamils were extremely successful, especially in the sciences, accusations by the Sinhalese of cheating and favouritism began to arise.[29] Out of distrust and suspicion, standard-ization and district quotas were born.[30] At approximately the time these measures were introduced, subsidies for foreign students in the United Kingdom, a traditional country of study for Sri Lankan (and especially Tamil) students, were abolished, suddenly making the cost of study abroad prohibitive and eliminating it as an alternative for many Tamils.[31]

The introduction of free education in the whole of Sri Lanka in 1945 and the explicit relationship of formal education to achievement and higher standards of living exacerbated the competition between Tamils and Sinhalese in the race for jobs.[32] The bursting school system produced far more graduates than the economy could absorb. In the face of widespread unemployment among the intelligentsia, the Tamils constituted a convenient scapegoat for the feelings of resentment that developed among the majority Sinhalese. Although standardization was abolished immediately after the elections in 1977, the damage had been done and even the inclusion of Tamil as a national language in the constitution of 1978 could not much help to undo it.[33]

The new system of district quotas established in 1978 which supplements allotted places according to merit and to 'underprivileged districts' has been opposed both by the low-country Sinhalese and the Tamils because it allegedly favours the rural areas against the urban (and it is meant to favour them since they are considered educationally backward).[34] Kandyan Sinhalese and a handful of Tamils from the educationally under-served Eastern province have been the ones to profit most from this system. It is interesting to note that although Tamils from Jaffna have a lower overall unemployment rate (10.9 per cent) than the low-country Sinhalese (18.5 per cent), their share of academic unemployment (i.e. unemployment following GCE A levels) is nearly one-and-a-half times as high as that of the corresponding Sinhalese group (41 as against 29 per cent).[35] This is a very impressive figure, and we will come back to its significance later.

Education, as stated, always held a very high place in the value system of Jaffna Tamils. It is considered the only worthwhile legacy to leave to one's children because all other inheritance is material and perishable.[36] The standardization trauma has encouraged and enhanced this view to such an extent that a virtual scramble for education and high marks is now going on from kindergarten onwards in Jaffna. Private tuition institutions have mushroomed all over the peninsula within the last two to three years. English is always a subject in the curriculum, whereas Sinhala is taught extremely rarely in Jaffna.[37] Jaffna is, moreover, educationally one of the best-equipped districts with respect to number of schools, size of classes and qualifications of teachers.[38] The availability of instruction in the Tamil language from primary education to university inclusively also helps create a favourable climate for educational achievement.

Nevertheless, the scramble for education by all means is, as Holmes very aptly pointed out, illusory. Only a very limited number of students are admitted to the universities. This leads to a host of very well-qualified young people who have no chance of ever getting into university and with slim chances of finding employment elsewhere.[39]

As the quality of education in Jaffna is generally high, people who cannot find employment in Jaffna or Colombo often try to go abroad, if not to the United States or Europe, then to Singapore or the Middle East. Their education in Tamil and their commitment to the language and the culture serve to maintain their identity even under adverse conditions, and form a sort of buffer against culture shocks and, most importantly, help them to retain links with and information about developments in Jaffna. They never cease to consider themselves as Jaffna Tamils and are never ambiguous or in doubt about this basic identity.

This identity, however, has suffered a considerable contraction over the last twenty years. During the 1950s and 1960s, Ceylonese Tamil meant ethnic (Jaffna) Tamil and citizen of Ceylon at the same time. The two concepts of identity did not conflict with each other but were rather considered as supplementary because the Tamils felt themselves to be legitimate citizens of Ceylon in their Tamil-ness. This feeling, however, has changed radically over the past ten to fifteen years. The more the Sinhalese made explicit their desire for a predominantly Sinhala–Buddhist Sri Lanka, the more the Tamils felt left out of this polity. Consequently, their identity as Jaffna Tamils more and more parted ways with their sense of themselves as Ceylonese citizens so that today these two identities are considered mutually exclusive by many, especially younger, Jaffna Tamils. Education cannot bridge this gap and is less and less intended to do so.

The national identity of the Sinhalese majority of Sri Lanka at no time included the Tamils, although the latter would have been glad to have been included at first. Sinhalese nationalism, however, was not secular but tied up with religion and, stemming from that, language, and thus could not act as a vehicle for integration.[40] The resurgent ethnic identity of the Sinhalese excluded the Tamils in a final way and made the Tamils yearn for the lost Tamil Īlam of their forefathers. Moreover, as education was the most prized achievement of the Jaffna Tamils, the sudden redundancy of this achievement after the introduction of 'Sinhala only', standardization and district quotas came as a severe shock. Highly qualified young people found themselves outside the gates of the universities where they felt they rightfully belonged. This group, disappointed in its aspirations and expectations, is the most fertile recruiting ground for the radical wing of the secessionists. The emergence of the so-called 'Tigers', mostly young men in their twenties who have failed to obtain university places, was in large part due to this situation.[41]

Indian (plantation) Tamils

Although education in the vernacular has fostered internal integration, self-assurance and social mobility among Jaffna Tamils and created a versatile, achievement-orientated and demanding younger generation, it has had virtually the opposite effect among the Indian Tamils on the plantations. Before examining this contemporary situation, however, let us first consider the historical development of education on the estates.

The Indian Tamils were brought to Ceylon in the early nineteenth century as plantation labourers. They were predominantly adult males who stayed in the country for a limited time.[42] Only when the plantation economy turned from coffee to tea and — to a lesser extent — rubber. where women and children could also be employed usefully and permanently or semi-permanently in menial jobs, did the composition of this group begin to change. There was thus no necessity for the provision of educational facilities for the plantation labourer until the middle or end of the century. Even then, when questions arose about the desirability of providing education for the plantation children, very few planters saw fit to respond positively. They feared that the work efficiency of children who went to school for the major part of the day would decline and were also of the opinion that Indian labourers should educate their children in India, if at all. and should only bring them to Ceylon after they had completed their education, i.e. at the age of 12 to 14.[43]

The legacy of this ambiguity and confusion of competence has dragged on virtually to this day. Although the desirability of teaching plantation children at least the three Rs — to enable them to be good workers(!) — was eventually acknowledged. education on the estates remained for a long time — until after independence — a private affair and the responsibility of the planters. In reality this situation often resulted in *Kanganies* doling out a minimum of 'education' to the labourers' children. The number and standard of plantation schools remained very low or even declined. Gnanamuthu claims that there were only 771 estate schools in 1976 for 76,237 children, as against 880 in 1972, and that no new schools have been established since 1948.[44]

As the Indian Tamils were disenfranchised after independence, there seemed no pressing need to provide educational facilities for them at that time either. Even when all schools were nationalized in 1961. the estate schools were excluded and are not totally nationalized even today; although after the land reform and nationalization of estates in the mid-1970s the government professed the intention of taking over all estate schools.[45] I have no information about the present government's policy with regard to the estate schools. The most recent statistics. however, still give a figure of 43.58 per cent illiteracy on the estates, compared to 23.40 per cent for the island as a whole.[46]

More important even than these statistics are the low standards of instruction and poor quality of equipment prevalent among the existing estate schools.[47] The classes never extend beyond primary school fifth or sixth grade. The teachers are the least qualified in the whole of Sri Lanka, and the pupil–teacher ratio (64:1) is the highest.[48]

The medium of instruction is exclusively Tamil. and no other languages are taught. Yet. when the 'Sinhala only' plan went through. a number of estate schools with almost exclusively Tamil pupils were transformed into exclusively Sinhala-medium schools since non-citizens were not counted in the school population for purposes of determining the language of instruction.[49] As these schools were then considered nationalized. Sinhala schools. the number of estate schools consequently declined statistically. and the Tamil children were deprived of instruction in the language they knew.[50] The language barrier in such schools creates an additional disadvantage for these Tamil children. although they would be ready and willing to learn Sinhala if doing so would assure them of the right to stay in the country and a modicum of personal safety and security.

Apart from poor facilities. the pupils from estate schools have virtually no opportunity of obtaining a higher. i.e. secondary or tertiary. education. In 1976. only 250 Indian Tamil graduates were to be found in the whole country. and one hundred Indian Tamils were enrolled in colleges and universities.[51] These statistics led the Ministry of Defence(!) to claim. in a publication about the Tamils in Sri Lanka. that 'Indian Tamils generally do not seek higher education'.[52] In fact. the geographical remoteness of the plantations makes enrolment in a far-away secondary school difficult as well as expensive. Furthermore. since no language besides Tamil is taught in estate schools in most cases. these children can follow neither Sinhala nor English courses. even were they to be admitted to university on the basis of their marks. In the Tamil University in Jaffna they would only be able to take courses in the arts since science courses there. as well as in the other universities. are still taught mainly in English. Moreover. the disadvantages of standardization and district quotas. intended for the Jaffna Tamils — and low-country Sinhalese — naturally affected the Indian Tamils most. because they had the lowest marks.

The few estate children able to leave the estate were usually the children of *Kanganies*. clerks and lower staff. They were sent to boarding schools specially founded for the purpose and reasonably well equipped.[53] The better Tamil primary and secondary schools were. however. as Gnanamuthu shows. often converted into Sinhala schools after 1961. with one Tamil stream (and this not in every case). Tamil children were sometimes expelled from these schools or not admitted to them on grounds of ethnicity and citizenship.[54] Free education brought more labourers' children to school after 1945 but paradoxically served to increase social distance rather than bridge it: labourers' children went to estate schools, others to English-teaching boarding schools.

The Sri Lankan government has continued to neglect education on the estates, as indicated by studies on the educational situation in Sri Lanka, which, though plentiful, nearly always state that the reported facts and dates 'do not apply' to the estate schools as 'these are excluded from the study'.[55] One explanation is that since Indian labourers are not citizens, the government does not feel any obligation to care for their children's education. In contrast to Jaffna, where a high standard of education can be maintained without government help, the Indian Tamils on the estates have been in no position to look after the educational needs of their children themselves. As they do not constitute a pressure group and were always expected to return to India one day, nobody consequently felt responsible for their educational needs. Even mission schools have been few and far between on the estates up to the present day.

Research material on the content and effect of this type of education or lack of it on the socialization and mobility of the estate population is virtually non-existent except for brief outlines in two slim volumes by Gnanamuthu.[56] But even he deals mostly with the number and standard of schools and says of the syllabus only that the three Rs are taught in most cases. He does conclude, however, that in nationalized estate schools where instruction is in Sinhala with a Tamil stream, the quality of Tamil instruction is nearly always at a very low level and assigned secondary priority.[57]

I venture, therefore, to apply the results of a study on the education of Tamils on estates in Malaysia, where the educational system on the plantations seems to be similar to the situation in Sri Lanka. Coletta[58] shows that Malaysian education of the type described guarantees ethnic and cultural internal integration and a stable identity at a very low level and at the expense of social mobility and quality of life. Instruction of Malaysian estate workers' children in Tamil transmits the values of Tamil culture, Tamil language and religion and at the same time the values of being a good, obedient worker who does not aspire to a higher station in life. A vicious circle is created where education does not lead out of poverty to a better job and a better life but rather conditions children from early on to be docile, efficient labourers, satisfied with what they get.[59] Instead of widening possibilities, this type of education narrows them. The preservation of ethnic identity in this case contributes to the preservation of poverty and low status. Since schools are provided on the estate itself, moreover, there is little incentive to venture out of the closed system of the estate and acquire additional skills.

Although the Malaysian and the Sri Lankan situations cannot be equated since in Malaysia three ethnic groups compete with each other, with the Malays in the ascendant, the situation on the estates is comparable since the Tamils in both cases live in a state of abject poverty and relative insecurity in a closed system. As staff children frequent schools in town, the estate schools often become ghetto schools for an underprivileged group (perhaps comparable to the Arabs in Israel). In addition, since so-called stateless persons are not admitted to government colleges and polytechnics.[60] those estate children who get as far as GCE O level have no further chance for advancement. They have, however, job expectations which cannot be met in the plantation situation, and this conflict creates resentment and unrest.[61]

Tamil schoolbooks in Sri Lanka

Before we come to a conclusion about the significance of the two types of education — Jaffna and estate — for ethnic identity, let us take a short look at the contents of the schoolbooks through which Tamil education is imparted.

K. Indrapala *et al.* show that Sinhala readers present an almost exclusively Sinhala or Sinhala-dominated country, nation and people.[62] I have been informed that secondary school readers in Sinhala present a somewhat more balanced picture.[63] However, as primary schools deal with a very decisive and formative phase of childhood, the presentation of such incompatible views of society is highly significant. In Tamil readers, on the other hand, an ideology of unity in diversity is upheld. Tamils as Tamils are part of a nation which comprises Tamils as well as Sinhalese, Moors, Burghers, etc., who live side by side and in harmony.

The authors of these Tamil readers, which appeared during the 1970s, belonged to or were identified with the group of leftist or left-orientated writers and intellectuals who created the concept of 'Sri Lanka Tamil nationalism', often in the face of strong resistance by conservative authors who had earlier compiled schoolbooks which projected an exclusively Tamil identity. Remarkably, this emphasis on unity and harmony, both subtle and overt, has had virtually little or no impact, at least in Jaffna, in spite of the good intentions of the authors. Both groups of Tamils remain increasingly aloof from the mainstream of Sinhala political and social life because the premises of the schoolbooks find no counterpart in day-to-day life.

Owing to the scarcity of available material. I am not sure whether schoolbooks for the plantations are the same as those for Jaffna or if they are perhaps imported from India. Such information is necessary before any evaluation can be undertaken. However, the fact that the syllabus of 1970(!) is still in force in the estate schools, virtually unchanged in over seventy-five years, is a strong indicator of what the content of instruction on the estates may be like.[64]

For Jaffna, despite its close links with Tamilnadu, education could never be India-influenced or India-orientated. Neither Tamil nationalism nor the content of Tamil education in India were ever considered applicable to Jaffna by the Jaffna Tamils. There was even strong resentment in the 1960s against the importation of literature of any sort from India. The import limitations under the United Front government gave a further impetus to the development of Jaffna Tamil literature and schoolbooks. The concept of 'Sri Lanka Tamil nationalism' called for schoolbooks which projected this desired national ideology and not that of Indian Tamilnadu.

Conclusion

Tamil education in Sri Lanka should be seen in its social context, not from a perspective of academic ideology. In both the Jaffna and estate cases the ethnic identity of the Tamils has been preserved largely by the form of the educational system. But whereas for the Jaffna Tamils ethnic identity was until recently coupled with high economic and social status, for the plantation Tamils just the opposite is true: on the estates ethnic identity equals poverty, low status, low quality of life and very restricted political, economic and social possibilities and rights. The explanations for these contrasting positions lie in the historical development of both groups, in their social environment and status, and in the political situation and development of Sri Lanka after independence. I would further single out two major points which, if applicable, also tell us much about the effects of educational systems on the ethnic identity of minorities in general:

1. In Jaffna, the preservation of ethnic identity was coupled with

social mobility because people became bilingual early on in the process. Did bilingualism produce social mobility or vice versa? This is rather a question of 'which came first, the chicken or the egg?' Jaffna Tamils had high status and economic positions to begin with. Thus, when English education was offered, they availed themselves of its opportunities. Unlike so many peoples, however, they suffered no cultural loss because education in the vernacular was always kept up, albeit at times very low key. The switch from Tamil to English and back was, therefore, connected with far fewer difficulties and less bitterness than elsewhere.

The demand for 'Sinhala only', on the other hand, created as much acrimony and opposition as the demand for Hindi in South India. This demand made the Tamils even more aware of the necessity to preserve Tamil. But it was essentially their bilingualism which enabled them to retain their ethnic identity at a high social and economic level.

Their language, together with their Tamil identity and perceived right to self-determination within or without the polity of Sri Lanka, turned out to be decisive. In the pursuance of self-determination, language became both an important vehicle and a symbol for the Tamils. The power of language found its ultimate expression in the educational field, which was already highly charged and tense because of its perceived role as a vehicle for upward mobility. In its quality as marker of ethnicity and identity, language acquired political significance and developed into a highly explosive issue. Education and language became part of a wider political issue, namely the identity, economic development and right of political self-determination of the Tamils as a nationality.

2. The Indian Tamils preserved their ethnic identity as well. But whereas the Jaffna system always included the option of enlargement (i.e. it possessed flexible boundaries), the closed system of the estate rigidified its borders. Segregation from the mainstream of Sri Lankan life became more and more pronounced on the estates as time went by and the status of the Indian Tamils grew increasingly insecure. Ethnic identity and cultural integration among the estate Tamils, maintained at a low level by a social and political system which had shown little concern for or recognition of them, have had the effect of severely limiting their cultural and religious life as well as their social mobility. The option of enlargement and widening of the circle does not exist for the

Indian Tamils. though many of them would welcome the chance to assimilate to a greater extent in order to obtain greater equality of rights and opportunity. Integration. though explicitly (statutorily) entitled. is implicitly (structurally) and firmly denied them by the Sinhalese.[65]

The political situation of which the language issue is a part is. thus. different for the two Tamil groups. Whereas the Jaffna Tamils consciously refuse to assimilate themselves into Sinhala society and elect to segregate more and more. the Indian Tamils are denied the assimilation they would otherwise choose. It is important. therefore. in discussing identity. integration and assimilation. to keep in mind at what level and under which conditions ethnic identity is retained.

If we agree with Karl Deutsch's statement that gradual assimilation with simultaneous retention of original ethnic and cultural identity achieves a slower but more complete and less stressful integration in the end. this hypothesis is obviously not working — or not being allowed to work — in the case of the Indian Tamils. and has only operated to a limited extent in the case of the Jaffna Tamils. Ethnic identity and its preservation in these two cases serves to close the ranks. increase differences and effectively prevent either integration or assimilation. This is so despite (or because of) strong cultural and ethnic similarities between Jaffna Tamils and Sinhalese. which even make it difficult physically to distinguish a Tamil from a Sinhalese. But precisely because these similarities call for differentiation. existing or perceived differences become overemphasized.[66]

The resulting stratification illustrates another of Deutsch's theses: every society creates for itself the groups. ethnicities or races whom it chooses either to emulate or to suppress. primarily for economic reasons.[67] This applies particularly to the form of the educational system as devised by the government of Sri Lanka and its policies to implement it. The form and rules of this system as defined and limited by the guidelines of educational policy are. in the case of the Tamils. more critical with respect to integration or segregation than the content of this education. This is shown very clearly in the case of Jaffna. where ethnic exclusiveness has been preserved despite the efforts of the proponents of an integrationist syllabus. Social reality and a lack of goodwill on both sides worked against it.

In summary. the main theses of this paper are:

1. The Jaffna Tamils were originally able to preserve their ethnic and cultural identity and integrate to a considerable extent because they became functionally bilingual, and, similarly, they could become bilingual because they possessed a secure and stable identity coupled with a secure territorial base.
2. On the estates, ethnic and cultural identity at a low ritual level were preserved at the expense of social mobility and quality of life and with an accompanying denial of the possibility of assimilation.
3. Thus we could conclude that maintenance of ethnic identity without loss of social mobility and quality of life is only possible when supported by *functional* bilingualism. Mere acceptance of an elite language or a lingua franca tends to lead to culture loss or to a phenomenon which has been called 'subtractive bilingualism' or, more colloquially, 'illiteracy in two languages'. These terms describe a situation in which a foreign tongue gains ascendancy over the native language, the latter then degenerating into a sort of 'bazaar language', and in which both languages function at rudimentary or at least limited levels of knowledge. Monolingualism in a minority language, on the other hand, leads to isolation and a nearly complete loss of mobility.
4. Sri Lanka constitutes a special case. Although Jaffna Tamils succeeded in developing a functional bilingualism to preserve both their high status and ethnic identity, their contact with the mainstream of Sinhalese life became more tenuous as English lost its hold on public life in Sri Lanka. Their bilingualism could not protect their high position because it consisted of Tamil and *English* and not Tamil and *Sinhala* or Tamil, English and Sinhala.

I have been informed that before independence, and even until 1956, many more Tamils spoke Sinhala in addition to English and Tamil than nowadays,[68] apart from the Tamils residing in Colombo, who all speak Sinhala as a matter of course. Political developments in Sri Lanka seem to have rendered the bilingualism of the Tamils less functional. Yet it remains an important differentiating characteristic and progressively so for those who go overseas. One could even say that this bilingualism enables them to open up opportunities outside Jaffna and Sri Lanka, which presents quite an interesting paradox. Bilingualism enables these Tamils to retain and reformulate their more radical goals of autonomy and secession even after the educational infrastructure in Jaffna itself has been destroyed for them.

Explanation of technical terms

Sinhala The language of the Sinhalese, derived from a Prakrit dialect and Elu, the language of the original inhabitants of the country.

Sinhalese The majority ethnic group in Sri Lanka. They are believed to be Aryan immigrants from India (*c*. 500 BC), but today are strongly intermixed with Dravidian Tamils, the largest minority in the country.

Tamils A Dravidian people who originally inhabited South India. Many Tamils migrated to Sri Lanka around the eleventh century and subsequently founded the kingdom of Jaffna. Tamils, however, are believed to have settled in Sri Lanka much earlier, even around the time of the Sinhalese immigration.

Kanganies (Tm. *Kaṅkāṇī*) Literally overseer. The term connotes the headman of a group of labourers in the plantations. *Kanganies* were employed to recruit labourers from India and were the social and professional leaders of workers' gangs.

(Tamil) Ilam The name of the Tamil secessionist movements demanding an independent state. Under the occupation of the Cōlas in the eleventh century, Sri Lanka was named Īlamaṇṭalam. Īlam is the ancient Tamil word for the island.

O levels and A levels These correspond respectively to the high school leaving certificate and nine credits in the American system. In the German system, *Mittlere Reife* and *Abitur* would be the equivalent exams.

Relevant dates

1945	Under Minister of Education Kannangara, free education from primary to university is introduced.
1948/49	Indian Tamils are deprived of their citizenship and voting rights by the Citizenship Laws.
1956	Under the MEP government, Sinhala becomes the sole official language of the country.
1961	All schools are nationalized under the SLFP government; Sinhala becomes the medium of instruction in all schools.
1971	'Standardization' is introduced.

1974	District quotas are introduced. The University of Jaffna is opened.
1975	All tea estates and some estate schools are nationalized.
1977	Standardization is being abolished by the UNP government. From
1978	onwards, a modified system of merit, district quotas and special quotas for 'underprivileged' districts is operated for university admissions.

Notes

1. See Chapter 1.
2. Donald L. Horowicz, Nathan Glazer and P. Moynihan, *Ethnicity: Ethnic Identity*, Cambridge, Mass., 1975, pp. 117–18.
3. See David L. Sills (ed.), *International Encyclopedia of the Social Sciences*, vol. 10, New York, 1968, pp. 365f.
4. See Chapter 1.
5. See Hans-Dieter Evers, 'Das Erziehungswesen als Faktor in der sozialen und wirtschaftlichen Entwicklung Ceylons', in Evers *et al.* (eds), *Erziehungswesen im sozialen Wandel*, Freiburg, 1962, p. 25.
6. See Chapter 1.
7. Ibid.
8. Ralph Pieris, 'Universities, Politics and Public Opinion in Ceylon' in A.B. Shah (ed.), *Education, Scientific Policy and Developing Societies*, Bombay, 1967, p. 192.
9. See Reggie Siriwardena, K. Indrapala, Sunil Bastian and Sepali Kottegoda, *School Text Books and Communal Relations in Sri Lanka*. Part 1: *Analysis of Text Books*, Colombo, n.d. (1982?).
10. Census of Population and Housing, 1981, quoted from *Sri Lanka's Ethnic Conflict. Myths and Realities*, Colombo, 1983, p. 1. Formerly the Indian Tamils constituted about 10 per cent of the population, but in the wake of statelessness and repatriation their number has declined.
11. Michael Roberts, 'Indian Estate labour in Ceylon during the Coffee Period, 1830–1880' in *Indian Economic and Social History Review*, vol. 3 (1966), pp. 1–52; 101–36.
12. K.M. de Silva, *A History of Sri Lanka*, London, 1981, p. 333.
13. A. Jeyaratnam Wilson, *Politics in Sri Lanka*, Colombo, 1979, p. 65.
14. De Silva, op. cit., p. 515.
15. Pieris, op. cit., p. 194.
16. Heinz Bechert, *Religion, Staat und Gesellschaft in den Ländern des Theravada-Buddhismus. Teil 1. Allgemein und Ceylon*, Hamburg, 1966, p. 208.
17. C.R. de Silva, 'Weightage in University Admissions: Standardisation and District Quotas in Sri Lanka 1970–1975' in *Modern Ceylon Studies*, vol. 5 (1975), p. 154.
18. K.M. de Silva, op. cit., p. 541f.
19. S. Arasaratnam, *Ceylon*, Englewood Cliffs, NJ, 1965, p. 115.

20. Ibid.
21. Bertram Bastiampillai, 'Educational Enterprise Among the Tamils in North Ceylon under British Rule in the Early 19th Century', lecture at the Fifth International Conference-Seminar of Tamil Studies, Madurai, 2–8 January 1981.
22. De Silva, op. cit., p. 334f.
23. Bastiampillai, op. cit.
24. Arasaratnam, op. cit., p. 115.
25. Michael Roberts, 'Elite Formation and Elites, 1832–1931' in Michael Roberts (ed.), *Collective Identities, Nationalism and Protest in Modern Sri Lanka*, Colombo, 1979, p. 188.
26. De Silva, op. cit., p. 513.
27. K. Sivathamby, *Ḻattil Tamiḻ Ilakkiyam* (Tamil Literature in Sri Lanka), Madras, 1978, p. 53.
28. De Silva, op. cit.
29. C.R. de Silva, 'The Impact of Nationalism on Education: The Schools Take-over (1961) and the University Admissions Crisis (1970–1975)' in Michael Roberts (ed.), op. cit., p. 483, gives a figure of 271 Hindu students admitted in Science as against 499 Buddhist ones, which reads as 52.2 per cent Buddhists against 28.4 per cent Hindus (Tamils). This is clearly an overrepresentation for the Tamils. Christians in the Sciences constituted 17 per cent, and it has to be kept in mind that this includes Sinhalese and Tamil Christians.
30. C.R. de Silva, op. cit., pp. 156–7. Standardization meant that to get a place in the university, a Tamil student had to have higher marks than a Sinhalese one in order to 'equalise' chances for an allegedly under-privileged group. The standardization was applied by subject.
31. Robert Holmes, *Jaffna (Sri Lanka) 1980*, Jaffna, 1980, p. 251.
32. Pieris, op. cit., p. 193.
33. C.R. de Silva, op. cit., pp. 489f, and especially p. 497.
34. K.M. de Silva, 'University Admissions and Ethnic Tension in Sri Lanka: 1977–1982' in Robert B. Goldmann and A. Jeyaratnam Wilson (eds), *From Independence to Statehood. Managing Ethnic Conflict in five African and Asian States*, London, 1984, pp. 102ff.
35. 'Report on Consumer, Finance and Socio-Economic Survey 1978/1979', and 'Labour Force and Socio-Economic Survey', *Sri Lanka's Ethnic Conflict*, op. cit., pp. 2–3.
36. Marai Malai Aṭikaḷ, *Tamiḻar Matam* (The Religion of the Tamils), Madras, 1974, p. 29.
37. See Holmes, op. cit., p. 266, who speaks of about 150 children learning Sinhala in Jaffna, most of whom, however, constitute special cases like Sinhalese living in Jaffna or children of mixed parentage. Government officials, however, are required to know Sinhala for promotions and permanency.
38. Marga Institute, *Needs of Children and Adolescents*, Colombo, 1975, pp. 26, 31, 36.
39. S. Arasaratnam, 'Nationalism in Sri Lanka and the Tamils' in Roberts, op. cit., p. 517. See also Holmes, op. cit., p. 261.
40. Wilson, op. cit., p. 237; Bechert, op. cit., p. 205.

150   *Dagmar Hellmann-Rajanayagam*

41. Arasaratnam, op. cit., p. 518.
42. Roberts, 'Indian Estate Labour ...', op. cit., p. 3.
43. H.P. Chattopadhyaya, *Indians in Sri Lanka*, Calcutta, 1979, p. 176.
44. George Gnanamuthu, *The Child in the Plantations*, Colombo, 1979, p. 9.
45. George Gnanamuthu, *Education and the Indian Plantation Labourer in Sri Lanka*, Colombo, 1977, p. 53, 102.
46. Gnanamuthu, *The Child in the Plantations*, op. cit., p. 13 and 'Report on Consumer Finance and Socio-Economic Survey 1978/79' in *Sri Lanka's Ethnic Conflict*, p. 6.
47. Gnanamuthu,*Education and the Indian Plantation Labourer in Sri Lanka*, op. cit., pp. 61f.
48. Chattopadhyaya, op. cit., pp. 197–8.
49. Ibid., p. 203n.
50. Gnanamuthu, op. cit., p. 9.
51. Ibid., p. 67.
52. 'Tamils in Sri Lanka', Ministry of Defence and Foreign Affairs, Sri Lanka, Colombo, 1976, p. 6. With regard to the educational situation in Jaffna and the East the pamphlet states that under the UF government expenditure for these regions was comparatively higher than for other districts (p. 7). However, the difficulties of getting Tamil teachers, the higher cost of Tamil books, and so on, confirmed the impression that Tamil education was neglected as against Sinhala (see p. 8).
53. Gnanamuthu, *Education and the Indian Plantation Labourer*, pp. 19, 26, 82.
54. Ibid., p. 65.
55. See Marga Institute, op. cit., pp. 27 and 42, and*Administrative Report of the Director-General of Education for the Year 1972*, p. 259, where the number of estate schools (738) is simply given with the hint that a special department for the management of estate schools exists (p. 259). See also C.R. de Silva, op. cit., p. 165.
56. See above.
57. Gnanamuthu, *The Child in the Plantations*, p. 15.
58. N.J. Coletta, 'Malaysia's Forgotten People: Education, Cultural Identity and Socio-Economic Mobility Among South Indian Workers' in Judith A. Nagata (ed.),*Pluralism in Malaysia. Myth and Reality*, Contributions to Asian Studies 7, 1975, pp. 87–112.
59. Ibid., p. 99.
60. Gnanamuthu, *The Child in the Plantations*, p. 16.
61. Ibid., p. 17.
62. Siriwardena *et al.*, op. cit., pp. 5ff and 35ff.
63. Personal communication from Ms. Radhika Coomaraswamy, 7 June 1984.
64. Gnanamuthu,*Education and the Indian Plantation Labourer in Sri Lanka*, p. 59, but see also p. 47.
65. See ibid., pp. 103–4.
66. Holmes, op. cit., p. 293.
67. Karl W. Deutsch, *Tides Among Nations*, New York, 1979, pp. 70f, 77.
68. See Holmes, op. cit., p. 269.

10 THE EDUCATION OF HISPANICS IN THE UNITED STATES: INADEQUACIES OF THE AMERICAN MELTING-POT THEORY

Isaura Santiago Santiago

Since the turn of the century American sociologists and anthropologists have strugged to describe and define what happens when two or more groups of people come together to live within a territory or natural boundary. An early term for the dynamic, 'social assimilation' was defined by Park (1930) as:

> the name given to the process by which people of diverse racial origins and different cultural heritages, occupying a common territory, achieve a cultural solidarity sufficient at least to sustain a national existence ... In the United States an immigrant is ordinarily considered assimilated as soon as he has acquired the language and the social ritual of the native community and can participate, without encountering prejudice, in the common life, economic and political ...

Glazer and Moynihan (1963) suggest that the origin of another term commonly used to depict assimilation was borrowed from the title of Israel Zangwell's 1908 play *The Melting Pot*. They assert that it was 'seized upon as a concise evocation of a profoundly significant American fact' (Glazer and Moynihan 1970: 289). Whether that assertion is valid or not, the sociological literature of the decades that followed is replete with the use of the term. Theoretical inquiry and debate of the early twentieth century centred on the concept of 'ethnicity' and the relative importance of various influences on the perceived extent to which different groups have or have not been assimilated.

As has also been acknowledged by Glazer and Moynihan (1975), even the term 'ethnicity' and the way we use it are still being defined. After a century of research there remains substantially little basis for prediction with respect to ethnic information. Even the best minds have been unable to predict when or the extent to which blacks or Hispanics in the United States will become part of the 'melting pot'. Glazer and Moynihan, for example, acknowledge the inadequacies of their predictions in the introduction to the second edition of *Beyond the Melting Pot* (1970).

Frustration resulting from the inadequacies of assimilationist theory have led some to reject it outright. Glazer (1982) and Liebman (1982), on the other hand, continue to romanticize it and cling to it. One consequence has been continued ethnic/racial conflict in the United States (Rose 1974). In recent years, leading educators have also romanticized the melting-pot theory and issued major recommendations for school reform based on its underlying ideology (Adler 1982, Sizer 1983, Twentieth Century Fund 1983, Ravitch 1985).

Perhaps no group in the United States has suffered more in recent years from this trend than Hispanics in the public schools. Educational programmes devised for them have largely been an outgrowth of assimilationist ideology. This chapter argues that it is because of this persisting ideology of assimilation that American schools have been unsuccessful in educating Hispanic youth. Given these trends and the relative powerlessness of Hispanics as a group to reverse it, there is every reason to be concerned that yet another generation of youth will be lost.

Language policy and language planning

Language planning in the public schools of the United States has suffered from the incongruencies and conflicts resulting from policies determining the education of ethnic minority children who speak a language other than English. Competence in a language other that English is viewed as a 'deficit' or a 'problem' which must be corrected (Cummins 1981). Schools often attempt to deal with this problem by excluding children from subject-matter instruction until they learn English. Wherever minority parents have rejected this practice and demanded that their children receive meaningful and substantive instruction, debate has ensued (Santiago Santiago 1978, 1983).

Particularly fierce has been the debate over the role of public schools. In most cases, the different positions taken are attributable to the social organization theory that the individual or group ascribes to, be it assimilation, pluralism, or whatever. Consequently, much like language policy on the national level, debate over language policy in the schools has largely been ideological and political (Otheguy 1982, Epstein 1977). This debate began when the writers of the Constitution were deciding what language to write it in (Kloss

1977). Today, the United States still has no national language policy, and the schools remain the primary arena in which the debate continues.

The Hispanic community in the United States has raised a loud voice in this debate. Many sectors of the heterogeneous group were responsible for the resurgence of bilingual education in the 1960s (Garcia, 1973). While many in the Hispanic community have supported the policy of compensatory bilingual education for limited English proficient students (LEPS) (Schneider 1976), a smaller but still substantial group has argued that maintenance bilingual education should not be precluded as a parental option (Cole 1983). Still others have gone a step further and argue that the federal government should support, if not ensure, the option of maintenance bilingual education for selected groups because of their unique historical relationship to the United States (Centro 1979; Gaarder, 1977). Hispanic educational leaders who have taken this position have included Mexicans, Puerto Ricans, and Cubans (Garcia 1983). They speak, however, for an undefined segment within their communities, and differences with respect to educational goals across and within Hispanic communities in the continental United States clearly exist. However, two goals seem to be shared by a majority of Hispanics in the United States: (1) having their children acquire a good command of the English language and (2) having their children receive a quality education (National Hispanic Educational Platform, 1984).

Within the context of the assimilationist melting-pot theory it would seem that the goals of the Hispanic and general public are consonant. Advocates of the melting-pot theory would agree that everyone should learn English and that education is the only appropriate vehicle for social incorporation. They argue that all immigrant groups have been subjected to the ethnic queuing process, and 'new' arrivals willing to give up their language and culture and attend school will ultimately reap the benefits shared by the mainstream. Very often, advocates of this view also take the position that English is the appropriate language of instruction (Epstein 1977). Glazer (1975) goes so far as to warn that providing 'special' remedies for some groups leads to 'affirmative discrimination' against members of other ethnic groups.

Why has conflict continued? This chapter will argue that the fault lies in the inadequacies of the melting-pot theory in explaining the experience of at least one group, Hispanics, and the continued reliance of educational policy-makers on goals and curricula based on assimilationist theory. It is also argued that the inadequacies of the theory preclude its use in defining future sociopolitical relationships and render it inappropriate for planning purposes. The substance of this argument is presented here in three parts. First, a demographic overview of Hispanics in the United States; second, an analysis of the historical and political relationships of selected subgroups of Hispanics to the United States; and third, an analysis of the education offered Hispanics in the United States. The chapter concludes with the assertion that major reform efforts are needed, an explanation why, and suggestion that a new theory of bilingual multi-ethnic/multi-racial education guide future efforts.

Demography of Hispanics in the United States

The Hispanic community in the United States is a heterogeneous one. Major subgroups include Mexicans, Puerto Ricans, Cubans and other Latin Americans. According to the 1980 Census, there were 14.6 million Spanish origin residents in the United States or 6.4 per cent of the total population (Bureau of the Census (Bureau) 1983). This figure, however, does not offer an accurate picture of the true Hispanic population because of sampling errors and because it does not include the estimated 6–10 million 'undocumented' aliens living in the United States — people who have entered the country without government authorization or the 3.1 million Puerto Ricans living on the island of Puerto Rico. The size of the documented Hispanic community rose from 14.6 million in 1980 to 15 million in 1983, and it has been projected that by the year 2000 this figure will reach 20 million. Furthermore, Hispanics have a low median age of 23 compared to the non-Hispanic median age in the US of 31 in 1980 (Bureau 1983). This means that they are more likely to have school-age children. The age discrepancy places Hispanics as a group in conflict with the majority at times (Hayes-Bautista *et al.* 1984).

Seventy per cent of the Hispanic community resides in five states: California, Texas, New York, Florida, and Illinois. Eighty-seven per cent reside in metropolitan areas, including 50 per cent in inner cities (Bureau 1983). As a result of their disproportionate presence in large urban areas and their further ghettoization within large cities, Hispanics today are frequently segregated with respect to the schools they attend (Noboa 1980; Cardenas 1975).

This growth in the size of the Hispanic community in the United

States has not gone unnoticed. One periodical acclaimed 'Ethnic Sleeping Giant Awakens' (Godsell 1980), another asserted 'It's Your Turn in the Sun' (*Time* 1978) and yet other articles evidence the public's concern, if not fear of the implications: 'Hispanics Make Their Move' (*US News and World Report* 1981) and 'Hispanic Voting Study Finds Sleeping Giant' (*New York Times* 1982).

The 1980 Census included a question on language spoken in the home. Results show that 11 per cent of the population spoke a language other than English. Of the non-English languages, Spanish was reported most frequently. Over 11 million persons (5 per cent of the total population) reported speaking Spanish in the home. Of these, 76 per cent also reported speaking English 'very well'. This and other sociolinguistic evidence suggest that Hispanics tend to retain the use of their native language across generations and that this pattern differs substantially from the experience of European immigrant groups of the nineteenth century (Bureau 1983; and see Ferguson and Heath 1981; Fishman 1956, 1980).

Indicators of social stratification

In 1982, the median family income in the United States was $23,433. For Hispanics, the median family income was $16,228. As with other social indicators there is substantial variance across Hispanic subgroups. Puerto Ricans, for instance, had the lowest median income of all subgroups at $11,148. The poverty rate for Hispanics was 29.9 per cent compared to 15.0 per cent for the total population (Bureau 1983). Furthermore, during the period 1979–82 Hispanic families experienced a substantial decrease (about 14 per cent) in real median family income (Bureau 1983).

In 1980, 43 per cent of all Hispanic families surveyed by the Census Bureau owned their own homes, compared to 67 per cent of the non-Hispanic population. Among Hispanics, 49 per cent of all Mexicans but only 21 per cent of all Puerto Ricans were home owners. There was no improvement between 1970 and 1980 in the rate of home ownership for Hispanics (Bureau 1983).

In 1983, 23 per cent of all Hispanic homes were headed by single women, up from 15 per cent in 1970. Of non-Hispanic homes surveyed, 15 per cent were headed by females (Bureau 1983). Here again there is significant variance across groups: 43 per cent of all Puerto Rican homes in New York City, for example, were headed by women (Association of Puerto Rican Executive Directors 1982).

Annual data on the unemployment rates of Hispanics, made available for the first time in 1973, have been consistently higher for Hispanics than non-Hispanics. In both 1979 and 1982, Hispanic unemployment was twice that of non-Hispanics. Between 1979 and 1982 Hispanic unemployment climbed from 8.3 per cent to 13.8 per cent (Bureau 1983). Unemployment rates for Hispanic youth are estimated at 37–40 per cent (Ginzberg 1980). Since this figure only includes Hispanics on the continent and documented workers, the rate is actually substantially higher.

Occupation statistics indicate that in 1982 about a quarter of all Hispanics held operative jobs, working as, for example, machine operators, service-station attendants and truck drivers. This was about twice the proportion for non-Hispanics. Although 9 per cent of all Hispanics were employed as professional and technical workers, almost double the proportion of non-Hispanics were employed in these jobs (Bureau 1983).

In summary, most traditional indicators of social participation show Hispanics are clearly not reaping a representative share of the economic and social benefits of American society. Hidden in much of the data is substantial variance among the four major Hispanic subgroups. Trends suggest that with respect to at least some social stratification indicators, Puerto Ricans are the least and Cubans are the most economically integrated of the groups.

Other trends suggested by the data give reason for alarm. With respect to each and every indicator discussed here, the condition of Hispanics as a group can be described as deplorable and in a rapidly declining state. The melting-pot theory is clearly not working for Hispanics and there is little likelihood that these trends will be reversed in the near future.

Education

Only in recent years have national data relevant to the condition of education for Hispanics become available. Even these data, however, are deficient in at least two key respects. First, in most cases they are limited to the quantification of a narrow number of measures of educational outcomes. Secondly, they are virtually devoid of any description of the content or context (much less the quality) of the educational experience of Hispanics and the institutions in which they are educated. Consequently, the available data serve only to blame the victim. Some suggest that this is because school systems do not want to be held accountable for the inequities that exist. In accounting terms, the insidious racial, ethnic and linguistic prejudice that is manifested in the curriculum and organizational structures of the schools is difficult to 'foot'.

While the validity and reliability of many of these data bases may be limited, there is one constant among them that sampling errors cannot explain: the overwhelming evidence that Hispanics are underachieving and leaving schools in large numbers (Santiago Santiago 1984a). Alan Pifer (1979), former president of the Carnegie Corporation, summarized educational outcomes for Hispanics as follows:

> Unfortunately, Hispanic children as a whole have not fared well in the public education system. Typically, they are two or three grade levels behind other students. A mere 30 percent manage to complete high school. Nationwide, in urban ghetto areas, the school dropout rate for Hispanics reaches as high as 85 percent . . . Less than 7 percent have completed college.

Hispanics comprise approximately 6 per cent of the population of public schools in the continental United States (that is, not including Puerto Rico). Between 1972 and 1978 the relative relationship between Hispanics and non-Hispanics in public schools remained constant while the actual numbers of Hispanic students rose from 1,299,000 to 1,480,000. The undercount in this data base may be as high as 40 per cent (Brown *et al*. 1981: 93).

The *Survey on Income and Education* (National Center for Educational Statistics 1976b) reported that in each grade Hispanic children enroll in greater percentages below grade level than white students, a disparity that increases with age. The survey also shows that delayed education for Hispanics correlates with family size, family income, parental education, membership of single-parent families, and limited proficiency in English.

Education, particularly the completion of high school, is valued by Hispanics (Coleman, 1966; Grebler *et al*. 1970). Indeed, it has been shown to be perceived as more important to Hispanics than to whites or blacks (Nielsen and Fernandez 1981). Nevertheless, in 1978 Hispanics aged between 14 and 19 were more than twice as likely as whites to have dropped out of school (Brown *et al*. 1981). The same report indicated that nearly 40 per cent of the Hispanic population between the ages of 18 and 24 left high school without receiving a diploma compared to 14 per cent of the comparable white population. The implications of this trend for the Hispanic community are devastating.

In some urban school districts, the data are even more appalling than the national averages. In a study entitled 'Social Factors in Educational Attainment among Puerto Ricans in [11] U.S. Metropolitan Areas', Aspira of America (1976: 16–17) reported:

> In Chicago ... 28 percent of Puerto Ricans aged 16 to 18 were not enrolled and had not graduated from high school, but this did not mean that the other 72 percent would graduate before their 19th birthday. On the contrary, many would continue to be enrolled and eventually drop out, making up the large proportion of young adults not enrolled nor high school graduates, 71 percent among those 19 to 24 years old.

A more recent report sponsored by the same group found that the drop-out rate for Hispanics in New York City was over 75 per cent (Calitri 1983). According to the 1976 *Survey of Income and Education* (National Center for Educational Statistics 1976b) Puerto Ricans have the highest non-completion rate of any Hispanic subgroup with women (as is typical of all Hispanic subgroups) providing the most distressing figures. Overall, Hispanics born outside the continental United States have less than one chance in two of completing high school (Brown *et al.* 1981).

King (1978) and others have studied the tragic labour market consequences of dropping out. In an insightful study, Mann (1982) describes Black and Hispanic youths' struggles first to stay in school and later to obtain the training necessary to obtain employment. This study lays to rest the myth of the lazy, uncaring minority youth.

One basic assumption of the melting-pot theory is that anyone obtaining a high school diploma has a better chance of getting a job — or of getting a better job — than those who do not complete high school. The data show, however, that in reality the theory is verified for all subgroups *except* Puerto Ricans. Puerto Rican high school graduates actually have a 30 per cent higher unemployment rate than Puerto Rican dropouts (Brown *et al.* 1981: 246–47). The implications of this are devastating. Why attend school if schooling does not make a difference?

Hispanics are not gaining equal access to high school academic or college preparatory programmes (Astin *et al*. 1982; Duran 1983). Only 29.3 per cent of all Hispanic high school seniors are enrolled in these programmes compared to the 45.5 per cent of white students (Brown *et al.* 1981: 60–61). Among full- and part-time college students in the fifty states and Washington, DC for 1980, only 3.9 per cent were Hispanics (National Center for Educational Statistics (NCES) 1982: 64). Hispanics were also far more likely to attend two-year colleges (Dearman and Plisko 1980).

Hispanics are not equitably represented in the professional (or non-professional) employee ranks in schools either. The proportion of teachers of Hispanic origin was only 1.8 per cent for secondary schools and 2.3 per cent for elementary schools in 1978 (NCES 1982: 51-52) according to the Equal Employment Opportunity Commission.

In summary, Hispanics have high delay rates, high drop-out rates and low college admission rates. Although some differentiation in achievement can be shown to be related to language background (Veltman 1980, 1981), and there is some variation in educational outcomes among Hispanic subgroups (NAEP 1982a and 1982b; Neilsen and Fernandez 1981), by and large Hispanics as a group are not receiving an adequate education and in many cases are being denied equal educational opportunities.

Historical–political relationships of Hispanic subgroups to the United States

An analysis of the historical–political relationship to the United States of each Hispanic national origin subgroup may help explain some of the differences in statistics and outcomes that have been mentioned. However, these historical and political antecedents are rarely taken into consideration when decisions related to language policy and education affecting these groups are made (Leibowitz 1971; Diamond 1983).

Mexican Americans

The largest subgroup, numbering approximately 7 million, consists of Mexican Americans (often referred to as Chicanos). Some segments of the complex Mexican American community are descendants of the Mexican society that inhabited the Southwest in the early eighteenth century, generations prior to the annexation between 1836 and 1853 of these territories by the United States. The Treaty of Guadalupe Hidalgo at the conclusion of the Mexican American War assured these inhabitants that their cultural life would be respected (Conklin and Lourie 1983). Presumably this guarantee included the right to continue to use the Spanish language.

The Mexican American population also includes many more recent arrivals and migrant workers. Some of them move in cyclical migration patterns between Mexico and the United States — and the number who do so without government approval has stirred considerable attention and misunderstanding. It has been estimated that there are between 5 and 6 million undocumented aliens in the United States. Of those counted in the 1980 Census, 45 per cent were from Mexico, 23 per cent from Latin America and 12 per cent each from Europe and Asia (Bureau 1983).

Despite the sometimes violent reaction against the so-called 'new' arrivals, Mexican *braceros* or migrant workers have for many years made an important contribution to the United States economy by doing agricultural work at wages United States citizens would very often not accept (Estrada *et al.* 1981). This exploitation of the migrant worker by the US farmer has been well documented. Their patterns of cyclical migration — so different from those of earlier 'one-way' European immigrants — requires more research and consideration in policy deliberations.

Puerto Ricans
Puerto Ricans comprise the second largest group of Hispanics. Three million Puerto Ricans live on the island of Puerto Rico and 2.3 million in the continental US. They have a unique political-historical relationship to the United States. As a result of the Spanish American War in 1898 Puerto Rico was colonized by the United States, cutting short its two-month taste of freedom from Spain. With the Foraker Act of 1917 the US granted Puerto Ricans a quasi-citizenship status.

Nowhere has the relationship between language policy and politics played a more compelling role than in Puerto Rico. The Commonwealth agreement established a unique relationship between Puerto Rico and the United States. Puerto Ricans are drafted to fight wars, but those living on the island are not allowed to vote for the President of the United States. A resident commissioner of Puerto Rico is allowed to sit in on meetings of the US House of Representatives, but he is not allowed to vote. According to the terms of the agreement, both Spanish and English were to be official languages on the island; however, many attempts to violate the agreement followed (Flores, 1978; Santiago Santiago, 1984a).

According to most demographers, the largest Puerto Rican migration to the US mainland took place after the Second World War when the island's economy had been devastated and many Puerto Rican soldiers lost. During the 1960s zero net migration was reported, but during the 1970s a substantial return migration to the island took place (Bonilla and Colon 1979; Flores *et al.* 1981). Today another wave of migration to the continent is underway (Gonzales 1982). However, since passports are not needed and islanders have freedom of movement between the continent and the island, it is difficult to maintain reliable data on the numbers involved.

Bonilla and Campos (1981) have documented the relationship between economic trends on the continent, their adverse effects on the island's economy and the consequent pressure on Puerto Ricans to leave the island (see also Bonilla 1983; Lindorff 1982). The struggles and discrimination faced by the Puerto Rican migrant, despite his citizenship, have been described poignantly by Nieves Falcon (1975). The argument that the Puerto Rican's place on the ethnic queue may be a function of race (since Puerto Ricans are a mix of white, black and Indian) has been discussed by Rodriguez (1973).

Researchers at the Centro de Estudio Puertorriquenas (Centro 1979) argue convincingly that Puerto Ricans are rendered unable to exercise their 'right to flight' (to move freely within national boundaries) if school systems where they constitute a critical mass continue to demand they refrain from using Spanish. Many spend a few years in cities such as New York, Chicago or Philadelphia only to return to Puerto Rico with the educational handicap of being unable to participate effectively in the instructional programme because it is conducted in Spanish (Curran 1985).

In summary, Puerto Rico was colonized and later incorporated (if only partially) because these acts served the political and economic interests of the United States (Maldonado-Denis 1969). The Commonwealth agreement, however, served to maintain Spanish as the official language of government and public life. Despite many efforts by the United States government to make English the language of instruction in Puerto Rico's schools, Spanish is still the official language of instruction today though English is taught as a subject beginning in the second grade (Santiago Santiago 1984a).

Cubans

Though only the third largest Hispanic group, Cubans have significantly influenced educational policies affecting Hispanics in the United States. Two major waves of immigration have been the source of a large part of today's Cuban community in the United States. The first major wave occurred as a result of the Castro revolution in 1959. The second wave of approximately 125,000 *marielitos* came in 1980 as part of the so-called 'freedom flotilla'.

These were clearly two different migrations. The first was largely middle class, anti-communist and white. More than half of the new immigrants settled in or near Miami. Many had been successful in extricating all or part of their wealth from Cuba. Under the Kennedy administration, federal legislation provided substantial economic aid in the form of scholarships, housing and other assistance in their refuge. These Cubans benefited from unprecedented support and ease of obtaining refugee status and later residence status and citizenship (Fagen *et al.*:, 1968).

One explanation for this special treatment is that both the Cubans and the United States officials fully expected that the refugees would not stay long (the Bay of Pigs invasion certainly supports such a hypothesis). Consequently, when this group demanded bilingual instruction so that their children could maintain their Spanish language skills until returning to Cuba, policy-makers acquiesced and the federal government supported the effort with the Bilingual Education Act of 1967 (Garcia 1973). The inclusion in that first wave of a large number of professionals, including teachers, may help explain the substantial success of programmes implemented for these Cuban children.

The 'Freedom Flotilla', on the other hand, was made up primarily of poor people. They came with few possessions, little education and during a period of economic decline in the United States. Consequently, this group has faced many obstacles, and it is unlikely that their experience will parallel that of their predecessors.

Other Spanish-origin groups

This 'catch-all' category includes people from vastly different socio-political backgrounds such as Spanish-speaking Europeans, South Americans and, more recently, those seeking refuge in the United States from the wars and upheaval in Central America. The United States is offering asylum to critically few from this region, however, so that the number is probably far smaller than might otherwise be expected. A highly diverse group, it includes approximately 1.5 million

Central and South Americans and 1.5 million individuals of 'other Spanish-origin' groups (Bureau 1983). Since the immigration and Nationality Amendments of 1978 restrict the number of immigrants from any one country to 20,000 per year, total Hispanic immigration is expected to drop substantially.

In summary, American colonial activity has led to the incorporation of large segments of the group that today forms the Hispanic community in the United States. US manpower needs were responsible for the inclusion of another segment. Outright intervention in other parts of the Western hemisphere have been responsible for creating yet another sizeable group of refugee immigrants. The numbers continue to increase. It would seem now more appropriate than ever to raise the question: does the United States have a moral or political obligation to these groups? The Treaty of Guadalupe Hidalgo and the Commonwealth agreement with Puerto Rico both postulated the viability of a pluralistic peace, yet neither has been honoured. Furthermore, does the United States have an obligation to provide for the social incorporation of those refugees displaced by its political and military interventionist policies in the Western Hemisphere? If so, the previous failure of massive assimilationist forces in American policies suggests that there should be an effort to develop new strategies to accomplish this objective.

Rejecting the melting-pot theory

If the melting-pot process were to work, American society should routinely integrate third-generation ethnic minority group members into the mainstream. The evidence presented regarding social participation and educational achievement, however, indicates that despite their long presence in the United States, Hispanics still have a long way to go to achieve educational, economic or social equity. Although sociologists and political scientists have pointed out the inadequacies of the melting-pot theory (Burkey 1978; Greenbaum 1974), many continue to believe in its viability (Castaneda 1975). But the painful introspective struggle to reach consensus on an ideological framework which will guide national policy-making in numerous areas is a process that the governments of many countries are engaged in today. Many nations are involved in efforts to respond to the demands made by indigenous minorities (Santiago Santiago

1982b). Many countries are struggling to adjust to the presence of ethnically diferent refugees, immigrants and guest workers (Ford Foundation 1982) and particularly school policies for these groups (Freudenstein 1978). Ironically, foreign policy-makers often perceive the United States as an example of effective ethnic incorporation. Noah (1983) has warned against such inclinations from a comparative education perspective. I would add the caveat that even if the melting-pot theory were viable in the US context, models are rarely transferable across national boundaries.

None the less, since the American public (encouraged by conservatives such as Glazer 1982; Epstein 1977; and Ravitch 1985) continues to maintain a romantic attachment to the theory, it is important to repeat here the inadequacies of the model with respect to Hispanics. Despite its inadequacies, the melting-pot concept is at the core of educational philosophy and practice in the United States, and its influence is having a devastating effect on Hispanics in the public schools.

The proposition that Hispanics can or will 'melt' into American society cannot be sustained for a number of reasons. First, and most obvious, Hispanics are not participating proportionately in the economic or social benefits of the society as assimilationist theory claims they should, given that sufficient time (most suggest it takes three generations) for social mechanisms to function has already elapsed for most subgroups. One problem is, however, that the theory was primarily devised to explain European ethnic and not racial incorporation. Hispanics are racially heterogeneous with differing degrees of Indian and/or black ancestry. The presence of this 'racial factor' makes comparisons with European immigrants unrealistic (Gordon 1964, 1978).

Furthermore, as already discussed above, the historical-political relationship between subgroups of Hispanics and the United States distinguishes them from other ethnic groups. That is to say, significant subgroups did not 'choose' to 'come' to the United States, but were part of a political incorporation or colonialization process over which they had no control.

Secondly, since the melting-pot theory assumes assimilation is a viable and appropriate goal, it requires the existence of a societal institution designed to achieve that goal: the public school. Yet, for Hispanics and others (Greer 1972), data on educational outcomes suggest that schools have not been viable mechanisms for social integration. Many, in fact, argue that the schools have only produced a highly segregated and stratified social structure (Spring 1976).

Assimilationist theory is inadequate on a third level. It was devised in order to explain the experience of 'one-way' immigrants, individuals who came to the United States and chose to remain there. While this is the case for some subgroups of Hispanics, a substantial segment of the community has been characterized by cyclical migration between Puerto Rico or Mexico and the US in response to work-force needs. While exploiting their labour, however, the United States has not devised social policies that meaningfully respond to the temporary nature of their stay.

The precedent of European immigration also fails to explain why a significant segment of the Hispanic community has maintained proficiency in Spanish — admittedly to different degrees (Ferguson and Heath 1981) — to a far greater extent and for longer than most other ethnic minorities retained their use of languages other than English (Conklin and Lourie, 1983). While this trend is probably related to cyclical migration, other factors such as the extent to which Hispanics are ghettoized with respect to housing and employment also serve to maintain cultural and linguistic identity. Assimilationists suggest it is necessary and appropriate for ethnic groups to give up their native languages and adopt English because a common language is necessary for a strong national identity (Fishman, 1972). The data on educational achievement, however, suggest that even where Hispanics are proficient in English, the schools have been ineffective (Byrne 1978).

The American public's insistence on the 'primacy' of English (*New York Times* 1983) has stirred much debate with segments of the Hispanic community over ethnicity and the role of schools as instruments of assimilation. Epstein (1977), Rossier (1983) and countless others have argued that assimilation is the primary function of the school and warned of the potential divisiveness of bilingual education programmes.

The inadequacies of assimilation theory as the basis for educational policy

When educational policies are based on the melting-pot theory, programmes developed are often incompatible with the educational (psychosocial, cognitive and linguistic) needs of ethnic minority students. Instead of providing a sound pedagogical basis for educational decisions they create individual and group insecurities,

166   *Isaura Santiago Santiago*

conflicts and dilemmas that push students out of school. In the case
of Hispanics in the US. assimilationist policies have resulted in the
practice of blaming victims for the failure of educational policies and
institutions and the implementation of deficit models of instruction.
Compensatory transitional bilingual education programmes are but
one example of these.

Blaming the victim
The underlying assumption of assimilationist theory is that underachievers are inferior and must assume the burden of responsibility
for becoming like the majority. This results in a vicious cycle,
psychoanalytically termed the 'self-fulfilling prophecy', which Rist
(1970) found to affect student performance as early as the third grade.
Students are expected to drop out, so they do. Society, in turn, views
these minority youths as lazy persons with little aspiration. Lucas
(1971), Carter and Segura (1979), Mann (1982), Estrada *et al.* (1981)
and others have offered greater insights into the plight of Hispanic
adolescents. All document the extent to which these youths feel that
schools do not offer enough. The degree to which such students have
incorporated a sense that schooling won't make a difference in their
lives is alarming. None the less, their perception is difficult to refute,
especially in light of the anomaly that for Puerto Rican youth
dropping out of high school is a higher predictor of employment than
high school graduation. This is contrary to everything assimilationist
theory promises. In this case, paying the price of giving up their
culture and their language to assume English-language skills and the
culture of the school does not produce for Hispanic youngsters the
expected rewards.

  Alarmed by these trends, Hispanic parents and educators have
consulted educational literature in an effort to gain insights into the
problem and identify solutions — only to find that researchers
frequently assert alcoholism. drug abuse. childbearing. family size
and socioeconomic status are the factors most frequently associated
with school attrition. Here again, the victim is blamed. While these
characteristics may correlate highly with the incidence of attrition,
they are probably symptoms of complex problems — including
student discontent with school. The prevailing language of educational
deprivation also blames the victim. The terms 'drop-out' and 'stay-
back', for example, imply these students are making a choice.
However, if one were able to identify inadequacies in the schools and
programmes these students attend that render futile their continuing

efforts to complete their studies and improve their situation, one would have to reject such a hypothesis. Newman (1981) and others have sought to explain the alienation students often feel in high school. Regrettably, researchers have more frequently focused their attention on the characteristics of students than on those of the schools, probably because they can readily gain access to the students, but school authorities are often reluctant to open their doors to investigation. Consequently, research in this area has added little to our understanding of school-related influences on attrition.

Deficit models of instruction
'Back to basics', 'minimum standards' and the 'Paideia proposal' (Adler 1982) are examples of deficit models of instruction that place the burden of responsibility for educational outcomes largely on the student. The burden is rarely, if ever, placed on teachers or administrators. On the contrary, teachers' unions have consistently fought against efforts to measure teacher effectiveness. The battles have been particularly fierce when efforts have been made to base teacher earnings on some measure of their effectiveness with their students. It is often argued that schools can't make a difference because the deficits these students come to school with are so great. The reality is, however, that many schools are effectively educating minority children (Edmonds, 1979; Goodlad, 1983, 1984).

Even where school systems have made efforts to address problems, they often have difficulty in surmounting the influence of their own prejudice, as evidenced by a study of New York City Board of Education's twenty-two drop-out prevention programmes. Researchers determined that there was substantial variance in the drop-out population with respect to three key variables — age, school performance, and language — but they found that programmes were not designed to address these factors. In fact, many drop-out prevention programmes screen out all but a narrowly defined group from among the schools' entire drop-out-prone population. Older students cannot participate, and minimum scores on English-language tests, irrespective of cognitive skills, are used to exclude other students. Clearly, these two criteria discriminate against Hispanic students because many Hispanics are delayed in their education and/or have limited English proficiency.

Perhaps the clearest yet most depressing analysis of the institutionalization of social disintegration or anomie in the schools is Sizer (1983). He suggests that teachers and students have subconsciously signed a pact to 'not bother one another' so that both can avoid a tedious exercise in futility — otherwise known as teaching and learning. Disturbing as this observation may be, his policy recommendations are even more upsetting. He proposes radical changes in high schools based on the argument that students, not teachers, are responsible for learning. Consequently, Sizer suggests placing the teacher in the role of 'coach' and admitting to high school only students demonstrating proficiency in language, mathematics and civics. However, only teachers and administrators should play a role in curriculum decisions, he concludes. These proposals would clearly result in excluding minorities that have not achieved.

Language background as a determinant
Consistent with the melting-pot theory, it is often argued that language background and socioeconomic status are determiners of educational outcomes. There is a growing body of literature which argues against these suppositions. For instance, although some data suggest that a non-English language background is a predictor of under-achievement (NAEP 1982a), this is not the cse for whites of non-English-language background born outside the United States. Why is a language background and birthplace a predictor of under-achievement for Hispanics and not for whites?

Veltman (1981), in analysing the results of the 1976 *Survey of income and Education*, also found that American-born English-speaking bilinguals have higher educational attainments than do American-born English-speaking monolinguals. The findings suggest that the maintenance of the Spanish language as a second language is related to positive educational attainment.

Cummins (1981), after reviewing research findings on the outcome of bilingual programmes, has shown the role primary language development plays in promoting educational success for language minority students. He suggests (1981: 38) that the apparent contradiction that bilingualism is associated with both positive and negative cognitive and academic outcomes can be explained as follows:

> An analysis of the characteristics of subjects in these two types of studies suggests that the level of bilingualism children attain is an important factor in mediating the effects of bilingualism on their educational development. Specifically, a large majority of the 'negative' studies were carried out with language minority children for whom L1 was gradually

being replaced by a more dominant and prestigious L2. Under these conditions, these children developed relatively low levels of academic proficiency in both languages. In contrast, the majority of studies that have reported cognitive advantages associated with bilingualism have involved students whose L1 proficiency has continued to develop while L2 is being acquired. Consequently, these students have been characterized by relatively high levels of proficiency in both languages.

Cummins (1981: 38) hypothesized that there may be threshold levels of linguistic proficiency that bilingual children must attain if they are to avoid cognitive delay and to allow the potentially beneficial effects of becoming bilingual to influence cognitive growth.

The Threshold Hypothesis assumes that those aspects of bilingualism that might positively influence cognitive growth are unlikely to come into effect until children have attained a certain minimum or threshold level of proficiency in the first language. Similarly, if bilingual children attain only a very low level of proficiency in one or both of their languages, their interaction with the environment through these languages both in terms of input and output, is likely to be impoverished.

Finally, reports from the National Assessment of Educational Progress (NAEP) (1982) indicate that some groups of Hispanics in the 11–13 age range have improved in reading more than whites and blacks over the same period. While at this point it is statistically indefensible to make the quantum leap in inference, it may very well be that for the first time we are seeing the effects of early bilingual education programmes. Given, however, the age of cohorts, the way bilingual education has been virtually limited to the early grades, the likelihood that the schools have not provided significantly during the last decade and the absence of other plausible explanations, the inference may well prove to be correct.

Consequently, what the Hispanic community has to reject is the notion that the schools cannot make a difference. Effective schools that have been found to be operating in urban minority communities around the country also refute this notion (Edmonds 1979).

The language overdose: the absence of substance in the curriculum
Throughout the 1960s and 1970s the major criteria of school effectiveness were measures of reading achievement. One consequence of this overemphasis on a single aspect of schooling was that

schools became language mills. Mathematics, science and history were relegated to positions of relative unimportance. While it is probably true that the results have been devastating for all children, they had proved a difficult disadvantage for Hispanics. From the melting-pot theory perspective, many schools viewed the Spanish dominance of Hispanics as the most obvious evidence of their 'deficiences' and proceeded to 'overdose' them with intensive English language instruction, often to the extent of giving limited or cursory attention to subject matter. In other instances children were placed in English-speaking classrooms with the expectation that this 'language submersion' would result in their learning English more quickly — another example of placing the responsibility for learning on the student. These practices, however, bored children and reduced their motivational levels, causing them to fall further behind their peers in cognitive skills and subject matter mastery.

Compensatory transitional bilingual education programmes
The only remedy other than English as a second language (ESL) instruction devised to meet the special educational needs of ethnolinguistic minorities in the United States has been compensatory transitional bilingual education, programmes that define competence in another language as a deficit which school systems must 'compensate' for by providing access to subject matter in the native language. To receive this instruction, children are set apart from their peers and segregated in special classes — to be 'cleansed' and prepared for re-entry into English monolingual instructional programmes. This emphasis on return, the transitional nature of the programme, is often abused. Participation in the programme, lasting two to three years, represents insufficient opportunity for a child to learn the English language. Consequently, participants enter the mainstream programme at a disadvantage.

In New York City, for instance, the criterion for eligibility for participation in the *Aspira* court-ordered consent decree transitional bilingual programme (*Aspira of New York* v. *Board of Education of the City of New York*, 1974) is that students must perform at or below the twentieth percentile on the Language Assessment Battery (LAB). The twentieth percentile, however, represents such a minimal level of proficiency that — since children learn some English in the early grades in Puerto Rico — it is likely that Puerto Rican migrant children will soare above it and therefore be excluded even from participation in transitional bilingual education programme grades.

A student entering the system at the high school level can hardly be expected to attain English proficiency in two to three years. Yet, at the high school level, the only service that schools are required to offer (and they often do provide this minimum) is intensive English instruction. Consequently, in 'general programmes' in most schools the only comprehensible instruction students receive is ESL training. Upper grade students, however, are likely to become bored by the combination of subject-matter instruction they cannot understand and substance-poor language training. Thus the push-out process begins to gather momentum (Santiago Santiago, 1984b).

Another measure of the inadequacy of policies for educating limited English proficient (LEP) students as reported by NCES (1982) is the fact that in those states where the need was greatest, only one-third to two-thirds of the Hispanic children that districts had identified as being limited- or non-English speaking were being served by special programmes. Barnes (1981) estimated the total LEP student population to be approximately 3 million.

Only in very recent years has the federal government allowed funds to be used in Puerto Rico to teach English speakers Spanish and to train and provide services by bilingual personnel. Such programmes are critically needed, given Puerto Ricans' cyclical mobility patterns.

The absence of a language policy
In general, Puerto Ricans and Mexican Americans in the continental United States have suffered from the absence of a coherent language policy. Despite the articulation of a policy by the Language Task Force of the Centro de Estudios Puertorriquenos in 1979 and similar efforts by Mexican Americans little attention has been paid to the question by policy-makers. Puerto Ricans' unique citizenship status requires the United States to recognize that education policies precluding the maintenance of a language other than English should be imposed on them (Centro 1979). Based on the special historical and political relationship between Mexico and the United States, one can make a similar argument on behalf of language maintenance for Chicanos (Macias, 1970).

Human impact on the economy
School budgets are particularly sensitive to fluctuations in the economy. During periods of inflation schools are pressured to do the same job with decreasing resources, a trick few are likely to

accomplish. What internal forces in school systems can do, however, is reduce the number of children in schools, particularly minorities who are viewed, accurately or inaccurately, as the most financially burdensome.

In the worst economic and political times we see social policy moving to the right as well. A recent article in *Esquire*, one of many appealing to even the most dormant xenophobic tendency, asks: 'The Latinization of America: What Does it Mean When You Walk the Streets of Your Own Country and You Don't Understand a Word of the Language?' (Morgan 1983). Another article specifically related to education appeared recently on the front page of the *New York Times* (1983): 'Panel Urges Stress on English Studies'. While the *Times* article was careful to use the word 'stress', a more accurate report of the phrasing of the Panel's recommendation would have read 'Panel reasserts the primacy of English' (*Chronicle of Higher Education* 1983).

The current administration's positions with regard to civil rights, immigration and education funding also reflect this swing to the right. Leibowitz (1971) noted a decade ago that language policy in the United States has for centuries reflected political-economic trends. Consequently, what someone asserted would become the Hispanics' 'turn in the sun' (Time 1978) has for economic and political reasons become another decade of oppression.

The testing fallacy

There is a fallacy perpetuated against students that suggests 'independent' testing provides an objective, valid and reliable method for school authorities to measure educational ability and achievement. These tests are also touted as capable of serving democratic and assimilationist ends by supposedly giving each student the same opportunity to demonstrate individual worth. In reality, the cognitive, cultural and linguistic limitations of tests often render them meaningless. Yet, school authorities rarely explain the limitation of any given test to youth and their families. Furthermore, tests are increasingly being used in schools — purportedly to maintain educational standards. But efforts across the country to establish graduation standards and institute competency testing have by and large not been accompanied by comprehensive efforts to ensure that students acquire basic skills. In fact, much testing has the effect of keeping Hispanic students out of the programmes they want and placing them in programmes where they will quickly lose interest and drop out.

Compensatory transitional bilingual education programmes: an outgrowth of the melting-pot theory

Bilingual education programmes offered by public schools in the United States today are by and large compensatory transitional programmes serving only a fraction of children in need (Bell 1984). Little is known about the substance and scope of these programmes. Consequently, much confusion exists about what bilingual education is and what it should be (Otheguy 1982). The Bilingual Education Act of 1967 making resources available to districts to experiment with bilingual methodologies is supported by funds capable of meeting the needs of only 15 per cent of all limited English proficiency (LEP) children. Even this act was recently revised to extend the eligibility criteria to English-only programmes (Bilingual Education Act 1967 as revised Public Law 98-511, 1984).

Under the Reagan administration, little or no pressure is being exerted by the federal government on behalf of LEP children. The Supreme Court Decision in *Lau* v. *Nichols* (1974) resulted in a set of programme guidelines requiring districts to provide compensatory instruction, preferably transitional bilingual instruction (except where a district can demonstrate that another approach is effective). Although the compensatory and transitional measures mandated by the *Lau* decree are consistent with assimilationist ideology, their implementation has largely been neglected. Except where the Office of Civil Rights or the courts intervene on behalf of LEP children, indifference or conflict prevails.

Where schools have been ordered to provide special programmes (usually compensatory bilingual instructions to ensure language minority children have access to the curriculum) or face the loss of federal funds, these threats have provoked strong reactions. The response has been particularly emotional among individuals who feel they are being forced to implement 'Un-American' policies by providing instruction in a language other than English (Rossier 1983; Epstein 1977). As a result, many programmes have been implemented half-heartedly. In other instances, school districts have conspired to limit the number of children eligible for special programmes (Santiago Santiago, 1982a). Some programmes have been successfully implemented, however, so the overall results have been mixed and the limited efforts to determine programme effectiveness have been inconclusive. Clearly the courts have acted within an assimilationist rather than a pluralistic context. They have not moved to make bilingual education a right. nor. it would appear, are they the proper policy-change mechanism to obtain such an end. Their role is to ensure access to and participation in the educational process. It could be argued. then. that the courts have served not to change the national policy that English is the language of instruction in American schools as many would charge but to support programme designs in which children of limited English-speaking ability are given access to the curriculum.

State law and the Hispanic

The majority of states with bilingual education statutes call for a transitional process with the sole goal of facilitating the entry of the LEP student into an English monolingual system as rapidly as possible. Many states and territories (twenty-eight in number) have no statutes at all. Others (fifteen) do not *require* that programmes be implemented and often have no provisions to monitor or ensure implementation.

Only two states. New Mexico and Texas. define bilingual education as the preservation of the native language and culture as well as the acquisition of English-language skills. In the case of Texas. the documented lack of implementation of bilingual education programmes served as the basis for continued litigation in *United States* v. *Texas*. In the end the Texas legislature. fearing the kind of programme the courts might impose. passed a more comprehensive state law with provisions for monitoring and enforcement (Santiago Santiago 1983).

Recently. a different kind of public reaction to the language rights of immigrants surfaced in Dade County. Florida. prompted by the 1980 influx of 160,000 Cubans and Haitians that formed part of the 'freedom flotilla'. Exclaiming 'I felt like a foreigner in my own country'. the founder of a group called Citizens of Dade United bragged (*Wall Street Journal* 1984) how the group had pushed through a referendum barring Dade County from doing official business in any language other than English. Nearly 60 per cent of the county's eligible voters backed the law. yet it had largely failed to speed up the immigrants' assimilation or improve their English-language proficiency. County government. in fact. has been forced to sidestep or violate the law in order to deliver vital services. and the business sector. unaffected by the law and with a Hispanic market of more than 40 per cent, goes on as usual — bilingually.

Although the law has proved a failure, several states and the United States Senate are considering similar measures. Since the Dade County ordinance went into effect, at least five states have declared themselves officially English-speaking: Kentucky, Indiana, Nebraska, Illinois and Virginia. Delegations from three more — South Dakota, North Dakota and New York — are considering similar laws. On 12 June, 1984 the United States Senate held hearings on a Constitutional amendment declaring English the official language of the United States.

Ironically, while all these steps are being taken to 'reaffirm the primacy of English' (Twentieth Century Fund 1983), the United States Congress and many states throughout the country including Florida, New York and Illinois are framing legislation for majority monolingual children that would make it mandatory for all students to learn a second language prior to high school graduation (President's Commission 1979; Comptroller General 1980). Though the present shift away from federal policy-making suggests that states will play a more important role in defining educational policy, the question is whether language minority groups will be more successful in the future than they have been in the past in asserting their interests through state-level policy-making structures. However, since there is little evidence that ethnolinguistic minorities today are more effectively participating in policy-making or governance structures, there is little reason to believe that there will be significant changes at the local level for minorities. In all probability, the shift of federal resources to the states will be accompanied by a drastic decline in resources and an increase in state bureaucratic structures and other barriers to minority participation thereby ensuring the perpetuation of the 'melting-pot syndrome' in American society.

Future perspectives

Bilingual education, even as a compensatory transitional measure, is under assault in the United States today. But as Fishman (1972) suggests, language differences alone are never sufficient cause for widespread conflict. At the root of the language-policy conflict in the US are issues that are complex and widespread. Inflationary economic trends are exerting pressures on the educational system. Coupled with decreasing enrolment trends, they are pitting one political interest group against another for control and resources. Furthermore, the national psychology of the crisis has resulted in witch hunts and ethnic white backlash. In this context, the search for unilateral models of bilingual instruction having high predictive value of effectiveness has been fruitless and serves only to convince the American public that bilingual education is not effective. C.B. Paulston (1980) offers an analysis of selected studies in bilingual education in the United States from the framework of R.G. Paulston's equilibrium and conflict paradigms. She demonstrates how seemingly contradictory findings can be explained when the appropriate questions are asked. The hidden agendas of the school system or those it serves must be unmasked as must the social, economic and political aspects of the context in which these programmes are being implemented. Only then does it become apparent why bilingual education is not effective in many contexts.

The reality is that in the political power struggle ethnolinguistic minorities remain just that — minorities. The economic crisis will undoubtedly affect them more negatively than others. Their interests will be served by schools no less than by probably any other sector of society. However, Hispanics may well be a positive force in 'megatrends' of the next century such as the increased need for competence in foreign languages (Naisbitt 1982). However, with respect to economic trends, as Bonilla (1983) has warned, the United States has moved in recent years through 'the first stages of transition to increasingly class-polarized, high-technology service-oriented economics, has fed on and reinforced preexisting class divisions and inequalities based on race, ethnicity and gender across and within national formations'.

As ethnic backlash has increased, so have concerns about issues such as the 'immigration problem' (*New York Times*, 1984). Historically this issue has surfaced most frequently during times of economic or political crisis. Reactionaries have led the witch hunt in the market place to 'recover' jobs held by undocumented workers despite evidence that these are jobs others do not want and will not take. Recently an entire State, Texas, attempted to close the school door to undocumented children (*Plyer* v. *Doe* (1982); see also *Los Angeles Times* 1981).   Glazer (1982: 149) gives voice to the resentment many Americans have felt at what they consider their government's inability to wipe out the threat of pluralism.

The 'melting pot' is now attacked not only on the empirical ground that it really did not melt that much or that fast but on the normative ground that it should not have been allowed to do so. And on the basis of this attack, Americanization becomes a dirty word, and bilingualism and biculturalism receive government support.

He goes on to argue:

I doubt that this is wise. Without endorsing the rigors of the Americanization programs of World War I and the succeeding decades, one can still see the virtue of forging a single society out of many stocks and can still see this process deserves some public guidance.

While some may find comfort in the notion of 'homogeneity', the experience of the United States and many other countries indicates that, despite many attempts, none has been successful in reaching the goal of a single 'stock'. Instead, nations throughout the world have increasingly sought answers through responsive multilingual/multicultural government policies buttressed by support for pluralistic values (Santiago Santiago, 1978; Freudenstein, 1978).

Is there a future for bilingualism and bilingual education in the United States in a time of economic crisis? The answer does not lie in the ability of minorities to muster sufficient political and legal power to force the country to continue to support compensatory transitional bilingual education. It is not likely that a society holding bilingualism and bilingual education in such low regard will change its values or perceptions either as a result of the pleadings of minorities or liberal calls for egalitarian democracy. Rather, hope for the future lies in the country's eventual recognition that it is in the interest of everyone that bilingualism be encouraged for all children. The President's Commission on Foreign Language and International Studies (1979) and the Comptroller General's (1980) report on the need for federal personnel with foreign language competence as well as the National Commission on Excellence in Education (1982) have found an appalling decline in the foreign-language skills of Americans. They argue that this is a threat to America's ability to play an effective role in international affairs and the international market-place.

Providing an environment in schools and society at large, however, that will encourage effective foreign-language learning and language maintenance will require that America establish a national language policy that will lay to rest old myths and fears and recognize the inadequacies of the compensatory programmes (including some transitional bilingual programmes) that are an outgrowth of the melting-pot theory. In so doing, however, policy-makers must examine critically the propositions for reform that are currently being advanced so forcefully (Adler 1982; Sizer 1983; Twentieth Century Fund 1983; Ravitch 1985) inasmuch as the theoretical underpinnings of these reforms are also deeply set in assimilationist ideology.

The public's interest would best be served by schools that implement comprehensive and effective models of bilingual/multi-ethnic education (Banks 1981). The multi-ethnic education model is based on an ideology incorporating ethnic, racial and linguistic considerations. It provides a framework in which schools can design curriculum, train teachers and administer programmes. It enables schools to incorporate ethnic minorities more successfully, improve cross-cultural and inter-racial understanding, and prepare all children to function in a pluralistic society.

Maintenance and enrichment bilingual education: the alternative

The best, and potentially most productive alternative to compensatory transitional bilingual education is maintenance and enrichment bilingual education. Maintenance bilingual education allows minority children to attain a level of proficiency in their first language which would permit them to learn a second language (English) and function in it effectively (Cummins 1981). These children would no longer be placed in the position of viewing their ability to use their native language as a deficit and thereby internalizing a sense of inferiority which erodes educational motivation. Providing enrichment bilingual education programmes to monolingual English-speaking children (a practice already operating in many private schools for the wealthy) gives children the opportunity to learn another language at the age when they are most receptive. Learning a language through studying subject matter also increases both the usefulness and retention of the language being learned. Providing both maintenance and enrichment programmes under the same umbrella, a natural outgrowth of the multi-ethnic theory of instruction offered by Banks (1981), is the most effective approach. It offers language-minority children the opportuniy to learn from majority children and vice versa. There is little hope that joint maintenance and enrichment bilingual public programmes will gain the support necessary for implementation unless the public is convinced that it is in the interest of everyone.

References

Adler, M. (1982). *The Paideia Proposal: Educational Manifesto*, New York: Macmillan.

Aspira of America (1976). *Social factors in the Educational Attainment among Puerto Ricans in the U.S. Metropolitan Areas*, New York: Aspira, Inc.

Association of Puerto Rican Executive Directors (APRED) (1982). *Puerto Ricans in SMSAs in New York City* (mimeograph).

Astin, A., Astin, H., Green, K., Kent, L., McNamara, P. and Williams, M. (1982). *Minorities in American Higher Education*, San Francisco, CA: Jossey-Bass.

Banks, J. (1981). *Multiethnic Education: Theory and Practice*, Boston: Allyn and Bacon.

Barnes, R. (1981). *Size of Eligible Language Minority Population*, Washington, DC.

Bell, T.H. (1984). *Th Condition of Bilingual Education in the Nation, 1984: A Report From the Secretary of Education to the President and the Congress*, prepared by the Office of Minority Language Affairs, Washington, DC: U.S. Department of Education, Inter America Research Associates.

Bonilla, F. (1983). *'Manos que sobran': Work, Migration and the Puerto Rican in the 1980s*, paper presented at the meeting of the National Puerto Rican Coalition, Washington, DC.

Bonilla, F. and Campos, R. (1981). 'A Wealth of Poor: Puerto Ricans in the New Economic Order, *Daedalus, 110*, 113–74.

Bonilla, F. and Colon, J. (1979). 'Puerto Rican Migration in the '70s', *Migration Today*, 2(2), 1–6.

Brown, G., Rosen, N., Hill, S. and Olivas, M. (1981), *The Condition of Education for Hispanic Americans*, Washington, DC: National Center for Education Statistics.

Bureau of the Census (Bureau), (1983). *Condition of Hispanics in America Today*, Washington, DC (mimeograph).

Burkey, R. (1978), *Ethnic and Racial Groups: The Dynamics of Dominance*, Menlo Park, CA: Cummings Publishing Company.

Byrne, D. (1978). *Chicano Students and Public Schools: A Descriptive Research Report*, ERIC Document Reproduction Service no. ED 144733.

Calitri, R. (1983). *Minority Secondary Education in New York State and New York City*, New York: Aspira Inc.

Cardenas, J. (1975). 'Bilingual Education, Segregation, and a Third Alternative', *Inequality in Education*, 19–22.

Carter, T. and Segura, R. (1979). *Mexican Americans in School: A Decade of Change*, New York: College Entrance Examination Board.

Castaneda, A. (1975). 'Persisting Ideologies of Assimilation in America: Implications for Psychology and Education. *ATISBOS: Journal of Chicano Research*, 79–91.

Centro de Estudios Puertorriquenos. (1979). *Bilingualism and Public Policy: Puerto Rican perspectives*, New York: Research Foundation, City University of New York.

Chronicle of Higher Education (1983). Panel Asserts the Primacy of English', 11 May.

180   *Isaura Santiago Santiago*

Cole, S. (1983). *Attitudes toward Bilingual Education among Hispanics and a Nationwide Sample*. New York: Colombia University, Immigration Research Program.

Coleman, J. (1966). *Equality of Educational Opportunity*. Washington, DC: U.S. Government Printing Office.

Comptroller General of the United States (1980). *More Competence in Foreign Languages Needed by Federal Personnel Working Overseas* (ID-80-31). Washington, DC: United States General Accounting Office.

Conklin, N. and Lourie, M. (1983). *A Host of Tongues: Language Communities in the United States*. New York: The Free Press.

Cummins, J. (1981). 'The Role of Primary Language Development in Promoting Educational Success for Language Minority Students' in Cummins, *Schooling and language minority students: A theoretical framework*. California State Education Department. Los Angeles, CA: Evaluation, Dissemination and Assessment Center, California State University.

Curran, M. (1985). 'Towards Understanding Interactions in High School Classrooms Containing Return Migrant Students in Puerto Rico', unpublished doctoral dissertation, Teachers College, Columbia University. New York.

Dearman, N. and Plisko, V. (1980). *The Condition of Education*. Washington, DC: National Center for Education Statistics.

DeWind, J. (1983) *The Organizing of Parents to Support Bilingual Education*. New York: Columbia University, Immigration Research Program.

Diamond, S. (1983). 'Historical Aspects of Bilingualism in the United States', unpublished manuscript, New York: Columbia University, Immigration Research Program.

Duran, R. (1983). *Hispanics' Education and Background: Predictors of College Achievement*. New York College Entrance Examination Board.

Edmonds, R. (1979). 'Effective schools for the urban poor', *Educational Leadership, 37* (1), 15–18.

Epstein, N. (1977). *Language and Ethnicity and the Schools: Policy Alternatives for Bilingual Bicultural Education*. Washington, DC: George Washington University, Institute for Educational Leadership.

Estrada, L.F., Garcia, F.C., Macias, R.F. and Maldonado, L. (1981). 'Chicanos in the United States: A History of Exploitation and Resistance', *Daedalus, 110*, 103–132.

Fagen, R., Brody, R., & O'Leary, T. (1968). *Cubans in Exile: Disaffection and Revolution*. Palo Alto, CA: Stanford University Press.

Ferguson, C. and Heath, S. (eds) (1981). *Language in the USA*. Cambridge, MA: Cambridge University Press.

Fernandez, R and Neilson, F. (1983). *Bilingualism and Hispanic Scholastic Achievement: Some Baseline Results*. Chapel Hill, NC: University of North Carolina.

Fishman, J. (1956). *Language Loyalty in America*. The Hague: Mouton.

—— (1972). *Language and Nationalism*. Rowley, MA: Newbury House.

—— (1980). 'Minority Language Maintenance and Ethnic Mother Tongue School'. *Modern Language Journal, 61*, 161–173.

Flores, J. (1978). *The Insular Vision: Pedreira's interpretation of Puerto Rican culture*, New York: City University of New York, Centro de Estudios Puertorriquenos.

Flores, J., Attinasi, J. and Pedraza, P. (1981). 'La Carreta Made a U-turn: Puerto Rican Language and Culture in the United States', *Daedalus, 110*, 193-218.

Ford Foundation (1983). *Refugees and Migrants: Problems and Responses*, Ford Foundation Working Paper, New York.

Freudenstein, R. (1978). *Teaching the Children of Immigrants*, Brussels: AIMAV.

Gaarder, A.B. (1977). *Bilingual Schooling and the Survival of Spanish in the United States*, Rowley, MA: Newbury House.

Garcia, G. (1973). 'An Analysis of the Bilingual Education Act', unpublished doctoral dissertation, University of Massachusetts, Massachusetts.

Garcia, S. (1983). 'Sociolinguistics and Language Planning in Bilingual Education for Hispanics in the United States', *International Journal of the Sociology of Language, 44*, 43-54.

Ginzberg, E. (1980). 'Youth Unemployment', *Scientific American*, 242(5), 44.

Glazer, N. (1975). *Affirmative Discrimination: Ethnic Inequality and Public Policy* New York: Basic Books.

—— (1982). 'Politics in a Multiethnic Society' in L. Liebman (ed.), *Ethnic Relations in America*. Englewood Cliffs: Prentice-Hall, pp. 128-49.

Glazer, N. and Moynihan, D.P. (eds) (1963), 2nd edn, 1970 *Beyond the Melting Pot: The Negroes, Puerto Ricans, Jews, Italians, and Irish of New York City*, Cambridge, MA: MIT Press.

—— (1975). *Ethnicity: Theory and Experience*, Cambridge, MA: Harvard University Press.

Godsell, G. (1980). 'Hispanics in the U.S.: Ethnic Sleeping Giant Awakens', *Christian Science Monitor*, 28 April.

Gonzales, J. (1982). 'Puerto Ricans on the Mainland', *Perspectives, 13*, 8-17.

Goodlad, J. (1983). 'A Study of Schooling: Some Findings and Hypotheses', *Phi Delta Kappa, 64*, 465-70.

—— (1984). *A Place Called School*, New York: McGraw Hill.

Gordon, M. (1964). *Assimilation in American Life: The Role of Race, Religion and National Origins*, New York: Oxford University Press.

—— (1978). *Human Nature, Class and Ethnicity*, New York: Oxford University Press.

Grebler, L., More, J. and Guzman, R. (1970). *The Mexican American People*, New York: Free Press.

Greenbaum, W. (1974). 'American in Search of a New Ideal: An Essay on the Rise of Pluralism', *Harvard Education Review, 44*(3), 411-40.

Greer, C. (1972). *The Great School Legend: A Revisionist Interpretation of American Public Education*, New York: Viking Press.

Hayes-Bautista, D.E., Schinek, W.O. and Chapa, J. (1984). 'Young Latinos in Aging American society', *Social Policy, 15*, 49-52.

King, R.H. (1978). *The Labor Market Consequences of Dropping out of High School* (monograph no. 9). Ohio State University, Center for Human Resource Research.

182   *Isaura Santiago Santiago*

Kloss, H. (1977). *The American Bilingual Tradition*, Rowley, MA: Newbury House.

Liebman, L. (1982). 'Ethnic groups and the Legal Systems' in L. Liebman (ed.), *Ethnic Relations in America. Englewood Cliffs, NJ: Prentice-Hall pp. 150–174.*

Leibowitz, A. (1971). *Educational Policy and Political Acceptance: The Imposition of English as the Language of Instruction in American Schools*, ERIC Document Reproduction Service.

Lindorff, D. (1982). 'The New Wave from Puerto Rico', *New York*, pp. 12–13.

Los Angeles Times (1981). 'Federal Judge Possibly the Most Hated Man in Texas', 12 April, p. 2.

Lucas, I. (1971). *Peurto Rican Dropouts in Chicago: Numbers and Motivation*, Final report to the Office of Education (Project O-E-103), Washington, DC.

Macias, R. (1979). 'Mexicano/Chicano Sociolinguistic Behavior and Language Policy in the United States', unpublished doctoral dissertation, Georgetown University, Washington, DC.

Maldonado-Denis, M. (1969). *Puerto Rico: Una interpretatición historico-social*, Mexico: Siglo Veintiuno Editores SA.

Mann, D. (1982). 'Chasing the American Dream: Jobs, Schools and Employment Training Programs in New York State', *Teachers College Record*, *83*(3), 341–75.

Morgan, T. (1983). 'The Latinization of America', *Esquire*, pp. 47–56.

Naisbitt, J. (1982). *Megatrends: Ten New Directions Transforming our Lives*, New York: Warner Books.

National Assessment of Educational Progress (NAEP). (1982a). *Students from Homes in which English Is Not the Dominant Language: Who Are They and How Well Do They Read?* (No. 11-R-50). Denver, CO.: Education Commission of the States.

—— (1982b). *Performance of Hispanic Students in Two National Assessments of Reading*. Denver, CO.: Education Commission of the States.

National Center for Educational Statistics (NCES). (1972). *National Longitudinal Study*, Washington, DC.

—— (1976a). *The Educational Disadvantage of Language Minority Persons in the United States*, Washington, DC.

—— (1976b). *Survey on Income and Education*, Washington, DC.

—— (1982). *Selected Statistics on the Education of Hispanics*, Washington, DC.

National Commission on Excellence in Education (1982). *A Nation at Risk: The Need for Educational Reform* (Report no. 065-000-0177-2), Washington, DC: U.S. Government Printing Office.

National Hispanic Educational Platform (1984). *Equity, Excellence, Involvement, and Pluralism: A New Day for America's Children*, Denver, Colorado: Center for Hispanic Educational Leadership.

New York Times (1982). 'Hispanics Voting Study Finds Sleeping Giant', 29 August, p. 39.

New York Times (1983). 'Panel Asks Stress on English Studies', 6 May, p. A1.

New York Times (1984). 'Bill on Aliens a Divisive Issue for Democrats', 22 April, p. 1.

Newsweek (1983). 'Can the Schools Be Saved?', 9 May, pp. 50–2, 54.

Newman, F. (1981). 'Reducing Student Alienation in High Schools: Implications of Theory', *Harvard Educational Review*, *51*, 546–64.

Nielsen, F. and Fernandez, R. (1981). *Achievement of Hispanic Students in American High Schools: Background Characteristics and Achievements*, Washington, DC: National Center for Education Statistics.

Nieves Falcon, L. (1975). *El emigrante Puertorriqueno*, Rio Piedras: Editorial Edel.

Noah, H. (1983). *The Use and Abuse of Comparative Education, Inaugural lecture*, Gardner Cowles, Professor of Economics and Education, Teachers College, Columbia University, New York.

Noboa, A. (1980). Trends in Segregation of Hispanic Students in Major School Districts Having Large Hispanic Enrolments (manuscript made available by author.)

Otheguy, R. (1982). 'Thinking about Bilingual Education: A Critical Appraisal', *Harvard Educational Review*, *62*(3), 301–14.

Park, R.E. (1930). 'Assimilation, Social' in E. Seligman and A. Johnson (eds), *Encyclopedia of the Social Sciences*, New York: Macmillan.

Paulston, C.B. (1980). *Bilingual Education: Theories and Issues*, Rowley, MA: Newbury House.

Pifer, A. (1979) *Bilingual Education and the Hispanic Challenge*, New York: Carnegie Corporation of New York.

President's Commission on Foreign Language and International Studies (1979), *Strength through Wisdom: A Critique of U.S. Capability* (no. 017–080–20653-3), Washington, DC.: Government Printing Office Stock.

Ravitch, D. (1985). *The Schools We Deserve*, New York: Basic Books.

Rist, R. (1970). 'Student Social Class and Teacher Expectations: The Self-fulfilment Prophecy in Ghetto Education', *Harvard Educational Review*, *40*(3), 411–51.

Rodriguez, C.E. (1973). 'The Ethnic Queue in the U.S.: The Case of Puerto Ricans', unpublished doctoral dissertation, Washington University, Seattle.

Rodriguez, R. (1982). *Hunger of Memory: The Education of Richard Rodriguez*, Boston: Godine.

Rose, P. (1974). *They are We: Racial and Ethnic Relations in the United States*, Random House: New York.

Rossier, R. (1983). 'Bilingual Education: Training for the Ghetto', *Policy Review* (The Heritage Foundation), 36–45.

Rotberg, I. (1982). 'Some Legal Considerations in Establishing Federal Policy in Bilingual Education', *Harvard Education Review*, *52*(2), 149–68.

Santiago Santiago, I. (1978). *A Community's Struggle for Equal Educational Opportunity*, Princeton, NJ: Educational Testing Service.

—— (1982a). 'Education: After Four Decades of Discrimination and Neglect a Call for Public and Private Sector Initiatives', paper presented at the First Conference of the Association of Puerto Rican Executive Directors, New York City, NY.

—— (1982b). 'Third World Vernacular/Bi-multilingual Curricula Issues' in B. Hartford, A. Valman and C.R. Foster (eds), *Issues in International Bilingual Education: The Role of the Vernacular*, New York: Plenum Press, pp. 113–38.

—— (1983). 'Political and Legal Issues in Maintaining the Vernacular in the Curriculum: The U.S. Experience' in L. Berg-Eldering, F. DeRijcke and L. Zuck (eds), *Multicultural Education: Challenge for Teachers*, Dorecht Holland/ US: Forris Publication, pp. 53–76.

—— (1984a). 'Language Policy and Education in Puerto Rico and the Continent', *International Education Research Journal*, 11, 29–60.

—— (1984b). 'Dropouts or Pushouts: The Crisis of Hispanic Youth in School', paper presented at the Wingspread conference center of the Johnson Foundation, Racine, WI.

Schneider, S.G. (1976). *Revolution, Reaction, or Reform: The 1974 Bilingual Education Act*, New York: Las Americas.

Silverman, L. (1976). 'The Educational Disadvantage of Language Minority Persons in the United States', *Bulletin of the National Center for Education Statistics* 78–84.

Sizer, T. (1983). *Horace's Compromise: The Dilemma of the American High School*, New York, Houghton-Miflin Co.

Spring, J. (1976). *The Sorting Machine: National Education Policy since 1945*, New York: David McKay Co., Inc.

Takai, R. and Fetters, W. (1982). *Language Proficiency of Hispanic High School Students: Descriptive Profile* (82–246b), Washington, DC: National Center for Education Statistics.

Time (1978). 'It's Your Turn in the Sun', October.

Twentieth Century Fund. (1983). *Report of the Task Force on Federal Elementary and Secondary Educational Policy*, New York: NY.

US News and World Report (1981). 'Hispanics Make Their Move', 24 August, pp. 60–64.

Veltman, C. (1980). *The Role of Language Characteristics of the Socioeconomic Attainment of Hispanic Origin Men and Women*, Washington, DC.

—— (1981). 'Relative Educational Attainments of Hispanic-American Children, 1976', *Metas*, 2(1), 36–51.

Wall Street Journal (1984). 'Law to Curtail Bilingual Aid Fails in Florida', 30 May, p. 1.

Court cases

Aspira of New York et al. v. *Board of Education of the City of New York et al.* 72 Civ. 4002 (SDNY filed 1974).

Lau v. *Nichols*, 414, U.S. 563 (1974).

Plyer v. *Doe*. U.S. App. 5th Cir. 80-1934 (1982).
United States v. *Texas*, 342 F. Suppl 24 (E.D. Texas 1971), aff'd per curiam, 446 F. 2d 518 (5th Cir. 1972). On appeals (5th cir.) July, 1982.

Laws

Bilingual Education Act of 1967, Statutes at Large, *81* (1968), US Code *20* (1968). Public Law 93-380 (1974). Public Law 95-561 (1978). Public Law 98-511 (1984).
Civil Rights Act of 1984, Statutes at Large 78 (1964), US Code *42* (1970).

11 BEYOND THE EDUCATIONAL SYSTEM: THE PROBLEMS OF MINORITY YOUTH

John Simon

The debate over whether educational systems are vehicles for stimulating social change or mechanisms for indoctrinating societies' existing normative values is neither new nor likely to be resolved clearly in any democratic society. My own experience during fourteen years working with New York City youngsters on the margins of society suggests that, at least in the United States, these two apparently contradictory activities have become so entangled as to be virtually inseparable, constituting a sort of yin and yang of tension within a deeply troubled educational complex.

For most of the youngsters I worked with, in any case, the educational system was certainly not a vehicle for entry into the mainstream of American society. In this chapter I will try to trace some of the historical roots of their exclusion as well as the impact of their presence in such large numbers on certain parts of the public school system. I consider some of the reasons why schools alone cannot be expected to deal effectively with all the problems created by the society that generated both the problems and the school system. And I suggest some ways in which it is necessary to look beyond schools to other resources capable of shaping an environment in which such youngsters can have a chance to live happy, healthy, productive lives.

The United States is a land of immigrants. Earlier in this century, immigration swelled the size of the population by more than 10 per cent in a single decade.[1] Although legal immigration has been restricted severely since that time, most Americans still identify with their ethnic origins. The most recent US Census reports three groups dominating the ethnic picture: the English (26.34 per cent), Germans (26.14 per cent) and the Irish (21.33 per cent). Then come Afro-Americans (11.13 per cent), Italians (6.47 per cent), Poles (4.37 per cent) and Mexicans (4.09 per cent).[2] If Puerto Rican and other

Hispanic groups are added to the Mexicans, the size of this group comes close to that of the Italians. If the number of Hispanic residents not counted in the Censes is also added, the group moves into fifth place behind the Afro-Americans.

The first immigrants were a rude collection of adventurers, thugs, debtors, landless younger sons of European gentry, and dissenters seeking escape from religious persecution. They established themselves by the end of the eighteenth century as beneficiaries of a constitutional government whose goals and standards were elaborated in eloquent and inspiring language but whose reality was an oligarchy with only white, male landowners sharing the franchise. Thus the initial promise of American democracy already embraced such contradictions as slavery, the oppression of women and the poor, and the genocide systematically waged against the original inhabitants of the North American continent.

The earliest educational institutions, designed to meet the needs of the new and self-proclaimed gentry, generally modelled themselves on English 'public' schools and universities. Although such models were in many ways poorly suited to the near-wilderness onto which they were grafted, they have persisted to this day as incubators for the nation's elite. As such, they offer a classical education for political and cultural leadership as well as scientific and mathematical preparation for technological superiority.

One should keep in mind, however, how rapidly America moved in its infancy from an agricultural economy into the Industrial Revolution. Within a century of the declaration of independence from England, factories were springing up throughout the American Northeast, drawing wave upon wave of European immigrants. These newcomers, as Lydia Anderson points out in her book, *Immigration*, had quite different origins from the young nation's first European settlers.

Up to 1882, 95% of the immigrants came from the British Isles, Germany, France, Belgium and Scandinavia ... Between 1881 and 1920, we received 4 million Italians and 4 million Austro-Hungarians, most of whom were Catholics, and 3 million Russians, almost all Jews.[3]

The educational needs of these immigrants — defined both by their immediate aspirations and the role which American society offered them — differed enormously from those of the earlier arrivals. They needed to learn the English language and familiarize themselves with American cultural imperatives so they and their children could become more efficient workers and eradicate the 'foreign' accents and customs that separated them from the cultural mainstream in their adopted homeland. Schools, meanwhile, were under parallel pressure to satisfy the expanding economy's needs for a competent and semi-literate working class.

One group, however, differed dramatically from the other immigrants. Africans, abducted from their homelands and sold into slavery by Europeans to work the farms and plantations of the American South, received no formal schooling whatsoever. Defined by an insidious compromise as three-fifths property for taxation purposes and three-fifths of a human for census purposes, slaves had neither rights nor protection under the law. An educated slave, furthermore, was a threat to the slave-owner class, so that teaching a slave to read became a crime.

The systematic diseducation of the slaves included efforts to outlaw the use of African languages (feared as languages of conspiracy), the imposition of Christianity, and the separation of parents from children so that even traditions of parenthood and nurturing were interrupted. In addition, since slaves were rarely trusted with equipment subject to sabotage, they had few opportunities to develop technical skills.

The abolition of slavery in the mid-nineteenth century at first did little to improve the lot of the still disenfranchised and immobilized blacks. While European iommigrants took whatever industrial jobs were created in the North, the former slaves remained bound by debts, ignorance, prejudice and political policies to the farmlands of the South. Despite the popular misconception that the Civil War was fought to free the slaves, the northern victors were only too happy to reinforce southern policies aimed at maintaining a docile, ignorant, unskilled and unorganized black labour force. Only when the First World War produced a critical labour shortage as workers went off to fight and the flow of immigrants was virtually cut off (from 1.2 million in 1914 to 111,000 in 1918) did northern industry actively welcome black workers. Factory owners sent recruiters into the rural South to lure black labourers to northern cities, and the number of blacks in industry nearly doubled (from 500,000 to 900,000) between 1910 and 1920.[4]

The economic threat of black non-union labour reinforced the racism introduced several centuries earlier to justify slavery. Racist unions rejected black workers on the one hand and attacked them on the other for taking white workers' jobs at lower wages. Faced with the alternatives of vilification or starvation, many blacks made the best of an ugly situation until the return of troops, union victories, or the onset of the Depression cost them their jobs.

Once significant numbers of blacks began settling in northern cities, the tempo of their migration quickened. Chicago's black population, for example, rose from 44,000 in 1910 to 134,000 in 1930.[5] As a consequence, black children began to appear in greater numbers in northern urban public schools.

Black migration was followed after the Second World War by an influx of Spanish-speaking job seekers and their families from the Caribbean, Mexico, and more recently Central and South America. This population shift, in some ways like the northward flow of black families in this century, is a form of post-colonial migration within a regional sphere of influence, contrasting with earlier patterns of immigration. Once these non-white Hispanic migrants arrived, moreover, they faced many of the same obstacles to advancement as blacks or native Americans plus the need to learn a new language.

As a nation of immigrants, America lacks a collective memory to bind its inhabitants to collective standards and goals. Except when faced with real or imagined threats, Americans find it difficult to conjure up a 'we' with which to define a national concensus. When Americans say 'we', they are usually referring to some identifiable subgroup (starting with self or family and working outwards through racial, religious and ethnic layers) rather than a national collective. And if 'we' represents only a fragment of the total population, everyone else falls by default into a 'they' category.

America's enduring romance with the spirit of capitalism further exacerbates this division. One of Americans' most cherished rights is the opportunity to 'get ahead' financially. The competitive nature of such a system encourages people to identify 'we' and 'they' with profit and loss, good and bad, and other pairs of polar (and often moral) opposites. It also leads to zero-sum thinking: if you win, I lose.

When such an adversarial system enables certain groups, identifiable by race, religion or ethnic origin, to benefit from inherited wealth and power while others suffer from chronic deficiencies in both, the education system is hardly likely to redress the inequalities. Yet many people have expected it to do just that.

The largely discredited melting-pot theory proposed that all second-generation Americans had to do was lose their accent identify with the dominant culture, and accumulate a little wealth. Those calling cards would open the gates to mainstream American society. Public schooling was charged with making sure its immigrant children accomplished the first two tasks and had a chance at the third.

This scenario worked well enough for certain groups. Certainly the public schools helped many immigrant families speed their children towards acculturation and middle-class status. The whole concept foundered, however, on the inability of large numbers of non-white Americans to achieve the same success obtained by European immigrants striving for affluence and social acceptance.

Much of the blame for this failure has been levelled at the public schools. First, segregation was blamed. Bilingual education has been charged with retarding the integrative process. Alternative education, compensatory programmes and other special efforts to help redress the evident imbalances in achievement have also been criticized for not achieving goals they were either not designed or not empowered to realize. And, of course, much of the blame has also been directed at the parents and the children themselves.

Although young people spend (or should spend) an important amount of time in school, other institutions and social forces exert a greater influence over their lives. Foremost among these is the family. In the past twenty-two years, the percentage of employed black males in the United States has dropped dramatically from 74 per cent to 55 per cent. During the same period the number of black families headed by a single parent more than doubled from 20.7 per cent to 46.5 per cent.[6] The overwhelming majority of these single-parent families are headed by women; of black families headed by women, 56.1 per cent are officially poor.[7] One in every three black families lives below the poverty level,[8] and 43.5 per cent of all families on welfare are black although blacks make up only 11.9 per cent of the total population.[9] These statistics have prompted many observers to speak of a crisis in the black family.

Furthermore, recent figures show that 30 per cent of all black students still attend schools whose student bodies are 90 per cent or more black.[10] There is nothing wrong with filling schools with black children, but there is something horribly wrong with dumping the offspring of the poorest and least powerful citizens into inferior educational institutions. There is little likelihood that such institutions will help those youngsters break the cycle of failure and frustration in which they are trapped. One might even suggest such institutions seem designed to preserve the status quo rather than alter it.

In most countries, national governments are responsible for education. In the United States the individual states retain the right to create their own educational systems. Much of the authority for running schools, however, rests with local school districts. Most of these districts derive their funds from local property taxes, so the wealthiest communities end up with the best schools while the poorest make do with poor facilities, outdated books, and whatever teachers they can hire on the meager salaries they can afford to pay. Since black communities are usually poor communities, schools where black children predominate have been among the worst equipped and most poorly staffed in the country. As the adage goes, 'Services to the poor are poor services.'

When non-white students look for work, these inequalities emerge in concrete financial terms. Unemployment for non-whites in 1982 was officially 18.9 per cent or 2.2 times that for whites.[11] In fact, 'the unemployment rate of 1982 black high school graduates (58%) substantially exceeded that of white high school drop-outs (36%)'.[12] Even when they find jobs, black males earn only 60 per cent of what their white male counterparts take home on an average pay-day.[13] Non-whites are overrepresented with respect to felony arrests and convictions, drug abuse and mental illness. Under these circumstances, why stay in inferior schools where teachers and administrators expect poor performances, tolerate high levels of truancy, and are often happy just to get through each day and escape to their suburban refuges?

The answer, not surprisingly, is that many youngsters do not. In 1979 the Chancellor of the New York City Board of Education admitted that 45 per cent of the students entering the city's high schools never graduate.[14] The figures for black and Hispanic students are substantially higher, with the drop-out rate for Hispanics in some school systems as high as 75 per cent. These numbers become even more shocking when one realizes many youngsters never even enter high school.

The young people I worked with at The Dome Project, a small community-based education programme in Manhattan, suffer terribly from society's perception of them as problems inherited from an earlier time. New York City lost over 600,000 jobs between 1973 and 1984, almost entirely of the unskilled or semi-skilled variety that originally drew so many black and Hispanic workers to New York

City from the rural South and the Caribbean. My students did not migrate to New York looking for a better life; most of them were born there. To them it was never a promised land but simply the scene of their day-to-day hardships.

It is not the fault of these youngsters that society, once slavery was abolished, resisted their forefathers' attempts to create more productive roles for themselves. It is not their fault that manufacturers have discovered it is cheaper to export factories than pay local labour a competitive wage. Now that the demand for cheap labour has abated, America cannot work out what to do with the roughly 17 per cent of its population that is non-white. Little wonder that few of those charged with educating these descendants of America's slaves and colonized peoples ever stop to ask: Educate them for what?

Much of what passes for schooling in many poor communities is little more than a custodial activity, keeping youngsters off the streets but little use in helping them acquire skills, self-confidence or independence. New York City's school system, for example, essentially shaped to serve immigrant children of a century ago who were eager to learn the language and rise into the middle class, now serves a population which largely despairs of either obtaining a useful education or passing into the American mainstream. Many of New York City's non-white students (74.1 per cent of the public school enrolment)[15] do not trust their white teachers (80.7 per cent of the pedagogical staff).[16] Similarly, many teachers manifest destructively low expectations of their pupils' capabilities. As a result, there is often a complete breakdown of the respect that teacher, student and parent must share to sustain an effective educational environment.

But is this breakdown primarily the fault of the schools? Or does it accurately reflect a breakdown in society at large? Writing in the *New York Times*, columnist Sydney Schanberg insisted recently: 'This city is as close as one can get to every-man-for-himself without being in a declared state of anarchy.[17] Schanberg was writing at the time not about violent adolescents but about City Hall politicians. Yet if *New York Times* readers recognize their society in Schanberg's lament, what must black and Hispanic youngsters feel who see the law flouted on every street corner and the rhetoric of equality mocked by the realities of their struggle to survive?

Young people pay a heavy price for discouragement. It has been estimated that New York City has between 163,000 and 177,500 heroin addicts, or approximately one in every forty residents.[18] Heroin does not attract people who feel they have something to lose in life. It only attracts those who feel any escape is better than the present, no matter what the price. Youngsters who reach that point are likely to have little respect for society or any of its members. They develop a predatory atitude which permits them to inflict violence and even death with chilling casualness. This process doubly devastates poor minority communities: their residents suffer disproportionately from crime, and their young people are disproportionately diverted from healthy development. How, for example, does a youngster who lives in an environment where life itself becomes so precarious (like Belfast or Beirut) concentrate on times tables and spelling assignments?

For schools to preach equality, respect for authority, and the advantages of the economic system (a student once asked me, 'How can they expect me to be a capitalist when I ain't got no capital?') to these youngsters when so much they experience contradicts these preachings, is a mockery that only makes some oppressed youngsters angrier. America has created a school system in its own image: private schools for the elite, competitive public schools for the middle class, minimally functional schools for working communities, and custodial schools for the rest. The wonder is that anyone should expect the youngsters not to recognize these distinctions and respond accordingly.

As bleak as this picture may be, I do not want to suggest that the situation is hopeless or that the only education these youngsters can acquire will be administered by the drug pushers and prostitutes who seem to be among their few neighbours with any money in their pockets. Some of these youngsters may be lucky or talented enough to escape their destructive environment before too much damage has been done.

For the majority, however, the only constructive way out is through a struggle to transform their world and thereby their role in it. I am not suggesting that they should not learn how and when to compromise but that compromise can only get them so far in a world where they have no power base from which to operate.

Even without a real power base, youngsters can often fulfil some of their dreams if they have effective mediators to help them. Wise and skilful parents are usually the best mediators, but parents of these young people are frequently unprepared to cope with the task. They have typically grown up in totally different environments from the one in which they are trying to raise their children. Many came from rural homes where the nearest town had fewer inhabitants than the forbidding urban school their children attend has students from communities where the support of extended family members made humiliating visits to hostile welfare centres unnecessary. They are poorly educated and feel the solemn weight of their inadequacies. Most of all they are beaten down by the constant struggle against all odds to create a decent life for themselves and offer their children a better life than the one they have known.

Most members of poor communities who acquire either power or access to power use it to leave those communities, making it even harder for poor youngsters to find proper role models and advisers. Without some kind of connection that extends beyond the broad underclass in which these young people find themselves, their world is bounded by passive, degrading experiences (welfare, custodial schooling, a decaying environment) punctuated by random and gratuitous violence. Along with that passivity comes a burning resentment which often finds its most pointed expression in racial hatred.

These youngsters need positive role models, including some whose characteristics (sex, race, life experiences), strengths and successes enable the youngsters to identify them with their own aspirations. They need to see those role models functioning in circumstances that demonstrate both self-respect and respect for others, for the street has taught them to equate respect with fear. Someone must also create a chance for them to experience multi-racial, multi-ethnic cooperation, for nothing in their lives even suggests such a possibility exists.

The Dome Project, which took its name from a geodesic dome a few good friends built with a group of truants and trouble-makers in 1973, has tried to create an extended family network that can reinforce the strengths already existing in inner-city families and provide access to the tools, skills, attitudes and connections their children need to compete in a society that generally holds them in low esteem. In addition to teaching these youngsters and creating a multi-racial, multi-ethnic staff of strong and competent men and women to serve as role models, we also have tried to give them a broader perspective on the world than their ghetto experience might otherwise permit. For example, we often engage them in community service projects. One of the most successful efforts involved transforming a rubble-strewn waste-ground into a beautiful park and garden. Youngsters must begin to believe in their power to transform the world around them. A vacant plot is a great place to begin and a garden a superb metaphor for the kind of healthy transformation that is possible.

No matter how good specific services for young people may be, we have discovered many of the neediest youngsters lack a coherent context in which to use them. Many doctors have recognized the same problem: proper diagnosis and appropriate prescriptions are ineffective if the patient does not have the prescription made up and take the medicine as directed. Birth control information, techniques and aids are only effective if properly and consistently applied. Similar examples exist in education, social services, legal assistance and virtually all interaction between poor youngsters and the institutions responsible for helping them. The Dome Project offers a range of services designed to create or strengthen a youngster's integrative resources.

The programme is open winter and summer from early morning until late in the evening. Activities range from alternative public school classes for children who cannot or will not function in regular school settings to ballet and basketball as alternatives to boredom and self-destructive activities. We have developed an extensive network of resources to help the academically oriented towards college and the vocationally minded into job training and permanent employment. Staff members work closely with parents and the various institutions serving their children to ensure that youngsters get the help to which they are entitled and parents learn how to make the system work for them in the future.

The Dome Project has succeeded in creating a real community — a sharing of feelings, experiences and support — for many young people and their families who were otherwise all too alone in the big city. Taking our cue from the Brazilian educator, Paolo Freire, we have tried to base our educational activities on coping with real problems in the real world our youngsters face. Whether the limitations obstructing their development are real or only perceived as such, they must learn to face and overcome them. Our job is to guide them through the process.

I like to think a proliferation of programmes such as the Dome Project would be a good thing, but it would hardly solve the problem of integrating America's minorities into society. Their exclusion is not a technical or pedagogical one but a social, historical and political one rooted in the desire of a dominant class to protect and perpetuate certain forms of privilege. These privileges undermine the mandated equality in educational opportunity guaranteed every youngster by law and constitute a serious threat to the American nation.

Notes

1. *Statistical Abstract of the United States*. US Department of Commerce. Bureau of the Census. Washington. DC. 1983. p. 88.
2. *Census of the Population, 1980*. US Department of Commerce. Bureau of the Census. Supplementary Report 'Percent of Population by Ethnic Origin'. PC 80–51–10. pp. 12–13.
3. Lydia Anderson. *Immigration*. Franklin Watts. New York. p. 15.
4. William H. Harris. *The Harder We Run: Black Workers and the Civil War*. Oxford University Press. Oxford. 1982. p. 61.
5. Otis D. Duncan and Beverly Duncan. *The Negro Population of Chicago*. University of Chicago Press. Chicago. 1957. p. 21.
6. *New York Times*. 20 November 1983. pp. 1. 56.
7. Kaiser. Robert. 'The Help for America's Poor Hasn't Been Enough'. *International Herald Tribune*. 14 November 1984. p. 4 (reprinted from *Washington Post*).
8. *Statistical Abstract*. p. 474.
9. Ibid.. pp. 32. 396.
10. Ibid.. p. 149.
11. Ibid.. p. 409.
12. 'Youth Employment Abstract'. The Roosevelt Centennial Youth Project. Washington. DC. 1984.
13. *Statistical Abstract*. p. 469.
14. 'High School Dropout Rate at 45%'. *New York Times*. 17 October 1979. p. 1.
15. *School Profiles, 1981–82*. New York City Board of Education. Fall 1983. p. A.
16. *New York Times*. 12 September 1982. p. 6E.
17. *New York Times*. 21 April 1984. p. 34.
18. 'Califano Cites 50% Increase in Heroin Addiction in City'. *New York Times*. 5 June 1982. p. 81.

12 ASSIMILATION AND INTEGRATION OF MINORITIES AND CULTURAL PLURALISM: SOCIOCULTURAL MECHANISMS AND POLITICAL DILEMMAS

Hans-Joachim Hoffmann-Nowotny

This contribution is devoted to the complex phenomenon of integration and assimilation of ethnic migrant minorities and to the problems related to the political notion of pluralism.

The theoretical framework which will be developed in order to deal with these phenomena claims to be of a universal nature, that is, is considered to be part of a general sociological theory. It refers thus not only to ethnic migrant minorities in Western Europe, with which this paper will deal and the studies of which form the empirical basis of the theoretical argumentation. It is postulated that the framework is applicable to minority problems in general and, beyond that, to a wide range of other societal problems. One must, however, keep in mind the methodological truism that in the application of a general theory to a special event, situation or problem the respective special marginal conditions have to be taken into consideration. Only then is it possible to make adequate use of a general theory. If this is well understood, it is completely appropriate to apply my theory to minority problems in Israel, India, Sri Lanka or Nigeria (see the respective chapters in this book), but it would lead to wrong conclusions and — even worse — to wrong political measures if one were simply to transfer conclusions from one context to another, even though both are being regulated by the same fundamental societal mechanism which one cannot escape.

In my analysis I shall restrict myself in the tradition of Max Weber to pointing out such mechanisms and social laws as determine the course of events in this world whether we like it or not. As a result we shall see that the field of our analysis consists of a complex set of unavoidable dilemmas.

The theoretical framework

The theory which I would like to propose for our analysis is methodologically based on a general systems-theory approach and has as its most abstract dimensions the concepts of structure on the one hand and culture on the other. These concepts are regarded as basic sociological categories in ordering social reality.

It is assumed that these dimensions are interdependent: structural factors and structural change influence cultural factors and cultural change, and vice versa. The idea of interdependence does not exclude the notion that the relationship between structure and culture might also be asymmetric; under certain conditions culture might be determined by structure to a stronger extent than structure is determined by culture. In addition we postulate the existence of structural as well as cultural self-dynamics.

Structure is defined as a set of interrelated social positions (or units) whereas *culture* is defined as a set of interrelated symbols (values and norms). This conceptual and pre-theoretical scheme may be applied to all levels of societal and social systems as is shown with respect to systems involved in the problems we are dealing with in Figure 12.1 (Hoffmann-Nowotny and Hondrich 1982: 602).

We further postulate the existence of collective interests on the different system levels in determining the conduct of groups and individuals (for the following see Hoffmann-Nowotny and Hondrich 1982: 603 ff.). These collective interests are seen as determined by different configurations of structure and culture and find an expression in the processes shown in Figure 12.1.

The collective interests that can be empirically determined will be dealt with in terms of three types:

- the ability of a group to take binding decisions free from outside pressure and to assert itself *vis-à-vis* other groups (political interests);
- interests relative to the production and marketing of goods produced by the group (economic interests);
- interests in social relationships based on the commonality of values, standards of behaviour and feelings (community interests).

We assume that these three sets of interests can be found to exist and be operative in all societies regardless of differences in age, sex, social stratum, occupation, language, religion, and so forth. In other words: we assume that the overwhelming majority of its members share an

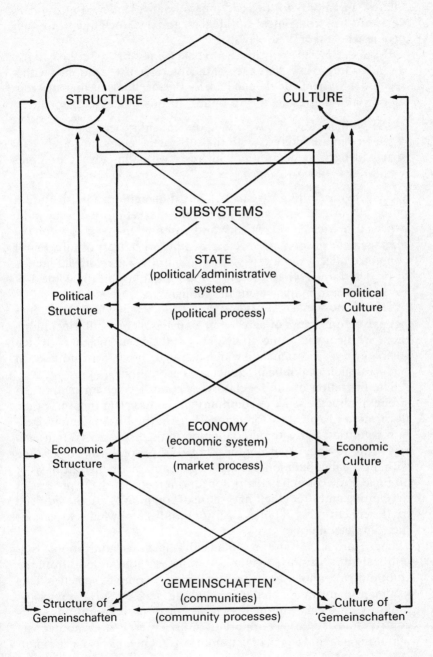

interest in improving their living standards, in making political decisions free from outside influences, and in associating freely with people who share their views.

If we continue to apply the theoretical framework described above, it is advisable to associate each of the interests just mentioned with a specific subsystem and then to look for the mechanisms that are set in motion and the results they produce. In this model we associate:

- the political interests with the political subsystem 'state';
- the economic interests with the subsystem 'economy'; and
- the identity or community interests with the subsystem 'communities' (*Gemeinschaften*).

As a general finding, it can be said that neither administrative, politically originated regulations nor the market mechanism can be expected to yield a satisfactory and comprehensive policy for the management of the issues we are dealing with, least of all when it comes to collective interests of the community. Therefore, it remains to be determined what role the community plays in the context of various tension-management mechanisms.

There is no social context and thus no society in which there does not exist a minimum of agreement, concensus, or similarity among those who constitute the group. This is the basic insight to which sociology owes its origin and which distinguishes it from older social sciences, such as political science and economics.

The operation of the regulatory or control mechanism through strengthening the sense of community becomes clear in terms of the illustration provided by foreign workers in the European immigration countries. For without adaptation to the host society, that is to say, in the absence of developing parallels to or similarities of attitude with the local population, attempts at integration on the sole basis of political and economic factors appear doomed. Thus, the process of developing and strengthening a sense of community is a prerequisite for the effectiveness of policy decisions and actually helps to smooth their implementation.

There are clear and sociologically justified indications that political-administrative regulations alone, without support from the community, cannot assure the functioning of complex societies. This would also mean that education alone cannot 'solve' majority-minority problems, although — under favourable conditions — its contribution can be very important (Gurny *et al.* 1983). Another way of putting it is that a lack of community (that means also a common identity) gives rise to problems of regulation by political-administrative means (as an example, see Chapter 7 of this book).

Integration without assimilation: the philosopher's stone?

Recently in several European immigration countries the idea has gained ground that immigrants (including the second or third generation) should be integrated and not be discriminated against on ethnic grounds while at the same time they should not only be allowed but be encouraged to preserve their culture and maintain links with their home countries. At the same time the population and the institutions of the immigrant countries should be taught not only to accept and tolerate cultural pluralism but to value it as an enrichment of the country's global culture and as a solution to all inter-ethnic conflicts (Colloque 1983: Giordan 1982; Ministère du Plan de l'aménagement du Territoire 1982). In short, what is seen as a kind of philosopher's stone is integration without assimilation. The same notion is also being suported by several associations of foreigners.

In the following we shall ask whether — from a sociological point of view — this notion is really the philosopher's stone. We will also have to ask which kinds of strategy seem able to secure immigrants a position in the immigration societies which is in accordance with their collective interests and with principles of social justice. This would mean both that foreigners would have the same opportunities for access to the goods and values of the societies in which they live as the members of the native population and that there would be no discrimination on grounds of ethnic origin.

Assimilation and structural distance

Immigrants in the highly developed countries of Europe come mainly either from underdeveloped countries such as Turkey, Algeria or Portugal or from the underdeveloped regions of more developed countries such as Italy or Spain. This means that they carry and bring with them characteristics of an achieved nature which distinguish them from the population of the highly developed immigration countries.

As a consequence they often lack those preconditions of life in modern societies which in the course of time have become minimum standards, such as eight to ten years of school attendance, for example. That is to say they often lack educational, vocational and social skills which belong to the normal outfit of all native members of the immigration societies. As a result there is a considerable structural distance between most immigrants and the native population. And it seems no wonder that such immigrants form a kind of undercast below the stratification systems of the receiving societies.

If the postulate of an interdependence of structural and cultural aspects holds true, it is not to be expected that the immigrants of the first generation have any noteworthy chance of becoming assimilated with respect to the dominant values of the immigration society. This is the more so if contacts with the native population are minimal because they work and live in places where they are mainly among themselves. But even if contacts with members of the majority take place, they are mainly with the native lower class, which has to be considered as relatively marginal with regard to the dominant culture. There exist thus strong structural barriers against the assimilation of a considerable — and from country to country varying — proportion of the first generation of immigrants. As long as their structural positions and their structural heritage remain unchanged, there is little chance that they can make any considerable progress toward assimilation.

Assimilation and cultural distance

There is not only structural distance between emigration and immigration contexts but also cultural distance. Furthermore, while structural distance lends itself to ratio measurement (level of income, years of schooling, degree of urbanization, and so on) and is subject to a world-wide consensus that it should be diminished(an indicator is the world-wide call for 'development'), the same cannot be said with respect to cultural distance. It seems that culture is regarded as a societal element which has to be valued immanently and must not be compared in an evaluative manner with other cultures, as was done, for example, when certain cultures were labelled as 'primitive'. Although there is no doubt that cultures can be compared with respect to a large number of dimensions (complexity, differentiation, stability, change, content of ethics, for example), it seems indeed problematic to apply to culture such terms as 'more' or 'less developed', which we do not hesitate to use in structural comparisons.

There is on the other hand no doubt, at least since Weber's essay on *The Ethics of Protestantism and the Spirit of Capitalism*, that cultural elements are decisive for structural developments (and vice versa). This implies, however, that it is not possible to combine just any culture with just any structural setting, at least not without creating anomie.

The question arises, therefore, to what extent certain cultural traits of immigrated ethnic groups are compatible not only with the culture of the immigration country but also with its structure, and, last but not least, with the collective and individual interests of the immigrants.

It is quite evident that there is no one single generalized answer to this question. I shall nevertheless try to arrive at some relatively general hypotheses starting from the assumption that migrants did migrate because they wanted to improve their economic and social standard of living.

Thus any development or behaviour on the part of immigrants would have to be regarded as dysfunctional if it represents an obstacle to reaching the mentioned goals. It would, therefore, appear as a functional necessity that migrants in Europe assimilate (at least in a functional way) into the dominant culture. The marginal conditions for this are that migrants be spread within and over the territory of the immigration countries (although there do exist some ghetto-like concentrations) and that these countries be culturally *relatively* homogeneous. With respect to the political culture this is even true for a country such as Switzerland, which otherwise (language, ethnic origin) is culturally truly heterogeneous, but preserves identities on a rather strict regional basis, dividing its population of only 6.4 million into 26 highly autonomous 'states' (cantons).

It seems that the mentioned (functional) assimilation has more or less taken place in European immigration countries as far as the economic system and its culture is concerned. Migrants from very different cultural backgrounds have proved able to fulfil their economic functions, although mainly in the lowest ranks of this system, which also means that the functionally necessary degree of assimilation can be low. With the exception of Switzerland (and some immigration countries with very small shares of foreigners, such as Sweden or Norway), whose immigrants mainly come from neighbouring countries (and which, with regard to integration and assimilation, has some unique traits), immigrants mostly did not acquire those characteristics which would have allowed them a noteworthy upward mobility. The reasons for this seem rather clear: the immigrants' structural and cultural origins and political and institutional barriers put them into structural positions in the immigration country in which the chances of integration and assimilation are low, which in turn leads to a vicious circle. This circle becomes reinforced by neo-feudal attitudes of the native population, which also tend to increase cultural distance by making cultural differences more conscious and more pronounced or by even (re)constructing them. This again leads to a vicious circle since the native population of the immigration countries feels itself legitimated in its behaviour and attitudes towards the immigrants because it can point to the 'large' cultural distance. One way out of the circle takes the form of return migration on the part of the immigrant minorities and demands for their repatriation on the part of the autochthonous majority, proving that it is not so much a question of whether or not immigrants would like to assimilate in order to reach the goals for which they emigrated but that there are structural and cultural mechanisms which function as severe barriers against assimilation. People who discriminate against immigrants because of their supposed cultural distance tend to forget that this distance is often created by the initial rebuff which the immigrants experience: this may lead to an explicit assertion of their identity (the 'black is beautiful' movement is an American example of this tendency) because they have been structurally as well as culturally rejected.

Integration and cultural heterogeneity

Integration without assimilation, integration of minorities which remain culturally distant from the majority, these notions we would propose to call 'ideological' because from a sociological point of view they obviously neglect the determinants and regularities which operate in social reality. But even if we would accept these notions as an at least partially realistic guideline, they obviously need a great amount of differentiation. From a cultural point of view they would also require the indigenous population to identify itself with what is different and foreign: with people who look different, have different traditions, customs, values and norms, lifestyles, family patterns, etc. (as, for example, with Muslims, with people who speak Turkish and with those who collect the garbage). This calls for either of two approaches: a redefinition of their identity as Germans, Swiss or French that would make it natural for Turkish or Algerian Muslims to become part of the German, Swiss or French national communities; or a definition of the community concept on a highly abstract level, which views Germans, Swiss or French and Turks, Muslims, Christians, labourers and intellectuals in terms of their shared characteristics — as human beings, and as interdependent individuals whose opportunities in life are enhanced by the pluralism of the society.

These redefinitions seem to make morally utopian demands on the community (*Gemeinschaft*) as well as on the political and economic system. And indeed they are utopian at least in a short-run perspective. But if one pleads for a truly culturally pluralistic society, one has to realize that these are the sociological requirements which would have to be fulfilled. Ideologists who would like to exploit the migrant's situation for power reasons or for the sake of their 'true belief' might perhaps not be interested in 'solving' the minority problem by integration or assimilation. A *Realpolitiker*, however, acting in the interest of the immigrants, would opt in the first instance for the removal of barriers against integration and assimilation, recognizing that their lifespans are limited and they would like to enjoy a higher status (which was the motivation to emigrate) during their lifetime, he would not want the immigrants to wait for the realization of a Utopia.

In a medium- and long-term perspective one would, of course, also work for a realization of the conditions mentioned for a cultural change, that is to say, try to dig the tunnel from both ends. In doing so one would be confronted with a series of problems. With regard to the political system one would have to ask oneself to what extent the indigenous population of the European immigration countries were willing (or could be influenced) to tolerate a deviating political culture, especially if it is expressed by foreigners. Or could and would European countries tolerate two legal systems regarding, for example, the position of women in society, one granting equal rights to them and another setting migrant women apart as a conservative Muslim group may demand in order to preserve its culture?

As regards the economic system, there seems to be more tolerance, but only in the small sector of ethnic restaurants, ethnic shops and the like. There would be very little tolerance if immigrants were to claim, for example, the right to a deviating work culture.

With respect to the community (*Gemeinschaft*) it has to be seen that it is based on similarities of its members and thus, by its very nature, cannot tolerate large deviations. To what extent such similarities could be made more abstract, making it possible to reconcile hitherto irreconcilable characteristics, remains an open question.

But even if one would agree that there is a movement towards a greater tolerance for people who look different or have different lifestyles, or that community interests and values are tending to become more abstract (which I doubt very much, considering, for example, the tendency towards an increasing regionalism), the question is not only whether individuals or systems of different levels can and will tolerate culturally different groups but to what extent cultural differences and certain cultural characteristics are compatible with a given societal structure, be it on the level of the political, the economic or the community system (Krause 1976; Korte 1982; Lebon 1983). Our model suggests that the cultures of the contexts from which migrants come are related to the structures of these contexts. A cultural change in the immigration countries aiming at a preservation of cultural traits of the sending countries and regions would thus probably require the structure of the receiving countries to move at least partially towards the structure of the emigration countries. Whether this is a realistic or desirable notion is not easy to decide.

Open versus closed societies: structural versus cultural policy

From a global point of view the existence of cultural heterogeneity necessarily implied structural segregation, and vice versa. If structure and culture are in a state of disaccordance, collective or individual anomie will be the consequence. This is a general and fundamental characteristic of all human societies. Structural and cultural segregation are institutionalized realities in caste and feudal systems, which therefore may be called 'closed societies'; but they are also — although to a much lesser extent — realities in modern Western societies, ideally regulated by universalistic norms, to which one can thus refer as 'open societies'.

It is theoretically and empirically stringent that structurally close societies imply cultural heterogeneity as far as the inter-class or inter-caste relations are concerned, and cultural homogeneity with respect to intra-class or intra-caste relations.

Closed societies can and do 'tolerate' cultural heterogeneity as an inter-class or inter-caste phenomenon, while they will not tolerate intra-class heterogeneity. The 'tolerance' of heterogeneity in caste and feudal systems is thus nothing but a necessity for the maintenance of their structural design. If this is so, and there seems to be no doubt about it, it follows that if a society wants to enforce cultural pluralism, understood as cultural heterogeneity, there will be also more structural segregation. And if there is a certain degree of cultural homogeneity but structural segregation (as seems to be the case as regards large segments of black Americans) there will be anomie.

If we agree that the redefinitions mentioned above cannot be realized within a short-term perspective, the acceptance of the notion of cultural pluralism would mean, with regard to the European immigration countries (if they would like to avoid an anomie situation), that open societies would become more closed. They would have to be refeudalized, 'polyethnically laminated', as William McNeill called it, and this at the cost of the immigrants. The latter, however, left their home countries because they wanted to escape from the constraints of a closed society.

A cultural policy, be it generated by the immigration countries or by the immigrants themselves, which aims at the conservation or even the enforcement of cultural heterogeneity (in a fundamental sense of the term) will thus definitively cement social inequality and structural segregation. A structural policy would instead be geared toward equal chances of participation in the goods and values of the immigration countries for all their members. It could, however, not guarantee to preserve the cultural identity of foreign ethnic groups if the term 'culture' is to be understood to mean anything more than 'folklore'.

The result of a structural policy will not be a harmonious society free of tensions and social problems, as the advocates of the mentioned cultural policy expect of their strategy, when they see 'la présence de communautés culturelles différentes . . . comme un moyen de renforcer l'unité nationale et d'aider la société à sortir de la crise qu'elle traverse' (Colloque 1983: 1). If it is historically true that stable closed societies generate and experience less social tension than open societies, then they may even be right.

Bibliography

Colloque (1983). 'Diversité Culturelle, Société Industrielle, Etat National', Communication Finale, Créteil, 9–11 May.

Giordan, Henri (1982), *Démocratie culturelle et droit à la différence*, La Documentation Français, Paris.

Gurny, Ruth, Paul Cassée, Hans-Peter Hauser, Andreas Meyer (1983) *Karrieren und Sackgassen — Wege ins Berufsleben junger Schweizer und Italiener in der Stadt Zürich*, Soziologishes Institut der Universität Zürich, Zürich.

Hoffmann-Nowotny, Hans-Joachim, Karl Otto Hondrich (eds) (1982), *Ausländer in der Bundesrepublik Deutschland und in der Schweiz. Segregation und Integration: Eine vergleichende Untersuchung*, Campus Verlag, Frankfurt and New York.

Korte, Hermann (coordinator) (1982), *Cultural Identity and Structural Marginalization of Migrant Workers*, European Science Foundation, Strasbourg.

Krausz, Ernest (1976). 'Ethnic Pluralism and Structural Dissonance', *Plural Societies*, 7, no.2, pp. 71–83.

Lebon, André (1983). 'Maintien des Liens culturels et Insertion des Migrants: Quelles Relations?' *Revue Francaise des Affaires Sociales*, 37, no. 2, pp. 89–114.

Ministère du Plan et de l'Aménagement du Territoire. Commissariat Général du Plan (1982). L'impératif culturel, La Documentation Française, Paris.

13 MODELS VERSUS REALITY, OR, LET'S CALL RACISM BY ITS NAME

John Simon

Most of the contributors to this book have focused on problems of how to integrate or how better to integrate ethnic minorities into the political and economic life of their respective countries. Underlying these studies is a widely held assumption that such minority groups should not have to renounce their cultural identity to share in the political and economic benefits of the society in which they live.

Professor Hans-Joachim Hoffmann-Nowotny argues in Chapter 12 that this assumption is naive and potentially dangerous. Cultural heterogeneity, he claims, can only be tolerated in closed societies, where the dominant class uses cultural differences to keep ethnic minorities segregated and subservient. Attempts to create pluralistic open societies in which ethnic groups retain their cultural integrity but achieve positions of political and economic equality are Utopian. They raise false expectations and ultimately hurt the minorities ostensibly being helped.

Professor Toru Umakoshi's description of the plight of second- and third-generation Koreans in Japan provides a good example of Professor Hoffmann-Nowotny's hypothesis at work in a contemporary society. Only by adopting Japanese names, language, and customs can residents of Korean ancestry hope to enter into the mainstream of Japanese economic and political life. Furthermore, their proven ability to advance structurally once they have taken the steps necessary to assimilate culturally strongly supports Professor Hoffmann-Nowotny's notion that cultural separatism is antagonistic to structural integration.

Professor Hoffmann-Nowotny's schema linking structure and culture through operative forces in every society's political, economic and community systems draws our attention to a perplexing conflict. But in his efforts to produce a configuration that 'is applicable to minority problems in general and beyond that to a wide range of societal problems',[1] he reduces *ad absurdum* some of the major issues facing ethnic minorities attempting to improve their plight.

Burying such powerful social determinants as ethnicity, religion and race in a catch-all category called 'culture' does more to obscure the problems of minority groups than clarify them. Just as the various minorities discussed in this book are often as different from each other as they are from the majority or dominant group in their respective countries, the problems obstructing their integration may vary according to the particular situation. For example, although the Korean immigrants in Japan willing to acculturate apparently have little trouble passing into the structural mainstream, the same does not hold true for Turks in Germany. Acculturation for the Koreans seems to consist primarily of learning to speak Japanese, wearing Japanese (Western?) dress, and adopting a Japanese name. It is unrealistic to suggest, however, that speaking excellent German, wearing the latest German fashions, and assuming German names will lead to the structural integration of Turkish guest workers and their families.

An acculturated Korean in Japan is indistinguishable from the majority population; an acculturated Turk is still an easily identifiable alien. Furthermore, Japanese society is apparently willing to assimilate a small percentage of Koreans, whereas Germany is clearly resisting integration of its larger Turkish population. The differences between the two cases, I suggest, outweigh the parallels drawn by Professor Hoffmann-Nowotny's model.

Before I test that model against some of the other cases presented in this book, I will digress briefly to discuss an important question of terminology. Professor Hoffmann-Nowotny relies heavily on European examples of workers emigrating from less developed countries to richer ones. He argues that cultural pluralism would require host countries to accept immigrant attitudes and behaviour appropriate in the countries of origin but which conflict with the norms of the country of immigration. The onus, therefore, is on the immigrants to conform or face continuing structural segregation.

Approximately half the studies in this volume, however, involve situations where no immigration was involved or where it occurred so long ago as to be meaningless in today's context. Can we call the Palestinians in Israel or the Ibo in Nigeria immigrants? What about the blacks in the United States, whose arrival pre-dates that of the so-called white ethnic minorities in that country by several centuries? In all three cases, curiously enough, as with the Koreans in Japan, these minorities were forcibly brought and included in or kept under the administrative control of a majority culture. They certainly did not emigrate in search of better opportunities as Professor Hoffmann-Nowotny's model assumes.

If these minorities are immigrants, then the term is being used loosely to describe groups of people different from (and thereby somehow inferior to) the dominant population who, because they have come from somewhere else (at some undefined time), have no legitimate claim to the full rights and privileges accorded the local (that is, legitimate) citizenry. Where such a mentality prevails, integrating the minority cannot proceed until the majority clarifies whether it wants to integrate them in the first place.

Germany, for example, clearly has never intended to assimilate its Turkish guest workers or their families. Indeed, it offers cash incentives to encourage their return to Turkey. At the other end of the spectrum, black and Hispanic citizens of the United States are guaranteed equal rights under the law, yet their struggle for equal opportunity has proved a bitter, prolonged and inconclusive one.

The European immigration context, therefore, where labourers are imported, exploited, and presumably repatriated when their labour is no longer needed, seems far too narrow to justify Professor Hoffmann-Nowotny's claim that a pluralistic open society is a contradiction in terms. Furthermore, his argument that minority populations 'often lack those preconditions of life in modern societies' which would allow them to compete as equals with the majority, while undeniable in some cases, runs directly counter to the realities in Malaysia, Sri Lanka, Nigeria, and other countries where so-called 'privileged minorities' have attained positions of disproportionate power and wealth. The current conflict in Malaysia, for example, as described by Dr Mary Somers Heidhues, has resulted largely from attempts to integrate the poorly educated, economically depressed *majority* Malays into the structural positions of privilege held by the Chinese minority. Far from being ill-adapted for success, the Chinese seem to have aroused the resentment of the majority population by succeeding too well.

I think we can get a clearer view of the forces resisting or opposing the integration of various minorities if we momentarily put aside Professor Hoffmann-Nowotny's broad cultural category and look at the impact of ethnic origin, religion and race on specific situations described in some of the preceding chapters.

Let us begin with ethnic origin. This book's only example of ethnic origin appearing in clear distinction to race and religion as an obstacle to integration is the above-mentioned case of the ethnic Koreans in Japan. Their ability to assimilate with virtually complete success when they choose to suggests that ethnic origin is not an insurmountable obstacle to integration. In fact, given enough time, full integration of the Koreans is probably inevitable. Separation from the sources of Korean culture, intermarriage, and conscious defections to the majority lifestyle will eventually erode ethnic ties until culture degenerates into folklore and the minority effectively dissolves into the dominant population.

A particularly interesting example of what happens when religious considerations intrude has been discussed by Professor Chaim Adler in his chapter on Israel (Chapter 6). In describing the difficulties Israel has experienced in integrating Jews from Africa and Asia, he reminds us that these immigrants face the same problems (emphasized by Professor Hoffmann-Nowotny) as any arrivals lacking the requisite educational, vocational and social skills are likely to encounter upon entering a modern technological society. In this case, however, religion acts as a powerful unifying force, motivating Israel to integrate these disadvantaged Jews despite the attendant difficulties.

The other side of the coin in Israel's case is the relationship between the Jewish majority and the Palestinians living in Israel. In terms of education, vocational skills and other cultural baggage, these long-time residents of the area are hardly distinguishable from most of the Jewish immigrants from Asia and Africa. If anything, they may be better off. But they are not Jews, and therein lies the root of their reluctance to integrate and the reluctance of Jewish society to integrate them. Israel is a Jewish state, not a secular one. The gap between the dominant (European-origin) Israeli culture and the culture of the Asian and African Jews may be difficult to overcome, but great determination and effort are yielding impressive results. Most of the determination and effort addressed to the integration of Palestinians into Israeli society has been, for better or for worse, aimed at preventing it.

The Israeli example, unlike that of the Koreans in Japan, is not a very clear one. The territorial struggles which have pitted the Israelis against their neighbours have made the integration of the Palestinian minority less a problem of national character than one of national survival. Still, it is a particularly interesting illustration of how two minority groups, in many ways very similar with respect to Professor Hoffmann-Nowotny's model, can encounter such different problems within the same society.

Moral imperatives often complicate the problems facing religious minorities. Judeo-Christian-Islamic religions, for example, are based on holy covenants granting their particular followers special status as defenders of the faith. Historically this status has often included the right to destroy, enslave or otherwise oppress infidels in the name of their particular heavenly mandate. As a result, religious segregation is often much more stubbornly rooted and harder to overcome than ethnic segregation. Moreover, religious minorities are often ethnic minorities. This double identification makes resistance to the integration of religious minorities considerably stronger.

As compelling a determinant of 'culture' as religion is in Professor Hoffmann-Nowotny's schema, it is not as compelling as race, a characteristic that one can neither choose, change, nor, except in rare cases, disguise. Although every respectable study on the subject has shown that race does not determine intelligence or even say very much about an individual's physiology, racial barriers remain extremely difficult for minority groups to overcome.

Ethnologists might not be happy with this application of the term, but I think racism is a major issue in the examples of the Chinese in Malaysia and Indonesia, as presented by Dr Mary Somers Heidhues, and the Turks in Germany, as described by Dr Ursula Mehrländer and Professor Antje-Katrin Menk. Although the Chinese are considered a privileged minority in the Malaysian context and the Turks are a disadvantaged immigrant group, they both differ from the majority in ethnic background, religion and race. As such, they are subject to multiple prejudice. As a Jew working among blacks and Hispanics in the United States, I have had plenty of opportunity to observe and experience the interaction of these three layers of prejudice. I have also had ample motivation to contemplate the ethnic, religious and racial role models that dominate the American self-image. They are summarized concisely by the acronym WASP (white Anglo-Saxon Protestant), which describes the dominant or majority group in the United States.

The 1980 Census of the US lists 83.15 per cent of the American population as white[2] and 52.48 per cent as being of English or German origin.[3] Religious questions are excluded from the Census, but of the nearly 140 million Americans affiliated with religious organizations, 55 per cent are Protestant.[4] Some of the Protestants are non-white, and some of the descendants of English and German immigrants are not Protestant, but the WASP profile still fits the largest and most powerful group in the United States and defines the dominant culture against which all minorities are viewed.

Looking at family income, one generally reliable indicator of how well a minority is fitting into the structure of society, we see some interesting figures. According to the 1980 Census, American families of Italian and Polish ancestry have higher mean incomes than those of English and German origins. Furthermore, the proportion of families of English (8.3 per cent) and German (8.0 per cent) stock living below the poverty line is far greater than that of families of Italian (5.4 per cent) or Polish (4.5 per cent) descent.[5] These figures suggest that the Anglo-Saxon part of the WASP label is no longer sufficiently potent to protect the economic privilege of its constituency.

Andrew Greeley has conducted a comparative study of the success of various religious groups in America with respect to educational attainment, job prestige, and family income. Non-whites were screened out to avoid the possibility that racial discrimination would distort the outcome of his investigation, as the 11.13 per cent of the American population that is black is heavily Protestant while Hispanics are predominantly Catholic. According to Greeley, Jews emerge on top in all three categories, and Catholics command second place in two of the three. Greeley concludes, 'both in stratification and mobility, all the Catholic ethnic groups seem to be more successful than all of the Protestant groups'.[6]

So it appears the 'P' in WASP is no more invincible than the 'AS'. Jews and Catholics have caught or surpassed the descendants of the Mayflower Pilgrims in educational attainment and family income. That leaves only the 'W'. Unfortunately, racial barriers appear to be much more effective predictors of success than religion or ethnic origin. James Davis compared the educational and occupational attainment and mobility of twenty-seven different minority groups. Of these, he concluded, 'a generation of "rapid social change" still shows ... blacks, Latins, and American Indians in the bottom six positions'.[7]

In her chapter in this book on Hispanics in the United States (Chapter 10), Professor Isaura Santiago Santiago reports that unemployment among Hispanic high school graduates is higher than among Hispanic drop-outs. In my chapter (Chapter 11) I show that unemployment among black high school graduates is 62 per cent higher than that of white high school drop-outs. What can education be expected to contribute to the integration of black and Hispanic youngsters in such a context? The message to them, no matter how hard their parents urge them to stay at school, is that education is not the controlling variable. Race is.

The United States, in contrast to most of the examples in this book, has been an unusually effective immigration society for many of its immigrant groups. It is understandably difficult for grateful ethnic minorities to look very critically at the society which gave them and their children the opportunity to escape poverty and social immobility. Religious minorities have been equally reluctant to criticize a society that offered them not only freedom of religion but an opportunity for educational and economic advancement and political participation. These successes, however, have only made it doubly frustrating for racial minorities to endure prolonged prejudice, lack of opportunity, and the perpetuation of their inferior status within an otherwise relatively open society.

I suggest the American example contradicts Professor Hoffmann-Nowotny's notion that cultural pluralism is a dead-end street leading to stratification and segregation. Rather, it raises questions about the kinds of diversity a society is willing to tolerate. The United States presently tolerates different religions more readily than different races. And while racism is particularly strong in many parts of the world, there may be societies where racial diversity is less a threat than religious nonconformity or even bilingualism.

The importance of ethnic or cultural differences, therefore, may depend largely on the national context. Dr Uma Eleazu and Professor Suma Chitnis, in their respective chapters on Nigeria and India (Chapters 7 and 8), specifically ask how one can create a modern liberal nation from the stratified remains of tribalism, caste discrimination, and colonialism. What policies will encourage everyone in a country to include everyone else in his/her definition of 'we'?

In Nigeria tribal, regional and religious differences divide the population. These divisions unfortunately correspond in many cases to inequitable distribution of wealth, power or privilege. In India, the divisions are perceived as regional, religious and of caste. How strong the feelings provoked by these differences can be was brought dramatically to our attention the day Professor Chitnis delivered her paper by the news that the Indian army had stormed the Golden Temple in Amritsar and killed many of the Sikhs holding it.

The problems facing ethnic minorities, whether privileged or underprivileged, are twofold: on the one hand they face the prejudices and misconceptions that people often develop about 'others' who are 'different'; on the other hand they must deal with difficulties stemming from the concrete inequities in wealth, power and related forms of privilege that frequently follow ethnic, religious and racial lines. Education's role in dealing with the former problem is not particularly controversial. Education should foster greater understanding of the history, customs and beliefs of different peoples. As the strange becomes increasingly familiar, misunderstandings decrease, fears subside, and cooperation becomes easier.

Defining the role of education in redressing structural inequalities, however, is much harder. While it is clear that education is an important ingredient in group progress, it is uncertain that education can produce group advancement in the face of other obstacles. So long as increasing educational opportunity means creating a larger pie for all to share, there is likely to be less resistance to including minority groups; but where increasing educational opportunities for one group means limiting access for another (cutting different-size slices from the same pie), the reaction is likely to be swift and possibly violent.

Should minority groups, therefore, limit their struggles for equality to those periods of structural expansion when additional wealth is being created? Such a suggestion hardly seems realistic or fair. Yet every gain made at the expense of another group, no matter how privileged or overrepresented by objective measurement, will produce a resentful backlash. Whether called 'affirmative action' or 'positive discrimination', such efforts are politically explosive.

There is no easy answer. The problems of ethnic minorities around the world display both similarities and contextual differences. Some of these conflicts have long historical antecedents; others are of relatively recent origin. Some seem likely to dissipate with the passage of time while others threaten to become more intransigent. Privileged groups have historically shown little willingness to surrender their privileges voluntarily. Yet all too often forceful attempts to dethrone privilege have merely replaced one oppressor group with another.

This book brings together the views of a number of skilled observers on education's role in dealing with the problems of integrating ethnic minorities in various societies. Their contributions suggest that although schools and universities may be excellent places to continue the struggle for a better world, such institutions are not generally equipped to recreate the world in the image of their teachings. They cannot guarantee their graduates a fair distribution of jobs nor equal access to anything but ideas.

But if education is not the answer, neither should it be the scapegoat. Solutions to the difficult problems discussed in this book will require prolonged struggle and commitment. Where can the roots of that commitment find more fertile soil in which to grow than in young people's belief that the world they create will be better than the one which they have inherited?

Notes

1. Hoffmann-Nowotny, Hans-Joachim, 'Assimilation and Integration of Minorities and Cultural Pluralism: Sociological mechanisms and political dilemmas', supra, p. 196.
2. Hacker, Andrew *A Statistical Portrait of the American People*, Viking Press, New York, 1983, p. 34.
3. 'Supplementary Report: Percent of the Population by Ethnic Origin', *1980 Census of Population*, US Department of Commerce, Washington, DC, 1983, pp. 12–13.
4. *Statistical Abstract of the United States*, US Department of Commerce, Bureau of the Census, Washington, DC, 1983, p. 58.
5. 'General Social and Economic Characteristics', *1980 Census of Population*, I, Chapter C, US Department of Commerce, Washington, DC, 1983, pp. 177–8.
6. Greeley, Andrew M. *The American Catholic, A Social Portrait*, Basic Books, New York, 1977, pp. 51–67.
7. Davis, James, 'Up and Down Opportunity's Ladder', *Public Opinion*, 5, no. 3 (June–July 1982), p. 51.

NOTES ON CONTRIBUTORS

Adler, Chaim, Ph.D., Professor and Head, Research Institute for Innovation in Education, Hebrew University of Jerusalem, Israel.

Chitnis, Suma, Ph.D., Professor of Sociology, Tata Institute of Social Sciences, Bombay, India.

Eleazu, Uma, Ph.D., Director, Manufacturers Association of Nigeria, Lagos former Director, Institute of Strategic Studies, Nigeria.

Heidhues, Mary Somers, Ph.D., political scientist, Göttingen, Germany.

Hellmann-Rajanayagam, Dagmar, Dr. phill., Research associate and part-time lecturer, South Asia Institute, Heidelberg University, Germany.

Hoffmann-Nowotny, H.J., Dr. phil., Professor of Sociology, University of Zürich, Switzerland.

Mehrländer, Ursula, Dr. phil., Head of the Research Division on Foreign Migrants in Germany of the Friedrich Ebert Foundation, Bonn, Germany.

Menk, Antje-Katrin, Dr. phil., Professor of German Philology, University of Bremen, Germany.

Rothermund, Dietmar, Ph.D., Professor of History, South Asia Institute of Heidelberg University, Germany.

Santiago, Isaura Santiago, Ph.D., Assoc. Professor at Teachers College, Columbia University, New York.

Simon, John, Founder-Director, The Dome Project, New York.

Umakoshi, Toru, M. Ed., Associate Professor, Research Institute for Higher Education, Hiroshima University, Japan.

INDEX

220 *Index*